PEOPLES OF THE PAST

MINOANS

PEOPLES OF THE PAST

MINOANS

J. LESLEY FITTON

THE BRITISH MUSEUM PRESS

The face of Crete is stern and weathered.
Truly Crete has about her something primeval
and holy, bitter and proud.

N. KAZANTZAKIS

Acknowledgements

My first and most heartfelt thanks are owed to Dr Olga Krzyszkowska, who has helped me with many aspects of this book. She will recognize some of her own words, particularly in the sections dealing with seals, sealings and administration. Her help has been invaluable: remaining faults are my own.

I would like to thank Nina Shandloff and her colleagues at British Museum Press for commissioning the book and patiently awaiting its completion, Kate Morton for maps and drawings, Susanne Atkin for the index, and Ruth Baldwin and Andrew Shoolbred for skilful editing and design respectively. Chris Power kindly lent me the drawing reproduced as figure 107.

John Allen, Dr Susan Woodford and Dr Dyfri Williams read the manuscript, in whole or in part, and I thank them for their encouragement and their comments.

I would like to thank Dr Alexandra Karetsou for many warm welcomes to the Archaeological Museum of Herakleion and Dr E. Grammatikaki for permission to publish material in that collection. Images were provided by P. Massouras, director of the T A P Service in Athens.

I have learned much from all the people whom I have met or travelled with in Crete over the years. These include friends, mentors and colleagues from the British School at Athens, other foreign schools and the Greek Archaeological Service, as well as my family, John, Rebecca, Stephanie and Madeleine, and groups organized by British Museum Traveller, usually in the company of Konstantinos Kakoudakis and Reggie Barnes. All of these, through their knowledge, their reactions and their discussions, have helped inform my view of Minoan culture. I have also benefited from the legendary hospitality of the modern Cretans, who have made me feel welcome in their lovely island. To them, too, I extend my thanks.

© 2002 J. Lesley Fitton

J. Lesley Fitton has asserted her moral right to be identified
as the author of this work.

First published in 2002 by The British Museum Press
A division of The British Museum Company Ltd
46 Bloomsbury Street, London WC1B 3QQ

A catalogue record for this book is available from the British Library

ISBN 0 7141 2140 1

Frontispiece: Gold pendant shaped like a Cretan wild goat, or *agrimi*,
and decorated with pendant discs. MM III–LM I (1700–1450BC).

Designed and typeset in Bembo by Andrew Shoolbred
Printed in Great Britain by The Bath Press, Avon

Contents

Chronological Chart   6

Map of Crete   8

Introduction   9

1 GEOGRAPHY, LANDSCAPE AND CHRONOLOGY   13

2 CRETE BEFORE THE PALACES   37

3 PROTOPALATIAL CRETE   66

4 NEOPALATIAL CRETE   109

5 FROM THE FINAL PALACE PERIOD TO THE END OF MINOAN CIVILIZATION 180

6 THE MYTHOLOGICAL LEGACY AND THE RECEPTION OF MINOAN CRETE   197

Notes   212

Further Reading   215

Illustration Acknowledgements   216

Index   218

Chronological Chart

EARLY BRONZE AGE	DATE	CRETE	
	7000BC	**Neolithic**	First substantial evidence of settlement in Crete by incomers, probably from Anatolia.
	3000	**Early Minoan (EM) I**	PREPALATIAL PERIOD (3200–1950BC) Minoan society grew and developed, though progress was not consistent throughout the island over this long period. A ranked society began to emerge, with concentration of wealth in the hands of certain people, whether clans, families or individuals.
	2900		
	2800		The island had contacts within the Aegean area. There is evidence for long-distance contacts towards the end of this period.
	2700		
	2600	**Early Minoan (EM) II**	
	2500		
	2400		
	2300		
	2200	**Early Minoan (EM) III**	
	2100		
MIDDLE BRONZE AGE	2000	**Middle Minoan (MM) IA**	
	1900	**Middle Minoan (MM) IB**	PROTOPALATIAL PERIOD (1950–1700BC) In about 1950BC the building of the First Palaces began. They were destroyed about 1700BC, perhaps by earthquakes, but the Minoans rapidly began to rebuild.
	1800	**Middle Minoan (MM) II**	
	1700	**Middle Minoan (MM) III**	NEOPALATIAL PERIOD (1700–1450BC) The period of the Second Palaces. Some disruption should be associated with Thera eruption towards end of LM IA. The extensive destructions throughout Crete around 1450BC were perhaps due to a combination of natural disasters and warfare, either internal or associated with the arrival of Mycenaean Greeks.
	1600		
LATE BRONZE AGE	1500	**Late Minoan (LM) IA**	
		Late Minoan (LM) IB	
	1400	**Late Minoan (LM) II**	FINAL PALATIAL PERIOD (1450–1375/50BC) Knossos survived as a palace and by the time of its final destruction was keeping records in Mycenaean Greek.
		Late Minoan (LM) IIIA1	
	1300	**Late Minoan (LM) IIIA2**	POSTPALATIAL PERIOD (1375/50–1200BC) Minoan culture continued to flourish, but was considerably influenced by Mycenaean Greece, now the dominant power in the eastern Mediterranean. The troubled twelfth century saw the Minoans seeking the safety of 'refuge settlements' in the mountains.
		Late Minoan (LM) IIIB	
	1200	**Late Minoan (LM) IIIC**	
	1100	**Sub-Minoan**	
	1000		

GREEK MAINLAND	CYCLADES	EGYPTIAN DYNASTIES	DATE
			7000BC
Early Helladic (EH) I	Early Cycladic (EC) I	I	3000
			2900
		II	2800
			2700
Early Helladic (EH) II	Early Cycladic (EC) II	III	2600
		IV	2500
		V	2400
		VI	2300
Early Helladic (EH) III		VII–VIII	2200
	Early Cycladic (EC) III		2100
		IX–X and XI · FIP	2000
		XII	1900
Middle Helladic (MH)	Middle Cycladic (MC)		1800
Rise of Mycenae		XIII and XIV · SIP	1700
Period of Shaft Grave circles at Mycenae	Flourishing of Akrotiri site on Thera	XV–XVI (Hyksos) and XVII	1600
			1500
Late Helladic (LH) or Mycenaean	Late Cycladic (LC)	XVIII (Amarna c. 1352–1323BC)	1400
Period of Mycenae's greatest influence			1300
		XIX	1200
		XX	1100
			1000

FIP – First Intermediate Period
SIP – Second Intermediate Period

7

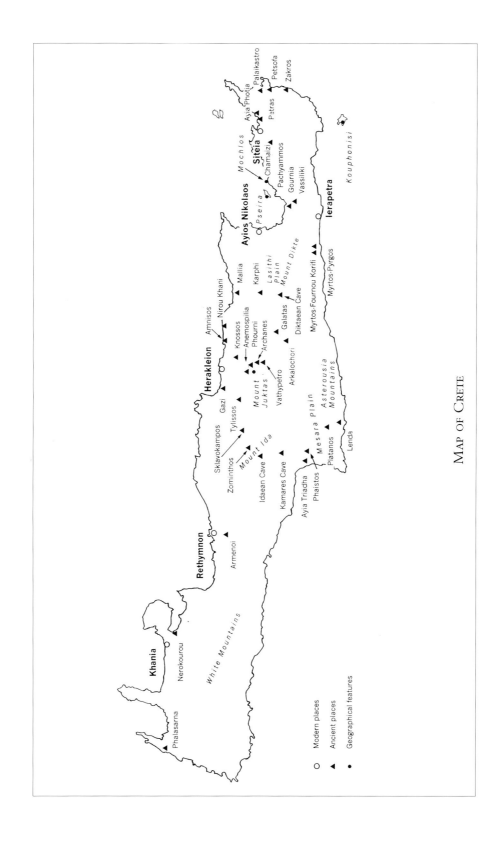

MAP OF CRETE

Khania

Rethymnon

Herakleion

Ayios Nikolaos

Siteia

Ierapetra

Phalasarna

Nerokourou

White Mountains

Armenoi

Sklavokampos

Zominthos

Mount Ida

Idaean Cave

Kamares Cave

Ayia Triadha

Phaistos

Platanos

Mesara Plain

Lenda

Asterousia Mountains

Tylissos

Gazi

Mount Juktas

Vathypetro

Arkalochori

Galatas

Diktaean Cave

Knossos

Anemospilia

Phourni

Archanes

Nirou Khani

Amnisos

Mallia

Karphi

Lasithi Plain

Mount Dikte

Myrtos-Fournou Korifi

Myrtos-Pyrgos

Pseira

Mochlos

Chamaizi

Pachyammos

Gournia

Vassiliki

Ayia Photia

Palaikastro

Petsofa

Zakros

Patras

Kouphonisi

○ Modern places

▲ Ancient places

• Geographical features

INTRODUCTION

THE PEOPLE whom we call 'Minoans', the inhabitants of Crete in the Bronze Age, occupy a special place in history. Their island home was big enough and sufficiently varied in landscape and natural resources to support them in independence, and to allow their society to develop in its own characteristic way. Minoan culture is therefore a distinct and unique phenomenon: Minoan architecture, arts and crafts are instantly recognizable. Yet connections with a wider world were important to the Minoans from early in their history. They needed some imports, particularly of metals, from abroad, while they themselves developed desirable products which were in demand from their neighbours. Such interconnections were not limited to exchange of material goods: we can chart the influence of what we might generally term the Minoan way of life in neighbouring lands – and recipro-cally their life at home was touched by outside influences.

We need to view Minoan Crete, then, both within the bounds of the island and as part of the nexus of lands in the eastern Mediterranean, and our understanding must mainly be based on analysis of material remains. Though this was a time when writing was known and used in Crete, Minoan culture has traditionally been classified as 'prehistoric' – before the time of written history. 'Protohistoric' may in fact be a better term, to reflect the fact that there is input to our picture from our understanding of the script called Linear B, and from our partial comprehension of the way the earlier Cretan scripts were used, even though the scripts themselves are not deciphered. Indeed we also have scraps of written evidence from Crete's neighbours. Evocative if historically unstable input comes too from the tales told about Crete by later generations and preserved in the literature of the ancient Greeks.

The lack of written history means that scholars have had to be ingenious in arriving at research methods that will extract maximum information from

1 A view of the Mesara Plain from the foothills of the Asterousia Mountains.

the archaeological record, and have had to beware of telling optimistic but unsubstantiated stories. Facts are plentiful. Excavations in the island have been going on to a greater or lesser degree of intensity since about 1900 (with some earlier researches) and workers in the field provide new buildings and artefacts for consideration each year. Secondary studies, on both a micro and a macro scale, provide further grist for the mill of synthesis. Yet synthesis remains a difficult process, showing up some really quite alarming gaps in even our basic knowledge and understanding of this once-great civilization.

That the civilization was once great, though, cannot be denied. To anyone standing at Knossos, outside the palace, contemplating the huge blocks of its walls, it is clear beyond doubt that the people who built it were powerful. To anyone standing in the Herakleion museum, examining the rich and finely wrought objects that they made, it is clear that they were sophisticated. And standing on the sun-baked site of one of the Minoan country houses that abound in the Cretan landscape, you can feel the presence of a simpler past, ruled by sowing, harvest, storage and all the needs of the land – the land that underpinned the whole of the Minoan achievement. There is much that we can see, learn, know, perhaps legitimately also feel about the Minoans when we stand among the remains of their material world. Our understanding may be only partial, but we are enriched by the experience.

This book is not aimed at the specialist reader, for whom, in this age of information explosion, an almost unencompassably vast literature exists in books and articles detailing the complexities of Minoan archaeology and the many unresolved issues that remain. Instead its target audience is the more broadly interested but non-specialist public – from the student beginning Minoan studies to the visitor who chooses a holiday in Crete and would like to know more. It aims to explain what can fairly be said about the people of Minoan Crete and their history, and to point out where consensus exists and what matters are still disputed. Its compass is not broad enough to create a complete gazetteer of Minoan sites, for which a good guide book remains indispensable,[1] nor can it detail in depth all aspects of Minoan material culture. In particular, the reader may feel the need to pursue the remarkable Minoan artistic achievements – in fresco painting, for example, or in the wonderful miniature worlds of the carvings on Minoan seal-stones – either in other, more highly illustrated literature, or, perhaps preferably, in the museums of Crete and elsewhere.[2] The intention here is to summarize, necessarily selectively, Minoan life and times, and to provide a background of information into which such experiences can be placed.

Above all, this is meant to be a book about people, and yet the Minoans remain difficult to summon to the mind's eye. We catch glimpses of them in their art – slim-waisted men going about their solemn tasks, pale women, elaborately dressed and coiffured, who sometimes allow us a glimpse of twirling hair or the steady regard of a large dark eye, yet still remain mysterious. This, moreover, is the equivalent of the art of court or church, and tells only part of the story. The ordinary Cretans, whether in the palace workshops or the vineyards and olive groves, are even more elusive.

2 Thousands of plain conical cups such as this are found on Minoan sites in Crete and abroad.

Perhaps what a book like this can best do is to try to provide a firm springboard for the imagination. We will always want to know more about the Minoans than the relics of material culture can tell. Take, for example, that most typical of Minoan objects, ubiquitous on Minoan sites, the small clay conical cup. The archaeological process is to excavate, describe, draw, date and publish the cup and then put it on exhibition in a museum. The human response is to think about the hand that last held the cup, or the hand that made it. It is, after all, such a palpably handleable, practical, usable, unpretentious little object – it calls to our common experience. Museums would be dead places indeed if we did not imagine the cup in a living hand.

We can and must, though, base such imaginative responses on knowledge, and on a rigorous regard for those facts that archaeology has been able to establish. Minoan society is incompletely understood, but that should not mean that it becomes a source for wild reconstructions or outlandish interpretations. The truth as we understand it is more subtle and complex and perhaps stranger than fiction: in so far as we are able, we must let the facts speak for themselves. Then, if elusively and only partially, the people will emerge from the works that they have left behind.

Chapter One

GEOGRAPHY, LANDSCAPE AND CHRONOLOGY

THE MOUNTAINS of Crete are the most noticeable natural feature of the island, and are responsible for creating remarkably varied landscapes within it, from snow-capped peaks to subtropical shores. Crete is long and narrow – some 250 km (155 miles) from west to east, about 60 km (37 miles) from the centre of the north coast to the south, but narrowing to only 14 km (8½ miles) at the isthmus of Ierapetra – and nowhere inland is very far from the sea. Yet because of the mountains such distances can be deceptive: a straight line on a map may in reality cover the most difficult terrain. In fact the sea itself must always have been the easiest way to link certain areas, and remains the only means of communication with a handful of places on the very rocky and precipitous southern coast.

Mariners approaching from the north and aiming for Knossos would have used as a landmark Mount Juktas, which stands in isolation at the southern end of the Knossos valley and is therefore noticeable, though its height is only 811 m (2,660 ft). A southern approach, perhaps with Phaistos as its goal, would be guided by the twin peaks of Mount Ida – Psiloritis, 'the high one', in modern Greek, actually 2,456 m (8,058 ft) and the island's highest spot. In the far west the White Mountains achieve 2,453 m (8,048 ft), while eastwards the circle of the Lasithi Mountains – where the peak of Dikte is 2,148 m (7,047 ft) – and the high table-land of the Siteia region complete the island's craggy backbone. Communication between north and south must always have been particularly easy at the narrow isthmus of Ierapetra, and relatively easy in the centre of the island where no great height is reached between Knossos and Phaistos. Crossing the island was also possible in the west, perhaps particularly south of Rethymnon, through the Amari valley.

3 Mount Juktas and part of
the Knossos valley, carpeted
with vines.

4 The northern part of the
Knossos valley, looking
towards the sea.

5 The Nidha plateau, high up behind the peaks of Mount Ida.

We no doubt see the enduring mountains much as the Minoans did, and the particular features of the limestone landscape, such as the caves, gorges and high upland plains so characteristic of Crete today, will scarcely have altered since their time. Nonetheless geological changes have taken place since the Minoan period. The neotectonic history of Crete accounts for the uplift of parts of the west of the island that has, for example, left the old Roman harbour installations at Phalasarna high and dry, while probable local downward movements in the centre and east have combined with a general rise in sea level to make former peninsulas such as Mochlos and Pseira into offshore islands, with the Minoan shoreline in many places submerged by several metres. Consequent changes in the water-table mean that the decorative water features of the coastal palace at Zakros are more fully and constantly filled (or flooded) than their designers could have foreseen. Soil erosion and deposition of sediments in valley bottoms have also altered the distribution and nature of fertile soils in some areas. An example is the northern part of the Knossos valley, where in some places erosion from the slopes of Ailias has resulted in the deposition of up to 5 m (16½ ft) of soil in the valley bottom at some stage during or after late Roman times.

Changes in climate and natural vegetation must also be considered in any attempt to evaluate how the island appeared to the Minoans, and what possibilities it offered to them. It seems that in the Neolithic (New Stone Age) period and Early Bronze Age (7000–2000BC) the climate was wetter than it is now, and the seasons less differentiated, though by the Late Bronze Age (from about 1600BC) the island was settling into the typically Mediterranean climate that it enjoys today. This is characterized by hot, dry summers and wet but not particularly cold winters, creating the same rhythm for the Minoan year as they do for the modern inhabitants. Another constant factor since Minoan times is the rain-shadow effect of the island's western mountains: the west is much greener, the vegetation lusher and large trees more common, while the eastern end of Crete is deprived of rain – an increasing problem for its inhabitants today.

The question of tree-cover and vegetation is an interesting one, discussed in detail by Rackham and Moody in their useful book *The Making of the Cretan Landscape*.[1] They caution against the wholesale acceptance of the idea that Crete was once covered with lush vegetation and extensive forests, describing the widespread belief that in many parts of the Mediterranean world the activities of man have destroyed a sort of demi-Eden as 'the theory of the Ruined Landscape'. It has indeed often been suggested that Crete was rendered more barren by activities such as building, ship-building, charcoal-burning and the like, combined with land-clearance for agriculture and the grazing of goats. Erosion and even a decrease in rainfall have equally been seen as consequences.

In fact, though, as the authors point out, this attitude owes more to the human tendency to describe lost Golden Ages than to an impartial assessment of the evidence. The real picture is only patchily recoverable, but shows much more variability over time and space. Thus while they generally conclude that the island has fewer trees now than in antiquity, they point also to periods of increasing tree growth (including, notably, the most recent past). Erosion, too, seems to be localized, depending as it does on underlying geology, and is much more likely to be a result of either heavy rain-storms or injudicious use of bulldozers than the effect of goats. Deforestation is most unlikely to have led to decreased rainfall: the Cretan climate is part of a bigger climate pattern which activities on this narrow island are unlikely to have affected.

The picture is complex, and certainly cannot be assumed to be one of steady decline. Indeed Crete is described by Rackham and Moody as a resilient landscape. They conclude that the aboriginal vegetation, before human habitation, was very different from the natural vegetation today. The aboriginal fauna, too, included species now extinct, among them pygmy elephant and hippopotamus, giant rodents and giant insectivores. Big changes in the Neolithic period and Bronze Age were partly dependent on climate change, partly on the activities of man. Subsequently, though, in spite of fluctuations, 'The main types of wild vegetation in Crete today would be recognized by any Cretan from Late Minoan times onwards.'

Agriculture, Animal Husbandry and the Use of Wild Resources

The same is certainly true of the three staples of agricultural production, grain crops, vines and olives, sometimes called the 'Mediterranean triad'. These have been cultivated on Crete for millennia, and the land cleared and prepared for them as appropriate. Wheat and barley arrived with the first settlers, while oats are first attested in the Early Bronze Age. The first evidence for vine cultivation is also of Early Bronze Age date. Olives may have been cultivated earlier, but seem certainly to have been established at this time. Both olives and vines are still prominent in the modern landscape, though cereal production has greatly declined in recent years. Citrus trees, which are now extensively grown in Greece as a whole, were introduced after the Minoan period.

Agriculture was at the heart of the Minoan success story, and the storage of agricultural products was a major preoccupation in the palaces and country houses of Minoan Crete. As well as grapes, olives and a range of cereals and pulses, figs were stored, as were almonds and pistachio nuts. Other fruits eaten included pears and quinces. Lettuce, celery, onions, garlic and a range of herbs seem to have been among the plants grown. Sesame and cumin are recorded in Linear B but have Semitic names and were perhaps imported. Flax was cultivated for the production of linen. Saffron gathering is shown on frescoes: the harvest could have been used for a number of purposes including as a dye, a foodstuff or a medicine, and had a place in Minoan ritual, as the Thera frescoes show.

Recent excavation results combined with studies of residues in cooking pots, storage vessels and table wares have brought interesting information on Minoan plant use and diet, confirming some general conclusions and adding greater detail.[2] It is now clear that olive oil was extracted at least as early as the Middle Minoan IA (MM IA) period (see the chronology on pages 6–7), and evidence for this comes from the building complex at Chamalevri in the area of Stavromenos, east of Rethymnon. Here olive stones seem also to have been burnt as fuel. In the same area an outdoor workshop was identified which seems to have been engaged in the production of perfumed oils. Hearths and specialist vessels were found, often showing traces of burning. Residues in these included olive oil and oil of iris, an ingredient in perfume. This activity also dated to MM IA, immediately before the foundation of the Minoan palaces.

Other analyses confirmed that the Minoan diet was quite surprisingly rich in meat, along with cereals, peas, beans and lentils, and a range of leafy vegetables. Drinking habits were fascinatingly illuminated, with evidence for

production of resinated wine as early as the Early Minoan period. Pine resin was used, as it is for modern retsina, while traces of resin from the terebinth tree were also found. It seems probable that barley beer was made from early times, and honey mead was later added to the repertoire.

Animal husbandry concentrated especially on the herding of sheep and goats, for which the Cretan terrain was particularly suitable. They first appear in the archaeological record in the Early Neolithic period. Flocks would have been kept not just for meat but also for 'secondary products'– milk, cheese, hides and wool. It has been argued that the 'secondary products revolution' was an important development of the fourth millennium, when animals started to be kept specifically for secondary products rather than primarily for meat, leading to different patterns of stock-breeding and animal husbandry and certainly necessitating the establishment of premises for the processes involved. The evidence from the Linear B texts for an extensive textile industry at Knossos in the Late Bronze Age can be seen as the ultimate extension of this.

Cattle were probably important to the Minoans not simply as a source of food, milk and hides but also as draught animals. Oxen could have pulled both carts and ploughs, and could have been used as beasts of burden. The Cretan terrain is not particularly suitable for cows, though breeds of cattle well adapted to a dry environment were numerous on the island until recently. The Cretan bulls so prominent in Minoan art and ritual must have been the largest animals that most Minoans ever saw.

Pigs were kept from Late Neolithic times onwards. Feral pigs, descended from domesticated animals, were perhaps hunted both for meat and their tusks. These were occasionally used in the Early Minoan period to make seal-stones (discussed more fully on pages 92 and 161), and later for the boar's-tusk helmets that were a prestigious possession of the Mycenaean warrior.

Donkeys were perhaps not present before, at the earliest, the Middle
Bronze Age. They must have been beasts of burden for the Minoans, as they
were until the age of mechanization in Crete. Horses were certainly used in
the Late Bronze Age, though they must always have been relatively rare.
The terrain was not particularly suitable for them, and ownership of a horse
was no doubt a symbol of the status of the owner. They are shown pulling
chariots in Minoan art from the neopalatial period onwards.

Dogs are represented in Early Minoan art, and were present from
Neolithic times. They presumably acted as guard-dogs, as pets and as helpers
in the hunt. Hunted animals included deer, which were introduced to the
island and appear in Minoan art from the protopalatial period onwards.
Fallow deer may have been introduced as park deer by the Minoans – there
is no positive faunal evidence for red deer until the postpalatial period, but
they too must have been introduced. Hares were also hunted, as was a
variety of birds such as partridge, quail and dove.

The *agrimi*, or wild goat of Crete, has been hunted from Minoan times
until the modern period, and is now very rare. It seems not to have been an

indigenous creature, but to have arrived with the first settlers, and would thus be a feral animal, descended from early escapees from herded flocks. It would then have adapted to the high, wild places that it inhabited. It is commonly shown in Minoan art, sometimes being hunted, sometimes decorating the rocky landscape around mountain-top shrines.

Cats appear in Minoan frescoes and on seal-stones, and domestic cats may have been known to the Minoans, though the evidence from bones is unclear on this point. Cats may simply have been depicted in art, along with other exotic animals, though it is possible that the real thing, not just the iconography, could have been imported from Egypt. The Cretan wildcat, still living in the island, is probably a feral descendant of the domestic cat, which was known from at least the Roman period.

Bee-keeping and honey are mentioned in the Linear B tablets, and bee-hives have no doubt been a feature of the Cretan landscape throughout history. Honey appears in Linear B among offerings made to the gods. The researchers working on analysis of residues in pottery suggest that honey was used to make mead, and that the drinking of this, along with beer and wine, may sometimes have been part of religious rituals. Honey would have been a significant source of sugar in the Minoan diet.

Snails were among the natural foodstuffs that could be gathered from the landscape, as well as a variety of edible greens. Herbs, too, were no doubt valued by the Minoans as they are today, for medicines, for infusions, for flavouring food and for their scent. Perhaps the Early Minoan vessels known as 'teapots' really were sometimes used for herbal tea. It has been suggested that the flail shown carried by pharaohs in Egyptian art is the implement used for gathering ladanum, the exudation of the rock-rose, *Cistus creticus.* This is an ingredient in incense, and may have been collected by the same method from ancient times.

Fishing and the gathering of shellfish were certainly practised by the Minoans. Their frescoes abound with marine motifs; octopods embrace their pottery, along with murex and cuttlefish; bronze fish-hooks have been found, and there is a certain amount of evidence from physical remains of bones and shells. As well as the use of fish and shellfish for food, there is evidence for the use of *Murex brandaris* to produce the purple dye later called Tyrian purple. Shells are found sporadically on various sites, but in the Middle and Late Minoan periods very large concentrations of shells occur at Mallia and Palaikastro and on the islet of Kouphonisi. This seems to indicate processing on the scale required to produce the dye. Very large numbers of shells are required for even a small quantity, which is partly why Tyrian (or imperial) purple was so valued in later times. It now seems that the Minoans were the forerunners in this prestige industry.

8 A well-preserved wine press in the 'country house' at Vathypetro.

9 An olive press in the 'country house' at Vathypetro.

As the above survey shows, our evidence for farming practices, animal husbandry and the use of wild resources comes from a variety of sources: from physical remains of bones, shells and plants, from representations in Minoan art and from written records. Surviving tools, vessels and installations such as grape or olive presses should also be added to this list. The uses of these can sometimes be understood through comparisons with more recent farm implements.

Indeed, the archaeological examination of modern practices to throw light on ancient ones is perhaps nowhere more fruitfully applied than in the consideration of farming and agriculture, since some agricultural aims in Crete have remained constant over centuries, with methods that have been similarly conservative, until the introduction of mechanization in the modern period.[3] Due caution must be exercised when it comes to the broader picture, since today Crete is part of a cash economy and there is no modern equivalent for palatial intervention or control, yet actual applied methods, and the tools used for them, can quite reasonably be thought to have changed little.

Raw Materials for Building and Crafts

Building materials were also an important natural resource. Timber was available, and charcoal evidence from Minoan contexts shows the use of cypress, juniper, evergreen oak and olive, though these may have been remains of furniture or fuel as well as of buildings. Cypress may have been used for the largest beams in the most important buildings, and traces occasionally survive. Cypress was available on the island, but it remains possible that some wood was imported. Egyptian records of Keftiu (probably Cretan) ships bringing timber to Egypt have been interpreted as indicating Minoan export of wood, though the ships may have been acting as carriers of wood from elsewhere.

The geology of Crete provided a range of stones. Limestone of various types was ubiquitous and was commonly used for building throughout the island. Sandstone occurred particularly in the region of Mallia, and gives the palace there its characteristically red appearance. Gypsum was also used, both in blocks and in thin sheets as a decorative wall veneer. Neatly shaped blocks of gypsum appeared in the First Palace at Knossos, which had a good local supply of the stone on nearby Gypsadhes Hill, just to the south of the palace. Limestone was more extensively used in the Second Palace at Knossos. The cutting of shaped blocks was a skill certainly known from the First Palace period onwards, and fine examples of ashlar masonry survive from the Second Palace period, but Minoan architecture often juxtaposed finely finished areas with stretches of walls that were less carefully built. Rubble was extensively used for walls, though these sometimes had neat facings, while timber and mud-brick were also common. Often only important rooms or areas were neatly finished, and even within the palaces fine architecture occurs side by side with much rougher construction techniques, though sometimes the walls have lost their finish of painted plaster.

Schists were occasionally used to build walls in those areas where they are common, but as schists naturally break into thin horizontal slabs they are a more natural choice for paving. Red and green schists were used in this way. Limestones of various colours, sometimes decoratively veined, were also used for such architectural details as column bases and paving. Other interestingly coloured local stones were similarly employed. The names used for these in the archaeological literature can be confusing: the stone called breccia by Arthur Evans is probably a veined limestone or dolomite; the greenish stone called serpentine by archaeologists is referred to by geologists as opheiolite; the stone called porphyry by the Cretans is a phyllite,[4] and so on. Some marble occurs on Crete, and was used for details in buildings, though it is usually of rather poor quality.

10 Stones of different colours make attractive paving in the Minoan town on the island of Mochlos.

Marls, sandstones and clays created some areas of dense, soft rock that were favoured by the Minoans for rock-cut tombs. Clay beds were also an important resource for the potters of Minoan Crete: their fine vases were admired and exported, and depended on the fairly widespread availability of good-quality clay.

Smaller-scale uses of attractive stones included the carving of stone vases, made of local stones such as serpentine and polychrome-banded limestones as well as some imported materials, and also the carving of seal-stones. Early in the seal-stone tradition soft local stones were used, while from the Middle Bronze Age harder stones were employed. These included agate, carnelian, jasper, rock-crystal and occasionally amethyst. Most must have been imported, though a Cretan source for rock-crystal has been noted.

One of the most important considerations for the success of any ancient culture was the availability of metals, which the island essentially lacked, and we might wonder how the Minoans managed, and flourished, without immediate resources. Two places in the island have copper ores in quantities that might have been usable in the Bronze Age, one in west Crete, one in the area of the Asterousia Mountains, but in fact it is not clear whether the Minoans exploited them. In all probability the island must always have been bronze-hungry. In the Early Bronze Age close contacts with the Cyclades allowed copper to be brought from Kythnos – at this stage it was alloyed with locally occurring arsenic to make bronze. At Chrysokamino in eastern Crete an Early Minoan copper-smelting site has recently been discovered, with a

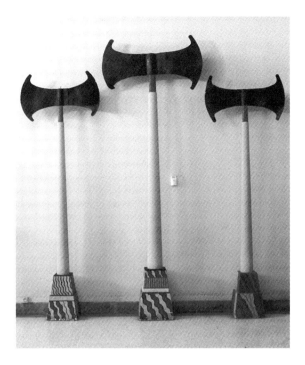

11 Very large votive double-axes and swords in Herakleion museum show the Minoan need for quantities of bronze.

hearth, clay pot bellows, clay furnaces and a quantity of slag. Some of the copper ore seems to have originated in Kythnos. Some copper may also have come from Lavrion in Attica on the Greek mainland: certainly from the Middle Bronze Age onwards Lavrion seems to have been an important source. Groups of copper ingots of Late Bronze Age date from Zakros, Ayia Triadha and Tylissos are a striking element in the display in the Herakleion museum and represent a considerable weight of imported raw material. Analysis has not pinned down their source precisely, though they may have come from Anatolia or Syria. Surprisingly, they are not from Cyprus, and in fact very little of the copper used in Late Bronze Age Crete is demonstrably of Cypriot origin, even though the island was a major producer at this time.

Sources of tin, alloyed with copper to make bronze from the Middle Bronze Age onwards, have also proved elusive. A possible source lies in Anatolia, though we do not know if it was exploited at this time. Further afield, tin also occurs in Afghanistan. Supplies from this source reached Mari on the Euphrates for onward shipment, and Crete may have been an ultimate destination (see page 99). Long trade routes with many intermediaries could well have characterized the importation of foreign raw materials into Crete.

The scale of some of the tools and weapons in the Herakleion museum is also striking, showing that even single items could use bronze in great quantity. Some of these may represent the wealth (perhaps the ostentatious display) of the palaces, but even the humblest tiller of the fields needed bronze tools to support him in his everyday life. All in all, bronze was essential, and it can be argued that the main motivation for the palaces sending ships abroad was the search for bronze. This need at the heart of Minoan life may paradoxically have become one of the mechanisms for Minoan influence – indeed, Minoan success – in the broader world of the eastern Mediterranean. It is possible that trade in precious metals occurred on the back of this: silver from the Cyclades and Lavrion could have been traded by the Minoans, as well as being used for internal consumption, while from the opposite direction Egyptian gold came into Crete. Egypt was probably also the source of precious stones.

Chronology

Minoan history, like that of Crete in more recent times, must have included specific, significant landmarks. We do not know whether, or to what extent, the people living in the palaces and great houses of Crete ever recorded their history, but we may surmise that they had a complex sense of their own past. This no doubt included memories of events that we can hope to see in the archaeological record, such as earthquakes and natural disasters, or man-made destructions as a result of conflict. Above all, though, it must have included people – named individuals whose stories could be told and whose actions were remembered in the islanders' consciousness, just as the stories of more recent heroes (and villains) are told by the Cretans today. These people, their histories or myths, and their effect on the Minoan sense of identity are lost to us: they are not recoverable by archaeology. Yet we should remember that they must have existed. We write contrasting accounts of ancient and modern Crete because of the different types of information available to us, but the contrast is essentially artificial. 'Prehistory' was not a time when people told their own story in terms of changes in pottery style. History was being created and recounted in Minoan times, but it is a history to which we now have only limited access.

Earlier generations of archaeologists, in the late nineteenth and earlier twentieth centuries, were less self-conscious about the limitations of archaeological evidence than we have learned to be, and were therefore very much inclined to attempt people- and events-based history, even on the basis of limited information. So popular literature on Minoan Crete evoked the figure of Minos, whether as an individual or as a title carried by successive kings, peopled his court with princesses and grand viziers, and generally used mythology, historical parallels and a good deal of imagination to create a rather *Arabian Nights*-like atmosphere. A backlash was inevitable, and certainly by the second half of the twentieth century the strong tendency was to eschew an imaginative approach and to refocus archaeological effort on the detailed examination of ancient material in its own terms. This could sometimes be purely descriptive in effect, but where wider questions were approached it was generally in the pursuit of broad processes rather than people. As archaeology came of age, it learned to construct the sort of theoretical models to which archaeological data would be relevant — in other words, to frame the sort of questions that archaeology could answer.

Nonetheless, the ultimate aim of archaeology must still be to write history. For this early, so-called 'prehistoric' period the type of history we can approach may seem disappointing: perhaps rather colourless in its lack of people, and frustrating because of the contrast with the material culture of ancient Crete, which is so vibrant and so full of colour. Of course not all problems are solved by the existence of texts. Archaeologists and historians face difficulties in reconstructing the history of the ancient world even where writing was used specifically for 'historic' purposes — for the recording of annals, king-lists and the like. The reasons need little elaboration: they include the partial preservation of texts, the problems of translation and interpretation, and above all, as in Minoan Crete itself, the fact that writing was used only for limited purposes. Matters of individual everyday experience, for example, were rarely written down, or at least have rarely survived. It is always going to be difficult to achieve the equivalent of the social history of more modern times.

Even with an awareness of these difficulties, it is tempting to look from Minoan Crete to the south and east, to the contemporary Egyptian and Near Eastern cultures that used writing, with some envy. In spite of problems of interpretation, there is undoubtedly a sense of added richness where extensive texts can be read and understood — a sense, too, of hearing some individual voices from the past which in Crete we lack. Moreover, there is one major aspect of history for which Minoan Crete has traditionally been dependent on foreign links, and that is the aspect of time.

The importance of dating is a rare matter for consensus in archaeological thought. Studies that ignore the dimension of time are few, while a complex literature covers questions of chronology. A chronological framework is certainly essential to our attempt to see the broad sweep of human history in

12 An Early Dynastic Egyptian stone vessel imported to Crete and adapted to Minoan taste by the addition of a spout and, originally, handles. It is unhelpful for chronology, as it was some 1500 years old when trapped in the destruction of Zakros in 1450BC.

the island of Crete in the Bronze Age. We want to date the sorts of events which we can see in the archaeological record, to know when sites were built and destroyed, to see how they articulate within the island and how they relate to developments outside it. The dates will of course be approximate, but we want as nearly as possible to know when things happened, in what order, and what was happening elsewhere at about the same time.

The relative chronology of Minoan civilization – the chronology dependent on changes in material culture within the island and expressed in archaeological phases – is quite well understood. A broad consensus exists, and can be outlined here. Problems arise when we come to absolute chronology, and the relation of the archaeological phases to calendar dates.

This has traditionally been achieved by links with better-documented cultures, particularly that of Egypt. So-called 'cross-dating' has been used – exports from Crete have been dated from their Egyptian context, or, conversely, dateable objects from Egypt have given a date for the Minoan context in which they were found. Near Eastern sites and objects also have a role in the complex series of links that has been built up in this way.

Recently, though, science-based dating techniques have been challenging dates arrived at by this method ever more vocally, and with increasing conviction. Controversy has arisen particularly over the date of the Late Bronze Age eruption of the island of Thera, a specific and much-studied event, of pivotal importance, for which archaeology and science might between them be expected to provide a firm date. This will no doubt come, but at the time of writing consensus has not emerged. In fact there is a difference of about a hundred years between the 'new', high chronology suggested mainly on science-based grounds and the 'traditional', lower chronology based on foreign links. After detailing relative chronology we must consider some of the arguments surrounding this divergence before attempting to outline a broadly workable chronological scheme.

RELATIVE CHRONOLOGY

The passage of time in Minoan (as in other) archaeology is marked by changes in material culture and particularly in pottery styles. Fired clay is practically indestructible, so fragments of pottery, often with painted decoration, are ubiquitous on Minoan sites. Styles in pottery changed quite quickly and they are therefore a sensitive chronological indicator. The basic principles of stratigraphy – the successive layers of habitation debris recovered in excavation – show the order in which the pottery styles developed. Often they can be related to major building phases and destructions, in the sense that typical pottery can be associated with these, though there is, of course, no reason why pottery styles should change in tandem with destructions and rebuildings.

Minoan chronology was first evolved by Arthur Evans during his excavations at Knossos, which began in 1900. He believed that Egyptian influence had been strongly felt throughout Minoan history and that there had from early (predynastic or Neolithic) times been an Egyptian element in the Minoan population that predisposed the two cultures to develop along similar lines. This view in no longer tenable, but it was one of the reasons for Evans' decision to divide Minoan history into an Early, a Middle and a Late stage, equivalent to the Old, Middle and New Kingdoms in Egypt. Each subdivision was itself divided into three.

The scheme was adopted in the Cyclades and on the Greek mainland, where the terms Cycladic and Helladic replaced Minoan. It is hallowed by usage, and most modern Aegean archaeologists retain it, though there are inherent problems; indeed it has been described by one recent author as a 'bed of Prokrustes, to which the material must be fitted willy-nilly'.[5]

Problems partly arise, as this implies, because of the difficulties of incorporating new material to a pre-existing scheme, but there are more basic weaknesses. The first is the fact that in the Evans system both pottery styles and periods of time are designated by the same names. The underlying logic should be that, for example, MM IA is the period of time when MM IA pottery was current. In fact, though, regionalism is a factor that needs to be taken into account. It has long been recognized that EM III pottery styles lingered in the east of Crete when MM IA pottery was used in the centre of the island. MM IA should be later than EM III if the terms refer to periods of time. It makes no sense for time to overlap, though pottery styles naturally can, and do.

Specialists make various accommodations, but the picture can become confused. Confusion is compounded by the fact that, in the Evans system, the major building periods of Knossos do not fit neatly with obvious points in the chronological terminology. Thus the First Palace was built after the start of the Middle Minoan period, and the major destruction that saw its end happened before the end of that period. Evans' broad chronological divisions have the advantage of tying in Minoan history to that of a wider world – the Middle Bronze Age in the eastern Mediterranean is a coherent, broader concept. Nonetheless, when describing developments in Crete, many writers have found it practical to use the terminology of First and Second Palace periods (sometimes expressed in the terms protopalatial and neopalatial) alongside Evans' more precise phases.

The chronological chart on pages 6–7 shows the relationship of the Evans phases and the palatial building phases, and ties in some of the major horizons briefly outlined here.

HISTORICAL OUTLINE

In the broadest possible terms, we can sum up what we know or surmise of the Bronze Age history of Crete in the following way.

While earlier groups of people may have reached Crete, our first substantial evidence indicates that the island was colonized in around 7000BC by incomers, probably from Anatolia.

Early settlement at Knossos represents the beginning of the site that was to be pre-eminent in Minoan history, but other favourable locations began to show the advantages of their position in the Neolithic period. Advances in agricultural practice enabled the exploitation of the island's rich natural resources that would be the basis for the Minoan achievement.

The Bronze Age is so called because bronze replaced stone as the main material used for tools and weapons. The Early Bronze Age was a period of more than a thousand years, and can overall be described as a time when Minoan society grew and developed, though naturally progress was not consistent over so long a time. A ranked society began to emerge, with some concentration of wealth in the hands of certain people, whether families, clans or individuals. The island had contacts within the Aegean area, and there is evidence for long-distance contacts towards the end of the period.

After the beginning of the Middle Bronze Age, in about 1950BC, the Minoan palaces were created, perhaps as a result of the fusion of ideas from abroad with the preceding internal developments in Crete. The destruction of the First Palaces in about 1700BC was probably due to an earthquake or a series of earthquakes. The devastation was extensive, but the people rapidly began to rebuild, and after some little time their culture re-emerged, arguably stronger and more sophisticated than ever before.

Some disruption must be associated with the eruption of Thera in the late LM IA period, still tentatively dated here to about 1530BC. The extent to which Crete was affected remains controversial, but Minoan Crete certainly was not directly destroyed by the eruption and Minoan culture as a whole shows continuity unbroken by the event.

The destruction of 1450BC was characterized by the collapse and at least temporary abandonment of almost all known Minoan sites. Knossos was a notable exception. The cause or causes of the destructions are uncertain: natural disasters must be one possibility, and the invasion of Mycenaeans from the Greek mainland another – indeed many commentators have suggested some combination of the two. It is also possible that Knossos used military force against the rest of the island at this stage, to reinforce her obvious cultural hegemony with real political control. In this case Mycenaeans need not have arrived as early as 1450BC, but could have come to the island somewhat later.

The destruction of the palace of Knossos has traditionally been dated to about 1375BC, though some scholars now suggest a date rather later in the fourteenth century. Mycenaean presence prior to this collapse is indicated by the presence of Linear B tablets in the ruins of the building. The causes of the destruction are again uncertain. Internal insurrection against the dominance of Knossos must be a real possibility, though mainland Mycenaeans might have felt that Knossos was too powerful and had to be subdued.

After the destruction of Knossos there may have been a shift of power towards western Crete; certainly Chania, where Linear B tablets have been found, became an administrative centre. Crete in the fourteenth and thirteenth centuries BC remained a prosperous place, but became part of an Aegean world dominated by the influence of the Mycenaean Greeks of the mainland. The material culture of Crete still retained an individual character, however, with roots going deep into its Minoan past.

The troubled twelfth century saw widespread disruption in the eastern Mediterranean. The collapse of social and economic systems in the Mycenaean world, and the unsettled and war-like movements of the people referred to in Egyptian texts as the Sea Peoples, brought chaotic times, and essentially marked the end of the Bronze Age in Greece. In Crete the people retired to the mountains, occupying so-called refuge settlements. These, often clinging precariously to the saddles of hills, provided relative safety, even though life in such places must have been hard. Coastal refuge settlements had long views of the sea, from which trouble might be expected.

In spite of these difficult times continuity of occupation can be seen on some Cretan sites. Knossos is a notable example, where cemetery material shows scarcely any break from the end of the Minoan period into later times. The eleventh and tenth centuries are known as the Dark Age in Greece: a time of relative poverty and depopulation when many of the arts and crafts that had been practised in the Bronze Age were lost. In some parts of Greece, though, tenuous threads of continuity can be traced from the Bronze Age to the Classical period and the later days of Greece's glory. Crete is an example, and although the island's history from the Bronze Age to the present has been turbulent, with lengthy periods of occupation by Romans, Arabs, Venetians and Turks, some Minoan blood may still run in modern Cretan veins.

ABSOLUTE CHRONOLOGY

A suggested absolute chronology for Minoan Crete, based on links with cultures that kept written records, was first attempted by Evans and his contemporaries, then slowly elaborated and refined over the decades of research and discoveries since Evans' time. The process was never easy. The number of exported and imported pieces is limited, so the sample is very small. The dates of objects removed from their place of origin must always allow some unknown and often unguessable margin of time to elapse for their travels or use before deposition in their archaeological context. Sometimes the contexts are vague – the stratigraphy may be confused, or, for earlier finds, the recording may be defective. Even in Egypt, for all its ubiquitous written texts, many contexts depend entirely on dates arrived at on archaeological grounds.

All these factors have to be taken into account in individual instances, and specific cases have often proved controversial. Both context and object should ideally be securely dated if they are to bear the weight of absolute chronology. Frequently the security of one or the other has given way under the intense scrutiny to which each has been subjected.

A major study by Peter Warren and Vronwy Hankey, *Aegean Bronze Age Chronology*,[6] provided a landmark. This reviewed the foreign links for Minoan Crete that had potential chronological significance and attempted to weigh up impartially how reliable the evidence was in each case, and how precise the chronological information could be thought to be. The study was gladly received by Aegean prehistorians, and the conclusions widely accepted. The dates arrived at were expressed within fairly broad limits, in recognition of the limited precision of the data available. Nonetheless, the whole was both felt by the authors, and generally accepted by the readers, to be greater than the sum of the parts. The chronology was viewed as articulating reasonably convincingly with that of Egypt and the Near East. It worked, which is why many scholars adopted it as a basis for their own publications.

Recently, though, the use of scientific methods to date the Thera eruption has given rise to a suggested revision backwards in time of about a hundred years in the heart of this chronology, and it is to scientific dating that we must now turn. On the face of it, it is perhaps rather surprising that science-based methods of dating have not already replaced the traditional

13 The sides of the caldera at Thera, formed during the Late Bronze Age eruption, show the thick layer of ash at the top that buried the site of Akrotiri.

archaeological approach. Radiocarbon dating has been used for some time, the techniques have been refined over the years and the corrections made to radiocarbon dates by the input from dendrochronology (the counting of tree-rings) have allowed much greater precision to be achieved. It has, however, been a long haul. Early enthusiasm from archaeologists working in the field or library for the results that their science-based colleagues could achieve was tempered by the difficulties encountered. For a long time precision was elusive. As a result, it has for many years been a commonplace in writings on Aegean prehistory to use dates based on radiocarbon dating for the Early Bronze Age, for which cross-references to other cultures are scarcely available, but to switch to dates based on such correlations for the Middle and Late Bronze Ages.

The future, and probably the near future, no doubt belongs to science-based dating, which will improve. In particular, large-scale dendrochronology projects continue to pour important new data into the picture. For the moment, though, the obvious way forward seems to be to attempt 'the marriage of science and archaeology', as Stuart Manning puts it in his important work *A Test of Time*.[7] This study sums up the scientific reasons for dating the Late Bronze Age eruption of Thera to 1628BC – a position already espoused by some scholars, but hotly disputed by others, who still maintain, as Warren and Hankey did, that a date late in the sixteenth century better fits the archaeological evidence. Warren suggests a date of about 1520BC.

The scientific evidence is from three main sources. First, the radiocarbon dates from the site of Akrotiri on Thera itself. Samples tested came from such things as seeds stored in houses and trapped there by volcanic ash. The dates given by these samples cluster impressively in the late seventeenth century BC, and Manning stresses that in all probability this is the correct date for the eruption. He admits, though, that the data are not unambiguous. Another clustering of dates in the mid-sixteenth century BC gives a second possibility for the date of the eruption, but in terms of probability it is much less likely. Manning states firmly that a date after about 1530/1520 is 'impossible' on the basis of the radiocarbon evidence.

Two other scientific approaches to the date of the Thera eruption have yielded interesting but tantalizing results. The second is based on the evidence for a volcanic event of some magnitude in the later seventeenth century BC that comes from certain traces, including particles of volcanic glass, trapped in the annual ice deposits in Greenland ice-cores. Is this glass from Thera? It has been analysed, but the significance of the results is disputed. Third, an anomaly in the growth patterns shown in tree-rings from various sites in the northern hemisphere indicates dramatic climatic change, also in the late seventeenth century BC. Emissions from a major volcanic eruption could have been the cause. Again, is this the Thera eruption showing up in tree-rings which are precisely dateable?

The scientists have had difficulty in linking these last two types of evidence specifically to the Thera eruption. If that connection is not accepted, we must conclude not only that a different volcano erupted at about this time (not in itself unlikely) but also that the Thera eruption itself left no mark in the tree-ring or ice-core record. No traces exist in either in the late sixteenth century BC.

Scientific approaches, then, can broadly be characterized as supporting a date of 1628BC, but also allowing the possibility of a date in the mid-sixteenth century BC, closer to, but still slightly earlier than, the conventional chronology. Let us now return to the archaeological evidence and the impact of these possibilities on our understanding of Minoan chronology.

The absolute date of the Thera eruption is important for two reasons. It provides a peg for the absolute chronology of Minoan Crete. It is widely accepted that in relative terms the eruption can be dated with confidence to a time towards the end of the LM IA period. A consensus exists, based on the study of pottery, that LM IA continued for perhaps another thirty years or so after the Thera eruption.

Its absolute date is also important is because of the implications for the articulation of the cultural sequences in the eastern Mediterranean and Egypt. On the conventional, lower chronology, MM III was connected with the Hyksos period in Egypt, LM IA had Second Intermediate Period links, while the succeeding LM IB period had connections with the time of Hatshepsut and Tuthmose III (1479–1425). This last series of links, detailed by Warren and Hankey, is, as Dickinson remarks, 'cumulatively impressive'.[8] LM II on this basis would have connections with the time of Amenhotep II.

Later synchronisms between LM IIIA1 and the time of Amenhotep III (1390–1352) are a matter for reasonable consensus. At about this time the 'traditional' and 'new' chronologies begin to get back into step. Manning brackets the end of LM IIIA1 to between 1390 and 1370BC.

In the succeeding period the chronologies truly reconverge with agreement about the Mycenaean pottery from Tel el-Amarna. A large number of Mycenaean vessels was imported to the site, and they are mostly Late Helladic IIIA2 in style, with some early LH IIIB. Although mainland Mycenaean, they are contemporary with Cretan LM IIIA2 pottery. This phase must therefore belong around the time of Akhenaten (1352–1336BC) or perhaps a little later, early in the reign of his successor Tutankhamun. The LM IIIA2 period has maximum limits of 1370 to 1330BC in Warren and Hankey's scheme, 1390 to 1300BC in that of Manning.

If, though, the higher chronology is correct, Thera erupted in about 1628BC and the LM IA period ended in around 1600BC or just a little later. Effectively the synchronisms of the LM I and LM II periods in Crete would have to be sought about one hundred years earlier in the sequences of Egyptian and Near Eastern cultures.

Some scholars have cited archaeological evidence in support of the high chronology. For example, Wolf-Dietrich Niemeier, excavating at Tel Kabri in Israel, found wall-paintings with clear stylistic associations with the Thera frescoes.[9] He argued that these should be dated to before 1600BC, and would therefore support the earlier dating for the Thera destruction.

This extends the argument on to the more difficult, if fascinating, ground of fresco painting, and here the site of Tel el-Dab'a certainly must be mentioned. Extraordinary frescoes of Minoan style were discovered on the site, unstratified, in a sort of rubbish deposit outside the building they originally decorated. They have stylistic links to the Thera frescoes, and therefore to the LM IA period, though some commentators have also suggested LM IB stylistic affinities. Their context is not precisely dated, and they must belong either to the late Hyksos period or to the early XVIIIth dynasty.

Manfred Bietak, excavator of this site, strongly upholds the low chronology. His argument is not based solely on the frescoes – and indeed it must be said that frescoes are not so chronologically sensitive as pottery, or at the very least the fine points of their development are not so well understood. Bietak cites the presence at Tel el-Dab'a of Thera pumice in an XVIIIth-dynasty context

14 Sherds of Mycenaean pottery from Tel el-Amarna.

as a piece of chronological evidence. Critics point out, though, that such pumice could have been floating in the eastern Mediterranean, or cast up on various shores, over any number of years. Perhaps more telling is the evidence from Cypriote White Slip pottery. Bietak argues that a type of Cypriote pottery known as White Slip I, found at Tel el-Dab'a in XVIIIth-dynasty contexts, is not found anywhere before the early XVIIIth dynasty. This is significant because a single example of White Slip I pottery was found in pre-eruption Thera. In Bietak's view this would strongly support an early XVIIIth-dynasty (i.e. late sixteenth-century) date for the eruption of Thera, and for the mature phase of LM IA.

The arguments continue to rage. Other experts maintain that Cypriote White Slip I pottery was made earlier in one part of Cyprus and later in the area that exported such pottery to Egypt. So the chronology of a different island, and the views of a different set of scholars, are drawn into the complex fray.

It is scarcely possible to do justice to such complexities in a short compass: for more detail the reader is referred to the specialist bibliography.[10] If we view the debate as polarized between the scientifically and the archaeologically derived dates, at the time of writing neither side can be said convincingly to have carried the field. In particular the 1628BC date poses very real problems for archaeologists studying the material culture of Crete during LM IB and LM II. The finds suggest that neither period was very long and that together they spanned no more than about one hundred years. The new dating for Thera, however, would make these periods stretch to some two hundred years and, at the same time, shorten preceding periods dramatically, squeezing earlier developments into an improbably short time-frame.

Because this is not satisfactory, because science has not yet carried all before it and made the late seventeenth-century date certain, and because the archaeologically derived synchronisms still carry much conviction, it seems that the best way forward is to adopt what Manning refers to as 'the compromise early chronology', which, as he remarks, is 'compatible with much of the large variety of scientific *and* archaeological data'. In essence the compromise position places the Thera eruption close to 1530–1520BC – the latest possible date allowed for by scientific methods, and one that does not greatly upset traditional synchronisms. In fact, it is very close to the 'traditional' view, and Warren's date of 1520BC. Perhaps, then, the two sides in the debate can be brought together on sixteenth-century ground.

We should in any case end this discussion by standing back for a moment from the search for precision, laudable though this is, to remind ourselves that before the challenge of Thera uncertainties about dating within ranges of some thirty to fifty years would have seemed commonplace. We should not be defeatist, but perhaps uncertainty is inevitable: when discussing chronological problems with colleagues working on the study of Roman pottery, from a truly historical period, it is salutary to learn that they would not expect precision within thirty years or so in the dates they are able to assign to particular pottery styles. Prehistorians have always accepted similar limitations. Even the Egyptian dates quoted here are given in Egyptological writings with the caveat that they are only approximate.

The chart on pages 6–7 shows the chronology adopted for this book. It basically derives from Warren and Hankey, though the date of the beginning of the Early Bronze Age is lowered, in line with recent scientific thinking. It also takes account of the 'compromise early chronology'. The result is schematic, and still requires the rubric that 'all dates are approximate'. We may hope that in the future, with the true marriage of science and archaeology, this will not be so.

Chapter Two

CRETE BEFORE THE PALACES

THIS CHAPTER surveys Cretan history from its earliest perceptible beginnings to the time at the start of the Bronze Age when the culture that we define as Minoan evolved, and takes the story through the period known as the Early Bronze Age, roughly the third millennium BC. The chapter ends at the beginning of the second millennium and the first phase of the Middle Bronze Age, with Crete poised on the brink of the First Palace period.

The long evolution of Minoan history that the prepalatial period represents is clearly fundamentally important, laying the foundation for the success story that, with the establishment of the palaces, Crete certainly became. Inevitably, then, the sorts of questions that are asked about the Early Minoan period seek to illuminate what came afterwards and why the island developed in the way that it did.

One obvious line of enquiry is whether the origins of the Minoan palaces, unique in the Aegean in their time, can be seen in this Early Bronze Age. At first investigators sought actual predecessors in the form of large and dominant buildings at various sites. More recently the question has been focused around the process of 'state formation' – the way in which certain places, notably the palace sites, became centralized controllers of various parts of the island. As we shall see in the next chapter, both the extent and the mechanisms of the regional control exerted by the First Palaces remain problematical. Nonetheless, they are certainly to be characterized as centres of power. Did Minoan society move at an inexorable, steady pace throughout the Early Bronze Age towards greater social stratification, and the emergence of elite groups who would control palatial power, or were fairly static periods interrupted by episodes of relatively sudden change?

A related question is that of regionalism in the island. It is possible to see in the Early Bronze Age archaeological record some distinct regional differences between various areas, and the extent to which these underpin later regionalism, or how or when they break down, are significant factors. We shall consider whether the First Palaces maintained or minimized such differences, but first must view the state of the island before their foundation.

Foreign interconnections are also important. Some scholars suggest that the idea of palaces is essentially foreign, imported into Crete rather than evolving from native traditions there. The Early Bronze Age relations of the island with the more developed civilizations of the Near East and Egypt must be considered. Closer to home, Cretan relations with the Aegean area are of interest too. The island's culture would become a major influence in the Aegean as the Bronze Age progressed: can we see the beginnings of this effect at this early time?

These lines of enquiry are not always easy to pursue. Essential evidence is often lacking, for two main reasons. The first is that many significant sites were excavated early in the twentieth century, when recording techniques were often insufficient. The second, more significant factor is that by definition from an archaeological point of view the earliest remains are going to be the most deeply overlaid and the most frequently destroyed in later building processes. This is particularly true at long-lived settlements such as the palace sites. Here scraps of evidence support a general conviction that much more must have existed. Places abandoned during the period under discussion give better evidence, and fill out our picture of what life was like in those that went on to further success.

These broader historical questions, which hope to tease out some sense of process and progress, should take us beyond simple description of material culture. Yet a close look at some of the sites and artefacts is well worthwhile. It would be wrong to view this period of a millennium purely as a precursor – an extraordinarily long overture. Instead it is a time that sees the Cretans in various parts of the island finding their feet in a remarkably steady way, producing objects that are interesting and admirable in their own right, and building various structures for both the living and the dead. Already, then, we are talking about a rich material culture, and a people whose way of life we can hope to evoke and at least partially understand.

The Earliest Inhabitants

While groups of people may have visited Crete, or even lived there, before Neolithic times, our earliest reliable evidence for the first populations in the island comes from around the beginning of the Neolithic period. Excavation at Knossos has revealed the existence of a settlement there from around (perhaps slightly before) 7000BC. This is the earliest known permanent settlement of an Aegean island. The inhabitants seem to have been colonists from abroad, who probably arrived with some prior knowledge that Crete was an agriculturally promising land. They used types of bread wheat which are attested in Anatolia, but not, so far as we know, on the Greek mainland at this time, and this may give a clue as to the direction from which they originally came.

The settlement of Knossos saw the beginning of a remarkably long and essentially unbroken chain of occupation of the area – amounting, indeed, to more than nine thousand years of human history, if modern Herakleion is viewed as the latter part of the same phenomenon. Knossos, then, was certainly destined to be a success; however, the area of occupation was at first small, amounting to only about 3 ha (7.4 acres). Early Neolithic sites have only rarely been recognized elsewhere in Crete, though some caves show signs of habitation, and the pottery from the Lera cave, on the Akrotiri peninsula near Chania, shows many similarities to that of Knossos, although it is about 100 km (60 miles) away.

It seems that for some generations settlements remained small, scattered and isolated, perhaps quite precarious in terms of survival. Only with the Final Neolithic period, in the latter part of the fourth millennium BC, do surveys show an increase in the number and types of sites, with evidence for both caves and built settlements in west Crete in the Chania region; in south central Crete on and around the Mesara Plain, including a relatively sizeable – some 5.6 ha (13.8 acres) – settlement at Phaistos; on the north coast not only at Knossos, where again Final Neolithic occupation seems to cover an area in excess of 5 ha (12.4 acres), but also further east in the Istron area and beyond; on the offshore island of Pseira; and, inland, on and around the Lasithi plateau. The pattern of sites in fact means that all the different types of Cretan terrain, from coast to mountain, were inhabited, though the sites that were to flourish later, such as Knossos and Phaistos, already show the advantages of their position.

We know something of life on Crete towards the end of the Neolithic period. People were living in very small communities, often only the size of hamlets or even sometimes just seasonally occupied camps. The settlements such as those at Knossos and Phaistos consisted of groups of simple rectangular houses of rubble, mud-brick and wood construction with beaten earth floors and earthen hearths. Burials have only occasionally been found, but were probably mostly simple inhumations, frequently using natural rocky crevasses or caves. Areas for religious ritual have not been identified, though figurines of terracotta and stone come from domestic contexts, often near the hearths in the houses, and perhaps show some form of house cult.

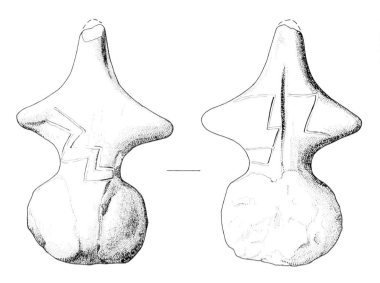

15 Drawing of a Neolithic figurine found at Knossos.

In view of the fact that even in the Final Neolithic period the settlements in Crete were relatively small and scattered, it is interesting to note that aspects of material culture, particularly pottery and figurines, have affinities not only among the sites on the island but also in the broader eastern Mediterranean world. Quite why there should be a sort of commonality of culture, and what is sometimes described as an 'international spirit' at this time, remains something of a puzzle. There may have been mechanisms for contacts which we cannot now reconstruct: the fact of colonization at Knossos itself presupposes the ability to make purposeful journeys over long distances, and we know, for example, that from the beginning of the Neolithic period the Cretans were using obsidian from Melos. This naturally occurring volcanic glass could be chipped to form blades and was therefore a desirable commodity, which must have been taken from Melos by ship. Similarities in material culture may thus in some instances be attributed to real contacts and to mutual influences, but in others it is possible that they are more or less coincidental, indicative only of common responses to a life that presented similar problems throughout the lands of the Mediterranean.

Early Minoan I

The Early Minoan I (EM I) period seems to have begun about 3200BC. A defining factor is the introduction of bronze technology, since the Early Minoan period is part of the Early Bronze Age in the Aegean as a whole. However, the production and use of bronze tools and weapons began gradually in Crete, overlapping with the use of stone, and particularly of obsidian, for some considerable time.

In pottery, too, certain traditions carried on seamlessly from Final Neolithic production, but the introduction of painted wares can be used to mark definably Minoan pottery styles. Similarly, while there was no revolution in building techniques, some types of construction that we can characterize as typically Minoan now appear: the tholos tombs of the Mesara Plain (see page 42) are a notable example. In fact our knowledge of the EM I period derives largely from burials, and information from excavated settlements is minimal. EM I was, though, a time of huge expansion. The number of sites revealed by surveys shows a big increase throughout the island.

EARLY MINOAN I SETTLEMENTS

What, then, were EM I settlements like? While some caves inhabited in the Final Neolithic period ceased to be used, others were still occupied. Open sites similarly often show continuity, but again new ones were created. Some sites continued to be seasonal, depending presumably on the use of summer pastures for sheep and goats. Pastoralism seems to increase from the Final Neolithic time onwards – the number of sheep and goat bones recovered archaeologically increases greatly. Other agricultural factors no doubt encouraged the formation of new settlements in previously uninhabited areas, or the expansion of older settlements as the population grew. These probably included the so-called 'secondary products revolution' – that is, the exploitation of herds not just for meat, but also for milk, cheese, wool and hides, the processing of which required fixed places dedicated to such purposes. Improvements in tools and the ability to plough heavy soils perhaps encouraged the cultivation of new crops, including olives and grapes.

Larger, open settlements near to good agricultural land are of course represented by the palace sites, and both the hill of Knossos and the Phaistos ridge no doubt saw flourishing occupation of fairly simple houses, though the precise nature of these is lost to us. It seems these major sites were noticeably bigger than the scattered settlements in their surrounding countryside. Evidence for the nature of a small farmstead or seasonally occupied camp comes from Debla, the single EM I settlement site that has been excavated and published. It lies in west Crete, in the mountains south of Chania, and consisted of only two or three single-roomed structures. The people there were processing wheat, barley and oats and herding sheep and goats.

The picture is of a simple lifestyle, mainly dictated by agricultural activities. The material from tombs adds more depth to the picture.

EARLY MINOAN I CEMETERY EVIDENCE

Evidence from EM I burials is of great importance because it is plentiful – much more plentiful than settlement evidence. It gives some idea of the

16 Remains of a pair of tholos tombs at Lenda in south-west Crete. The tombs seem to have been used from EM I to MM IB.

probable location and size of nearby settlements even where these are not known, and it includes well-preserved artefacts indicative of the arts and crafts of the time. Regional differences, too, emerge clearly from EM I burial practices.

In north Crete burials were mainly simple inhumations grouped together in caves or rock shelters, accompanied by a small number of vases, obsidian blades, sometimes copper artefacts and occasional stone figurines. In southern Crete communal inhumation accompanied by a range of artefacts was also practised, but in a very specific tomb type – the circular tholos tomb. Keith Branigan, whose studies are fundamental to our understanding of these tombs, has defined a Minoan tholos as a 'circular, thick-walled, above-ground structure with a single doorway'.[1] He thinks that many, but perhaps not all, were fully vaulted in stone. Some had a complex of regular ante-chambers, some a single ante-chamber, some none at all.

About seventy-five tholoi are known in southern Crete in and around the Mesara Plain; on an island-wide basis, and counting all possible scraps of evidence, the total rises to ninety-four. Roughly one half of the southern examples which preserve dating evidence (some twenty-five tombs) were built in EM I, and these are generally the southernmost ones, clustering on the south side of the Mesara Plain and the north slopes of the Asterousia Mountains. Tholoi were often long-lived, with burials being made in them for periods that could be as lengthy as eight or even ten centuries. Those built in EM I are relatively small – often less than 5.5 m (18 ft) in diameter. EM II tombs include larger examples, while those begun in EM III–MM I tend to be smaller again.

The preservation of skeletons in the tholoi is not usually good, partly because of tomb robbing and partly because of their treatment in antiquity. Older bones were disturbed each time a new burial was put into the tomb; the charring of certain bones perhaps indicates fumigation processes, and various other ritual activities seem to have resulted in selective storage of skulls, removal of some bones and chopping or even grinding of others.

The paved areas that are a feature of some cemeteries may have been the site of funerary rituals accompanying a new inhumation, or involving the secondary processing of bones from previous burials. It is possible, too, that they were an important focus of the life of the community. We do not always have evidence for the settlements served by the tombs, but where we do it is clear that the cemeteries were generally very close. It may be, then, that these long-lived tombs near to the village were important for the sense of continuity in the community, and their paved areas were the setting for ritual activities both funerary and perhaps also non-funerary. Pavements may, for example, suggest areas for dancing, and we know from later representations that dance was an important element in Minoan ritual.

Interestingly, though, the doorways of the tombs usually face to the east, and the settlements lie to the west of the cemeteries. The living are therefore not overlooked by the dead, perhaps in a conscious effort to separate the two realms. The doorways of the tholoi are also quite small and constricted – inconveniently so, it might be thought, for the process of making burials within them, but perhaps again with some underlying notion of keeping the dead in their proper place. The limited evidence indicates that bodies were laid in the tombs on an east–west alignment, their heads to the east. It may be that the doorways were specifically aligned to face the rising sun.

We shall return to tholos tombs later, but, before leaving EM I, might mention that one tholos of this period has been found in north Crete, at Krasi. This is of interest to scholars who suggest that Cretan tholoi derive from Cycladic grave types – though the resemblance is not close. Perhaps more convincing is the argument that sees them as akin to artificial caves. They appear to be a Cretan invention, and those in the north of the island are mostly later: tholos building really does seem to begin in the Mesara region.

In marked contrast, Cycladic influence is pervasive at the cemetery site of Ayia Photia, on the north coast of Crete east of Siteia. The differences between tombs at this site and the Mesara tholoi clearly show regional variation within Crete at the beginning of the Early Bronze Age, and this presumably extended to the land of the living as well as that of the dead.

Ayia Photia is a very large and important cemetery. It contained 252 tombs that have been excavated, and the excavators estimated that about 50 more originally existed. In form the graves were generally simple shallow oval shapes cut into the bedrock, with a small doorway on the north side and therefore facing out to sea. An upright slab closed the door, and a small paved elliptical area in front of this sometimes contained a single vase, usually a chalice of so-called Pyrgos Ware. In the tomb chamber sea-pebbles covered the floor, and on these the body was laid, accompanied by pottery and sometimes other things. Bronze daggers, knives, fish-hooks, chisels, a single sword and a single socketed axe, two lead zoomorphic amulets, obsidian blades, stone axes and a few stone vases were among the finds.

The Cycladic character of the cemetery is very striking. The type of grave is found in the Cyclades, but differs from contemporary Cretan graves elsewhere, and the objects from the cemetery are in many instances either Cycladic imports, or strongly influenced by Cycladic types. In fact about 90 per cent of the pottery is technically and stylistically indistinguishable from Cycladic products.[2] Mineralogical analysis has not yet proved Cycladic manufacture, but the probability must be that the pottery was imported from the Cyclades – or if made in Crete, made by Cycladic potters.

The metal objects, too, mostly look Cycladic, and include a very typically Cycladic kind of dagger with raised mid-rib. Analysis indicates a Cycladic source for the copper, but this is not so significant – analyses show that the Cyclades, and particularly the island of Kythnos, seem to have been the main source of both copper and silver for Crete at this period. Nonetheless the graves also included crucibles for metal-working. Not only are these of a Cycladic type, but the inclusion of such artefacts in graves is a Cycladic custom. In addition the 'killing' of daggers seems to be a Cycladic practice: the weapons were bent and deformed before burial so that they could not be of further use.

The chronological span of the cemetery is mainly – and it has recently been suggested perhaps exclusively – EM I, though the excavators dated some finds to EM II. In any case it may not have been used for much more than a century in absolute terms. This relatively short time-span is of significance since, with some 300 burials, the Ayia Photia cemetery is the largest excavated cemetery in the first phase of the Early Bronze Age Aegean, and is much larger than any known burial site in the Cyclades. A fairly large settlement would have been required to lead to so many burials within a century, and it has been estimated that a minimum of fifteen families must have lived in the settlement. This would make a larger village than appears to have been characteristic of Crete at this time. The settlement has not been found, but may lie under the nearby modern village.

It seems that Ayia Photia should certainly be described as a Cycladic 'colony'. Presumably Cycladic traders took advantage of a previously uninhabited but agriculturally quite rich area of Crete, and formed a settlement. The reason for the demise of Ayia Photia is not clear, but it may have been in some way overtaken by native Cretan developments. The growth of Mochlos as a major trading centre may have challenged its position, and the Cycladic element in the population was presumably either expelled or subsumed. Certainly, as we shall see, in the succeeding EM II period Cycladic imports and influences were also marked at Archanes in central Crete, and even penetrated as far south as the Mesara region – many Cycladic figurines and artefacts have been found in the Mesara tholoi. These finds are different from those of Ayia Photia, however, in that they were found within a thoroughly Minoan context. They are therefore consistent with trade, but do not imply a Cycladic element in the population, as Ayia Photia does.

Early Minoan II

The Early Minoan II (EM II) period can be seen as one of consolidation of what had gone before, with a balance reached between fully developed agriculture and herding. The new crops, particularly olives and grapes, were established. These conditions encouraged the development of the relatively large open settlements near to arable land. Sites such as Knossos and Phaistos therefore became established in their position at the top of local settlement hierarchies, though the evidence does not show them increasing in size at this time. However, the number of settlements continues to grow, though at a slower rate than before, throughout the island, and the size of the settlements lower down the hierarchy also often increases.

The technology of metal-working advanced at this time, with bronze-working becoming fully established and a wider range of objects being produced. Other areas of craftsmanship also developed, implying the existence of craft specialists, on either a full- or part-time basis. Seafarers, too, must have been engaged in procuring the raw materials needed for such activities, and using them for barter or exchange. Society was obviously developing a level of complexity beyond that involved simply in sustaining life from agricultural activities, though life for most people must still have depended very directly on the demands made by the cultivation of the land.

EARLY MINOAN II SETTLEMENTS

At Myrtos-Fournou Korifi, a hamlet in south-east Crete that was built and destroyed by fire in the EM II period has been excavated. This site provides some of our best evidence for life in Crete at this time.[3]

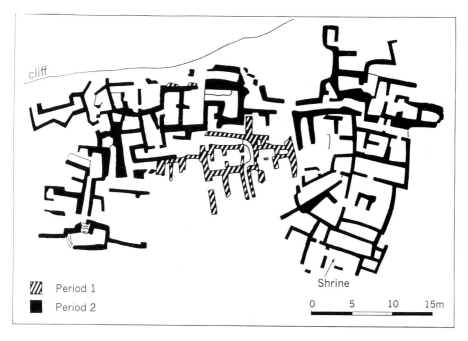

cliff

▨ Period 1
■ Period 2

Shrine

0   5   10   15m

17 Plan of the settlement of Myrtos-Fournou Korifi.

Built on a low hill on the south-east coast of Crete, overlooking the Libyan Sea, the hamlet was about 50 m (164 ft) from north to south and 25 m (82 ft) from east to west, and was surrounded by a wall on all but the east side, where the ground fell away precipitously. The main entrance was a door protected by a small tower on the southern, seaward side. Some five or six irregularly shaped and single-storeyed houses seem to be represented by the densely packed cluster of rooms that the excavations revealed. They were built of undressed stone, sometimes with mud-brick superstructures, and had flat roofs of timber, reeds and coarse plaster.

Within the houses some rooms had cooking areas including a hearth or cooking hole and some had built-in benches and cupboards for pottery and other household items. Storage rooms with large jars or pithoi presumably held quantities of agricultural produce, and are thoroughly typical of residences, from the palace to the simple village house, throughout Minoan history. Loom-weights indicate domestic textile production, and turntables show that pottery was made at Myrtos too. Rooms at the south-west corner of the settlement were identified as a shrine, their contents including the engaging terracotta 'goddess', who holds a water-jug. Water would presumably have had to be fetched from some distance to the arid hill-top site of the village, since there is no evidence of cisterns there, and this might explain why the figurine cradles her water-jug in the crook of her arm like a baby.

The people of Myrtos had grain crops, grapes and olives in their store-rooms, and their animals included cattle, pigs and a predominance of sheep and goats. They presumably farmed the reasonably favourable and fertile land in the immediate vicinity of the settlement, which would have been more well-watered in antiquity than it is today. Estimation of the population is difficult, with suggestions ranging from as few as twenty-five to thirty inhabitants to perhaps fifty or a hundred people.

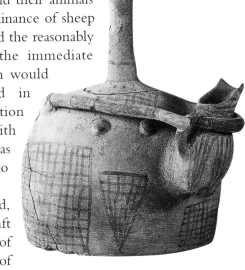

18 The 'goddess' of Myrtos.

Life must have been very hard, with farming, fishing and craft production taking up the majority of everyone's time, but the presence of two *kernoi* – the stones with circular depressions that again feature at all Minoan sites both great and small – may be a sign of leisure activity. Such stones are sometimes identified as offering tables for small quantities of agricultural produce, but an alternative idea is that they were gaming boards. Their position at the edge of a communal courtyard at Myrtos-Fournou Korifi makes this an attractive suggestion, conjuring up a picture of leisure at the long day's end – perhaps particularly for the very old or the very young.

While life was characterized by an essential simplicity, one aspect it had at Myrtos that begins our knowledge of another typically Minoan phenomenon is the use of seals and sealings to secure, identify and control the storage and movement of goods and commodities. The system became both complex and sophisticated when used by the great Cretan palaces on an island-wide basis. At Myrtos stone stamp-seals and one clay sealing – a lump of clay from a fastening with the seal impression preserved – are the first securely dated examples of this practice that we know from Minoan Crete.

The Myrtos-Fournou Korifi settlement was destroyed by fire at the end of EM II, so we cannot tell how the site might have developed. The fact that it was not re-inhabited may partly have been due to the difficulties of its position, and particularly the lack of a truly convenient water supply.

A similar site at Trypeti, also on a hill-top on the south coast of Crete, is currently being excavated, and some forty-six rooms have been revealed in houses around a broad central street. The houses had large central rooms with hearths, storage cupboards and benches, and these were surrounded by smaller store-rooms. Finds included evidence for the food of the inhabitants, with bones of sheep or goats, cattle and pigs, along with birds and hare. Vegetable remains were of wheat, barley, figs, peas and vetch, while snail-shells, sea-shells and fish-bones added to the picture of a varied diet. Two seals and a sealing have also been found at this interesting site, which was apparently founded in EM I and went on to MM I, but flourished in the EM II period. The completion of excavation and publication will add considerably to our knowledge of prepalatial settlements.

At more favourable sites, including Knossos, Phaistos, Mallia, Ayia Triadha and Gournia, remains of EM II houses have been found, but in these instances the later success and development of the settlements mean that this early phase is only patchily recoverable. No specific architectural evidence for the kind of building that might later turn into a palace has been found. The identification of such a building was, though, claimed by Richard Seager, an early excavator of the Minoan settlement of Vasiliki on the isthmus of Ierapetra.

Excavating here in 1906, Seager thought that he had found a sort of primitive palace, flourishing in the EM II period, which he called 'the House on the Hill'. A reassessment by Antonis Zois over many years of excavation in the 1980s and 1990s, has shown, however, that Seager was conflating a group of houses on the hill-top into one. In fact two distinct phases are represented within EM II, and in both EM IIA and EM IIB up to about six houses were clustered together in the excavated area. Vasiliki should therefore be viewed as a village rather than a single building. The houses of EM IIA are arranged touching each other in a close-knit formation. In EM IIB the paved court at the heart of the site seems to act as a sort of village square, with houses grouped round it. The excavator suggests that up to about two hundred people may have lived in the village, with agriculture, of course, as their main occupation. The characteristic mottled pottery known as Vasiliki Ware, though first identified on the site, was not necessarily made there: recent work suggests that the pottery may have had two main centres of production, their precise location as yet unknown, from which it was distributed widely around the island in EM IIB.

Vasiliki continued to be occupied in both the First and Second Palace periods. It cannot now be used as evidence for an early palace, and indeed is described as showing a sort of egalitarian arrangement of houses. Nonetheless some of the architectural remains are substantial and impressive. This is particularly true of the basement structures of the 'Red House', so called because of the coating of red-painted lime-plaster that still survives in places on the walls. These were solidly built, with thick walls of rough rubble construction which still preserve the holes where timber beams must have

19 Part of the 'Red House' of Vasiliki, showing the thick rubble walls, the red plaster and the holes left by timber beams.

been. Perhaps constructed with earthquakes in mind, they have withstood exposure to wind and weather remarkably well. While the evidence may not indicate any hierarchical ranking within the houses at Vasiliki, those areas which are well preserved give an impression of substance, as though the whole group of houses was inhabited by people of more-than-average wealth. Certainly the houses seem larger, more spaciously constructed and more rectilinear in layout than those of Myrtos-Fournou Korifi. The evidence for upper storeys also indicates greater complexity.

The position of Vasiliki allowed it to dominate the isthmus of Ierapetra, where the island of Crete is narrow and the journey from north to south easily made. The position of other sites of the period may also have been determined by communications rather than by strictly agricultural consider-ations. Mochlos, now an island but a peninsula in the Bronze Age, is a case in point. First settled in EM IB, perhaps by groups of people from central Crete, it became an extensive settlement in EM II–III, and remains of substantial houses have been found in places beneath the settlement of the LM IB period. The inhabitants had the advantage of rich agricultural land nearby, but it is clear that Mochlos was important as a harbour. Its position allowed ships to shelter on either side of the peninsula, depending on prevailing winds. Recent studies have characterized Mochlos as a 'gateway community' for eastern Crete, its ships bringing imports from the Cyclades and the eastern Mediterranean. Among these were very large quantities of obsidian from the island of Melos. Manufacturing also seems to have flourished there, with evidence for the production of stone vases and gold jewellery. The rich tombs of the Mochlos cemetery suggest the wealth of some inhabitants, and provide good evidence for the emergence of social ranking in prepalatial Crete, as we shall see.

EARLY MINOAN II CEMETERY EVIDENCE

Burials in the EM II period still show marked regional variation. The tholos tomb continues to be typical of southern Crete and the Mesara region, while in the north rectangular house-tombs are the norm. These are built tombs that were constructed like houses of stone, wood and mud-brick. They contained a room or rooms in which the dead were originally buried in the ground, though later large jars and terracotta larnakes or coffins were used to contain them. The very important and extraordinarily long-lived cemetery at Phourni on the outskirts of Archanes in central Crete begins in this period, and here a certain amalgamation of tomb types and burial customs occurs.

Some tholos tombs can be shown to be EM II constructions, and the average size of these is greater than those of the preceding phase. The argument about whether such tombs were fully vaulted in stone, as Branigan and others believe, remains essentially unresolved due to lack of evidence. Few of the excavated tholoi apparently contained enough fallen stone to have vaulted the space completely. However, this could easily have been the result of plundering, and the removal of stone for other building purposes. Moreover, corbelled lower walls, where the courses of stone are arranged to overhang inwards, would not have been necessary if a plain enclosure wall were intended, with roofing of different materials such as wood and packed earth. Such roofs may have existed, but it remains perfectly possible that some, perhaps most, of the tholos tombs were fully vaulted in stone.

The tombs, many with paved courtyards and ancillary buildings, received an array of offerings during the EM II period, though their long-lived nature, combined with the fact that many have been plundered, means that it is not always easy to isolate these specifically. Nonetheless, we can work out that the dead were usually accompanied by a few pottery vases: jugs, cups or bowls apparently of an everyday nature; items of personal adornment in gold

20 The remains of a large tholos tomb at Platanos, probably used between EM II and MM II.

and other materials including beads, pendants and diadems; seal-stones; bronze tools, toilet articles or weapons – daggers are frequently found – stone vases and sometimes a stone figurine.

In the house-tombs of the north, too, long usage for communal burials makes specific dating of finds difficult, and often only a rather generalized EM II–MM I bracket can be quoted. At Mochlos, the largest and best-studied cemetery of such tombs, social differentiation seems to be apparent between the wealthy tombs of the west terrace and the smaller, less elaborately built and provided tombs of the south slope. Fine jewellery of the EM II period comes from Mochlos tomb I, which included beads of various shapes in gold, amethyst and rock-crystal. Pottery, stone vases and bronzes were among the other finds from this tomb. Elsewhere in the Mochlos cemetery elaborate jewellery in sheet gold, often in flower shapes, has been attributed to this phase, as has an extensive range of stone vases. Some gold jewellery tucked into a small silver vase was found next to tomb VI. Recent restudy of the Mochlos tombs combines with new evidence from the EM II–III settlement to confirm the significance of the site in the prepalatial period.[4]

We should at this point visit another important site, indeed one of the most remarkable archaeological sites in the whole of Crete. On a hill-top near to the town of Archanes lies the Phourni cemetery. Excavated from 1964 onwards, the cemetery contains burials of various types, beginning in

21 The rectangular house-tombs of the west terrace at Mochlos were solidly built. This seems to have been the richest part of the prepalatial cemetery.

EM II and continuing until the very end of the Minoan period, thus representing an astounding and continuous 1,800 years of Minoan history. It is a rich source of information.[5]

Tholos tomb E at Phourni was built during EM II. Its upper part had been damaged by later cultivation of the area but the lower part survived, including the doorway on the east, flanked with two monolithic stones. Inside an undisturbed EM IIA stratum was found, with above it an MM IA–IIB level (which followed after a gap of some two hundred years).

The EM II burials were levelled for the formation of the upper burial layer, and so were not individually preserved, but the number of interments must have been considerable as no fewer than 117 funerary offerings were found. These included stone and ivory seals, ivory amulets, gold jewellery and other rich finds. Two clay larnakes or sarcophagi came to light, but most bodies must simply have been laid on the ground.

Construction of tholos tomb C at Phourni was dated by the excavators to EM III, but a recent study has shown that the earliest burial layer in the tomb is of EM IIA date, underlying an EM III–MM IA level. The tomb was of the Mesara type, and it is certain that it was fully vaulted in stone. It had a low doorway on the east side and, uniquely, a window and a built hearth. The window was used to make offerings to the dead in the LM IIIA2–B period, about a thousand years after the tomb ceased to be used. These offerings were apparently pushed through a window, showing that the tomb was still intact at this time and the dead within it were considered worthy of reverence.

Finds in the lower level lay among a layer of stones that covered the floor of the tomb, and included pottery, bronzes, jewellery in gold and silver and some seals and pendants. Perhaps most remarkable, though, was a group

22 The southern area of the cemetery of Phourni at Archanes, with part of one of the rectangular burial buildings, the badly preserved remains of tholos tomb E and the modern buildings of Archanes in the background.

of about twelve Cycladic marble figurines, two intact, the others fragmentary. Most of these were probably imports from the Cyclades, though it has been suggested that Cycladic craftsmen may have worked at Archanes. Certainly a figurine in bone could have been made in Crete in imitation of Cycladic examples.

EM II emerges from both the settlement and the cemetery evidence as a long and productive period, which saw the island of Crete flourishing. Contacts abroad, particularly with the Cyclades, were firmly established at this time. Life seems to have differed from region to region, but movements of pottery show that communication routes within the island were established. There is little direct evidence for internal warfare, though the planning of some sites

23 Tholos tomb C in the Phourni cemetery, showing the low door. The vault was originally completed in stone.

may have included considerations of defence and control. Destructions by fire occurred at the end of the EM II period, and some sites, such as Myrtos-Fournou Korifi, were abandoned at this time. Elsewhere, including at Knossos, the transition to EM III was not marked by any episodes of destruction.

Early Minoan III and Middle Minoan IA

Early Minoan III (EM III) seems to have been a relatively short period. It has been closely defined at Knossos, and indeed remains of three substantial houses beneath the West Court of the palace show clearly that a flourishing town existed on the Kephala hill at this time. Elsewhere, too, EM III has been recognized as a distinct phase, though material belonging exclusively to it has sometimes proved difficult to isolate. Groups of material from indefinite and long-lived contexts are sometimes designated as EM II/III, while studies of various types of artefact, such as seal-stones, often use an EM III/MM IA classification. This latter grouping partly also reflects the fact that EM III pottery styles continued in use in east Crete after the new polychromy characteristic of MM IA had been introduced in the centre of the island.

While, then, there is no doubt that EM III exists as a stratigraphically distinct period, there is something to be said for viewing it together with the following period. Between them EM III/MM IA constitute a time of quickening of culture in Crete before the foundation of the palaces at the beginning of MM IB.

As we have noted, one of the peculiarities of the Evans chronological system as actually applied to Minoan Crete is that the foundation of the palaces occurs at the beginning of MM IB – not at the apparently more important-sounding divide between the Early and Middle Minoan periods, when great changes might be expected to take place. This is largely due to the borrowing of the tripartite chronological system from Egypt. The beginning of the Middle Bronze Age, and the MM IA period, actually continues seamlessly from EM III and in some types of material no real division can be seen.

Pottery, as usual, is the most sensitive indicator, and at Knossos MM IA pottery has recently been closely defined. Inheriting the use of light paint on a dark background from the EM III period, the beginnings of polychromy, with added red and white paint, are a Knossian phenomenon, and much slower to catch on elsewhere in the island. Pottery is not at this stage thrown on a wheel, though some turning devices seem to have been used for certain shapes.

EARLY MINOAN III AND MIDDLE MINOAN IA SETTLEMENTS

Crete occupies a unique place in the Aegean Bronze Age because the island enjoyed more or less peaceful cultural continuity from the Early to the Middle Bronze Age. Signs of destruction and abandonment in EM III have been emphasized by some scholars, who feel that the island was subsequently re-invigorated by foreign influences leading to the foundation of the palaces there, but in fact it seems that disruption was much less marked than in the Cyclades and on the Greek mainland. The Cyclades experienced some turmoil in the Early Cycladic III period, and the Greek mainland suffered a reverse at the end of Early Helladic II from which it would take centuries to recover. In Crete, though, in spite of some destructions and abandonments at the end of EM II, it is possible to argue for a general trend of population growth and developing richness and prosperity in the EM III period, and for a time of expansion in MM IA.

This is certainly the case at Knossos, where progress throughout the Early Bronze Age can be seen as cumulative, even if not evenly paced. Here the EM III period seems to have been one of relative isolation, perhaps due to problems in the Cycladic islands with which the site had previously been in contact. The settlement in MM IA, however, grew in size. It is known only from scraps of excavated evidence, but was clearly a well-established and flourishing place, which provided a springboard for the foundation of the palace. Phaistos and Mallia similarly were extensive sites by the MM IA period, providing suitable support systems for the foundation of the palaces.

Some settlements that were to become important, though they would not develop major palaces, were also quite substantial: in east Crete evidence comes from Palaikastro, Gournia, Vasiliki and Mochlos. Smaller sites include villages: Myrtos-Pyrgos on the south coast of the island and Patrikies near to Phaistos are examples. Some smaller sites that are essentially single buildings of the MM IA period are, though, unusual. We might mention in this context the substantial building at Ayia Photia, east of Siteia, and the so-called Oval House at Chamaizi, also near to Siteia but lying to the west.

The large, neatly laid-out, rectangular building at Ayia Photia is of MM IA date, situated on a headland and fortified by a strong wall around its seaward side. Some thirty-seven rooms and areas are arranged around a primitive central court, in a layout suggesting to some observers a sort of short-lived and experimental prototype for a palace. The excavators surmise that the building could have been a dwelling for a number of families or a small clan, with agricultural wealth deriving from nearby fertile land.

Ayia Photia is unique in layout for its time, and so, for different reasons, is the building crowning a small peak at Chamaizi. Here a substantial oval wall encloses a series of well-built rooms. Because of its location Chamaizi used to be regarded as a possible peak sanctuary – though a very untypical one. (Peak sanctuaries are described on pages 58–60.) Restudy has shown that in fact it is much more likely to be a house, perhaps, like the building at Ayia Photia, inhabited by an extended family or clan. Its contents – pottery, storage jars, loom-weights, tools and so on – were essentially domestic in nature and its unusual form was dictated by the lie of the land.

The Cretan landscape in the period immediately before the emergence of the palaces, then, was filled with a series of sites, from towns to villages and hamlets and occasional substantial but apparently fairly isolated structures. Fortification or defensive considerations may have figured in the siting or construction of a number of these sites: as well as the fortification of isolated structures Gournia and Mallia have traces of what seem to be defensive walls.

EARLY MINOAN III AND MIDDLE MINOAN IA CEMETERY EVIDENCE
The long-lived Phourni cemetery has important burials of both EM III and MM IA date, and it is to this site that we must turn first for evidence for the burial customs of the time. Tholos tomb C in the Phourni cemetery had an upper burial layer attributed by the excavators to the EM III period, though some of the finds may be of MM IA date, illustrating the difficulties of separating the two phases. Eleven sarcophagi were found in this upper level, all rectangular apart from one bathtub-shaped example and a single burial pithos. Eighteen people were buried in these containers: most singly, but the pithos and one sarcophagus contained two bodies and two of the sarcophagi contained three bodies. Other burials had been made between the sarcophagi and near to the entrance of the tomb, bringing the total of dead to forty-five. Pottery and bronze items were found with these burials, along with some seals and pendants. The funerary objects were not put inside the burial containers, but accompanied them in the ground.

Tholos tomb E at Phourni came back into use in the MM IA period, and burials were made in it throughout protopalatial times. Other rectangular funerary buildings at this site began to be used in MM 1A. Phourni therefore shows remarkable continuity from late prepalatial into protopalatial times, with an amalgamation of the use of tholos tombs and rectilinear funerary structures.

Elsewhere in Crete both tholos and house-type tombs continued to be used during MM IA. In the south many of the rich objects from the Mesara tombs must date from MM IA, though their contents were unstratified and are therefore usually more broadly dated. The same is true of the house-tombs at Mochlos.

By the end of MM IA the main period of use of the tholos tombs of Mesara was over, perhaps partly because of depopulation of more marginal

24 The corner of the rectangular funerary building at Chrysolakkos, north of the palace at Mallia, showing the fine ashlar construction contrasting to the jumbled remains of walls within.

areas as the population moved to bigger centres. A change in burial customs, though, is also a factor here: the increasing popularity of pithos and larnax burials show an increased sense of individuality in interments, though these were still made in group tombs.

We might end this brief survey of EM III–MM IA burial customs by mentioning a unique burial building, the rectangular Chrysolakkos funerary complex at Mallia. This was essentially constructed in MM IA, though there was evidence within it for an earlier phase. The complex lies near to the sea, north of the site later occupied by the palace and in the area of rocky coastline that had traditionally been used for burials by the inhabitants of Mallia from the earliest times. It is a well-built structure on an impressive scale, and its limestone ashlar facade can claim to be the earliest example of this style of masonry on Crete. The interior consisted of small rooms or compartments, within which burials were made. The internal arrangements suffered, though, at the hands of plunderers. The name Chrysolakkos – 'gold pit' – clearly shows that the location had a reputation as a source for rich finds, and so the way in which it was used is now scarcely recoverable. The bee-pendant was one of the few precious objects to evade the plunderers' eyes: we will return to this later as it is of protopalatial date, and the Chrysolakkos complex certainly continued in use at the time of the First Palaces.

Religion in the Period before the Palaces

We have already noted the evidence indicating the use of paved areas near to tholos tombs as centres for group ritual activity in the Early Minoan period.

Such rituals may have grown out of some sort of cult of the dead, and were perhaps extended to include the whole village community in rituals or festivals that were independent of funerary rites. Elsewhere we may suppose that shrines and sanctuaries existed in both natural locations and within the built environment, as they did in later Minoan times. Shrines such as that identified at Myrtos-Fournou Korifi begin the tradition of what seem to be essentially 'private' cult-places within domestic settings, their use presumably confined to a small number of people. Group cult activities probably occurred in the sanctuaries in natural locations, particularly peak sanctuaries and sacred caves.

It would seem probable that certain caves were regarded as sacred from the earliest times, though in fact evidence for Early Minoan cult use of caves is sparse. The picture is also complicated by the fact that caves were used as habitation sites in the Neolithic era, and for burials in the Early Minoan period. However, where Early Minoan pottery is found in caves that would go on to be important as sacred caves in the Middle and Late Minoan period, it is certainly possible that earlier activity, too, was of a ritual nature. Examples include the Psychro cave, the Kamares cave and the cave of Eileithuia at Amnisos.

The hill-top shrines known as peak sanctuaries were established in the period before the foundation of the Minoan palaces, mostly towards the end of the Early or the beginning of the Middle Minoan period. That on Mount Juktas, for example, was founded in MM IA, and thus predates the palace at Knossos, with which it seems later to have been quite closely associated. The hill-top cult activities must, therefore, have originated independently of the palaces' concerns, even if they were later subsumed into palatial spheres of influence. What was the motivation for the foundation of these establishments?

It seems that across Crete the Minoans shared a commonly held belief that deities were particularly present or approachable in the high, wild areas of their mountainous land. Peak sanctuaries were therefore situated in such high places – though not in fact on the very highest peaks of the island. They were usually fairly readily accessible, and near to grazing grounds. Perhaps originally they served the local herders of sheep and cattle, though later they must have had a broader catchment among the population, who may have visited them for festivals at particular times of year. It has been argued that most were widely visible from the area which they served, and that mutual inter-visibility was a factor in their location.

Most peak sanctuaries had a wall enclosing an open sacred area known as a *temenos*: this could be oval, rectangular or irregularly shaped. Cult activity seems generally to have centred on altars in the open air. Shrine buildings were perhaps of secondary importance to the craggy hill-top itself: they were

25 Terracotta votive figurines from the peak sanctuary of Petsofa, near Palaikastro.

often fairly simple, and though dating can be difficult the buildings seem in some cases to be later than the enclosure wall.

Natural fissures in the rock were used to receive votive offerings, typically small models made of fired clay. Some are human figures, and these also include parts of bodies. A variety of animals includes bulls, sheep, goats, pigs, dogs, birds, scarab beetles and, occasionally, weasels. Miniature vessels and representations of foodstuffs are also found. The choice of dedications varies noticeably from place to place.

The human figures clearly represent worshippers, as they are shown in formalized attitudes of prayer. Body parts may have been dedicated with prayers for a cure for affliction of the part represented, as they were in later times. Animals and vegetable representations were presumably dedicated with prayers for the protection of flocks and crops. Wild animals are not common, though where scarab beetles are found they perhaps had some symbolic significance, as they did in Egypt.

The concentration of certain types of models at particular peak sanctuaries may show that the deity worshipped was not the same in each sanctuary. It remains the case, however, that the similar situations of the sanctuaries imply a connection with the natural world of weather and the landscape, while the dedications often reflect human activities dependent on these natural phenomena, notably agriculture and animal husbandry. Aspects of ritual practices in many of the sanctuaries also have much in common. Extensive ash deposits show, for example, that bonfires were lit, and votive offerings put into them.

It seems, then, that there is a certain unity in the way peak sanctuaries were made and used, indicating common religious ideas throughout the island. The choice of offerings may, though, have been made according to the specific deity worshipped at each place, implying a polytheistic religion.

The peak sanctuaries flourished particularly in the period of the First Palaces, and we shall return to them below. Some continued in use in the Second Palace period, but by this stage a change of emphasis perhaps indicates concentration of cult practices within the palaces, as we shall see.

Prepalatial Arts and Crafts

The settlements, cult-places and particularly the tombs of prepalatial Crete have provided a wealth of examples of the work of prepalatial artists and craftsmen, and we might try here to draw together some of the major strands in craft development in this long and fruitful period.

Various styles of pottery were produced. The black or grey vases of Pyrgos Ware had decorative burnishing and simple incised patterns that essentially carried on the Neolithic tradition. Shapes included chalices and cups, small jugs and double or triple vases. However, painted pottery styles also began in EM I, including the so-called Ayios Onouphrios style, usually with reddish paint on a buff background, and the Lenda style, in which white paint was applied to a brown or red-brown ground. In both these styles decoration was essentially linear, and some fine, well-controlled effects were achieved. Shapes included jugs, jars, *pyxides* (boxes) and multiple vessels.

Both Ayios Onouphrios and Lenda style pottery carried on into the EM II period. The former seems to have developed into the so-called Koumasa style, where the same sort of linear decoration was presented in more complex ways. In contrast, the EM IIB phase was particularly characterized by the mottled vases of the Vasiliki style. Differential firing of the vessels was used to create a decorative mottled effect. Shapes included vessels known as teapots, with extraordinarily exaggerated spouts. Both the mottled surfaces of the vases and such features as applied blobs of clay resembling rivets perhaps indicate a debt to metal vessels. The way such blobs are sometimes positioned to look like eyes on each side of a large beak must surely represent one of the few pieces of evidence we have for a Minoan sense of humour.

It should be noted that the pottery styles are generally named after the sites where they were first found, and these should not be taken to indicate place of manufacture. The latter can sometimes be proved by analysis, and it has been shown that Early Minoan pottery was not just used near to where it was made, but moved around the island to a remarkable extent.

26 'Teapot' of Vasiliki Ware.

Towards the end of the period, in EM III–MM IA, the White style developed. Vases in this style have a range of linear or curvilinear motifs, including spirals, painted in a creamy white paint on a black background. The addition of red paint characterized the period directly before the foundation of the palaces, creating a forerunner to the Kamares style. This period also saw extensive use of barbotine decoration, where the surface of the vase was either roughened or decorated with applied knobs or pellets of clay to create a three-dimensionally textured surface.

Some prepalatial vases were made in the form of animals and birds. An interesting example is the bull vessel from Koumasa that has three small acrobats clinging to its horns. Such plastic vases overlap in technique with terracotta figurines, of which the Myrtos 'goddess' is an example.

The range of pottery vessels was joined by vases carved in stone. The EM II period saw the firm establishment of this craft, which would continue to be a particular Minoan speciality. Many different small jugs, bowls, boxes and multiple vessels were produced in a range of decoratively mottled and veined local stones. The techniques may have been learned in the Cyclades, though influence from Egypt is also a possibility.

After a relatively slow start in EM I the working of metals progressed greatly during the EM II period. A range of tools was made, as were daggers of various types. The EM III–MM IA period saw further technical advances and an increased range of products. By this time tools included axes, double-axes, saws, chisels, mattocks and personal items such as tweezers. Bronze daggers became more robust at this time.

Elaborate jewellery was produced in prepalatial Crete, as the finds from Archanes and Mochlos amply testify. Gold jewellery included diadems, pins, bracelets, pendants and ornaments designed to be sewn to clothing, along with hair ornaments and a wide variety of beads. Beads were also made of other materials such as ivory, faience and various stones. Techniques of gold-working

began with the use of simple hammered gold, cut out into various shapes and with repoussé decoration. Silver was also used for jewellery, and occasionally for silver vases: two examples were found in the Mochlos cemetery.

The earliest prepalatial seals were made of bone, soft stone and boar's tusk. Relatively simple shapes included conoids or irregular pyramids, and decoration was often a simple lattice pattern, sometimes quite roughly incised. The arrival of imported hippopotamus ivory in the EM II period seems to have given the impetus towards more elaborate shapes and designs. Animal-shaped seals became popular, and designs included spirals, floral patterns and some pictorial motifs. Human figures were rarely shown, but animals, including lions, now occurred. A group of cylindrical seals with sealing faces at both ends belongs to the so-called 'parading lions and spirals' group. Foreign influence can be detected in the choice of lions as a motif, but it is interesting to note that the Minoan cylinders were essentially used as stamp-seals, with sealing surfaces carved at one or both ends and not around the circumference. They were not rolled to make an impression, as their Near Eastern counterparts were.

27 Drawing of a seal showing 'parading lions'.

Towards the end of the prepalatial period the importation and imitation of Egyptian scarabs began, and this is discussed below.

Foreign Relations in the Prepalatial Period

Before the beginning of the Early Bronze Age sporadic contact with the Cycladic island of Melos is indicated by the presence of Melian obsidian on sites in Crete. During the Early Bronze Age Crete was in contact with the Cycladic islands to the north, and, as we have seen, interchanges seem to have been particularly frequent in the long EM II period, when the Cycladic islands also flourished. Subsequently, in EM III, evidence for contact dies away, reflecting the fact that this was a time of relative poverty and isolation for many of the Cyclades. Contacts began again in MM IA, a period which was characterized by the islands beginning to flourish once more. From that time forwards they would be increasingly influenced by Minoan Crete.

The settlers who created a Minoan settlement at Kastri on the island of Kythera in EM IIB may have been fishermen from western Crete who used the island as a seasonal base. It forms a natural stepping stone between Crete and the Greek mainland, and this would become important later in its history, but it seems not to have been used in this way at first. Indeed evidence for contact between Crete and the Greek mainland is very slight throughout the Early Bronze Age, with only the most sparse handful of small portable objects – amulets and the like – suggesting any contact. This again was to change at the beginning of the Middle Bronze Age, when Minoan pottery began to be exported to the mainland of Greece.

The earliest substantial contacts between Crete and the civilizations of the Near East and Egypt can be attributed to the EM III–MM IA period, and take their place as an element in the sense of acceleration and diversification of Minoan culture in the time immediately preceding the foundation of the palaces. Stray exotic imports came to the island even earlier, and the presence there of raw materials such as gold, ivory and precious stones indicates sporadic and perhaps sometimes indirect contact, but at this time an intensification of exchanges appears in the archaeological record.

The first good example lies in the realm of Minoan seals and Egyptian scarabs, and from the Cretan point of view the story is quickly told.[6] Seal-stones of various shapes are known from EM II onwards, made of soft materials such as ivory, stone and bone. The designs are various, but from an early stage spirals become popular. Much of our evidence for such seals comes from the tholos tombs of the Mesara Plain. In one of the Mesara tholoi, at a site called Lenda on the south coast of Crete, Egyptian scarabs of First Intermediate Period to early Middle Kingdom date were found in a context dated by the excavator specifically to MM IA. The chronological link indicated by this find is accepted by most scholars.

These imported Egyptian scarabs are part of a most interesting phenomenon, because in the same MM IA period workshops that were probably situated in the Mesara Plain were producing Minoan scarabs. These copy the Egyptian scarab beetle form, but are cut in a totally distinctive way and could never be mistaken for Egyptian products.

The scarab type does not emerge in Egypt until the First Intermediate Period, about 2050BC. If MM IA ended in about 1950BC, we have here evidence of a fairly rapid sequence of events: the invention of Egyptian scarabs, their importation to Crete and their imitation there. This seems to imply a certain intensity of contact between Crete – particularly the south of the island – and Egypt at this time, though the possibility of scarabs coming to Crete via the Syro-Palestinian coast should not be discounted. Moreover, the adoption of spiral ornaments on scarabs in Egypt adds a fourth

28 Designs on three imported Egyptian scarabs (first and second left) from the Lenda tholos tombs compared with two scarabs of Minoan manufacture, probably made in the Mesara region.

stage to the story. While spirals are not unknown in early Egyptian art it is very noticeable that they suddenly become the main motif on scarabs made in Egypt at the same time as the phenomenon of imports and imitations of scarabs in Minoan Crete. It seems more than likely that this is a reciprocal influence on Egyptian art from Minoan Crete, transmitted in the medium of ideas about small glyptic – even though known imports of Minoan seals to Egypt are sadly lacking at this time.

A further isolated but intriguing piece of evidence for Egyptian contacts may be mentioned here. A clay model of an Egyptian sistrum or rattle was found in the Phourni cemetery, apparently in an MM IA context. Sistrums were used in Egyptian ritual. They are not common in Crete but the idea clearly caught on: the figure leading the procession on the Harvester Vase from Ayia Triadha is shown rattling a sistrum.

Contacts with the Syro-Palestinian coast and Cyprus also began in the phase immediately preceding the foundation of the Minoan palaces. Indeed, while the scarab evidence outlined above seems to indicate fairly intensive contact with Egypt, it must often have been the case that material from Egypt came back to the Aegean indirectly, via various points on the eastern Mediterranean shore. This is because ancient trade in the eastern Mediter-ranean tended to follow an anti-clockwise pattern, dictated by prevailing winds and currents. These meant that it was always easier to go from Crete to Egypt than vice versa, and meant, too, that trading vessels travelling from the Aegean would tend to return via the Syro-Palestinian coast and perhaps Cyprus or southern Turkey. Coastal entrepots such as Byblos, Ugarit and so on became increasingly important as the Bronze Age progressed.

Conclusions and the Genesis of the Minoan Palaces

The period of intensified interchanges immediately before the foundation of the Minoan palaces provided a climate in which the 'idea' of palaces could have been transmitted to Crete. Were the Minoan palaces themselves an import?

Their genesis has been a matter for controversy. On one side are those who claim that internal developments within Crete are sufficient to explain the phenomenon. They point to the increasing size and complexity of the major settlements in the island and of individual buildings within them, and the evidence for an increasingly hierarchical or 'ranked' society. The advances in agriculture that allowed surpluses to be created and then used as a means of wielding power, the growth of wealth of particular groups (clans or families) or individuals – all of these things created a suitable background for the emergence of the centralized palatial system.

Critics of this type of analysis would argue that such circumstances pertained elsewhere in the ancient world, but did not always result in palaces. They claim that the idea of the palace had to come from elsewhere, either from the Near East or Egypt. We tend (because of its later Greek history) to see Minoan Crete as the south-easterly extreme of early European culture, whereas in fact it is quite possible to see its palace-based administration as the north-westerly extreme of an essentially Middle Eastern phenomenon.

It seems clear that this argument has been polarized in a way which, while useful in focusing attention on the question, does not necessarily represent the only two possibilities. In fact, both the increasing prosperity and complexity of Minoan society and the quickening influence of foreign contacts may have been necessary to result in the palaces. Certainly the Minoans would have learned from other lands of large buildings that were religious and political centres, with complex administration systems based on seals and writing. But if the idea came from elsewhere, no blueprint did. The Minoan palaces were unique, both in their architectural form and in their purpose, combining religious, political, economic and administrative power. Temple and palace were generally separate entities in contemporary cultures.

We cannot doubt that the Minoans were aware of and inspired by developments abroad. It is clear from their achievements that they were a lively-minded people, with the outward-looking, adventurous spirit of an island race. What they created at home certainly assimilated foreign influences, from artistic ideas to the running of a complex administration. Essentially, though, these became part of a system and a way of life that was entirely their own.

Chapter Three

PROTOPALATIAL CRETE

TOWARDS THE END of the period known as MM IA, in about 1950BC, a remarkable development took place at Knossos. The top of the habitation mound or 'tell' which had built up over the centuries of occupation of the hill was levelled and the building of the First Palace was begun. Large-scale predecessors may have existed – it is possible that the north-west corner of the palace incorporated an earlier structure – but essentially the First Palace swept away what had been there previously. It took its place in the heart of a flourishing settlement, its approach roads and courtyards sometimes encroaching on earlier parts of the town. Though the remains of the First Palace are only partly recoverable from beneath the now-visible remains of the Second Palace we can surmise with some confidence that it was on a large scale and architecturally sophisticated, with impressive facades and entrance-ways. Construction must have taken some time; indeed we should perhaps think of the First Palace as evolving over a period of some 250 years towards the 'canonical' architectural form represented by the Second Palace. Nonetheless, it must have been a remarkable sight, quite unlike anything seen on Crete before.

The palaces of Phaistos and Mallia were begun at about the same time. Both similarly took their place in already prospering settlements, extending over earlier structures. We can still see today that the First Palace of Phaistos was impressive, as extensive parts of the west side of the building survive. Zakros, too, may have had a First Palace at this stage, though as at Mallia its remains are scarcely visible. There was probably also a similar new foundation at Chania, though palatial remains there are difficult to excavate because they lie under the modern town.

Although the palaces were built in prosperous towns, and therefore in some sense depended on the pre-existing success of their various sites, we should not underestimate the extent to which they must have revolutionized those sites, and Minoan society as a whole. They were big, well-planned and well-organized; they represent a very considerable investment of resources in both labour and materials and their dominance indicates the existence of a powerful elite – or of several elite groups in various localities. The people in the palace towns and their surrounding countryside must have supported the building of the palaces, whether by coercion or consent. The palace-centred 'state', whatever the problems of precise definition, thereafter became the characteristic social and political unit of Minoan Crete.

The regionalism previously typical of Crete does not end with the First Palaces, nor is their foundation necessarily part of a single system of island-wide control. Knossos was from the beginning the biggest and most elaborate of the palaces, though by the end of the First Palace period they seem all to have conformed to a similar plan, indicating mutual influences and perhaps cultural unity at some level. Some commonly shared religious beliefs are also suggested by the similar finds and practices from shrines and sanctuaries throughout the island, as we shall see. Nonetheless, Knossos perhaps began as a 'first among equals', and the relationship between the powerful groups that built the palaces may not have been entirely friendly. Separate territories (or 'states') can loosely be defined around each, mainly on the evidence of localized pottery styles. Some evidence for fortifications along major routes perhaps suggests uneasy relations between these territories. The situation may be contrasted with Crete in the Second Palace period, where Knossian styles in pottery and architecture become island-wide in their spread, and Knossos really does seem to be pre-eminent in the island as a whole.

Protopalatial Crete, then, was characterized by palaces and palace towns of some size at Knossos, Phaistos and Mallia, perhaps also at Zakros and Chania. While much of Crete must have come under palatial control, people in the wilder parts or the extremities may have had a looser relationship to the palaces than the inhabitants of their immediately surrounding areas. Moreover, some areas were apparently controlled from smaller centres that had buildings with palatial features in which centralized storage and administration took place. Evidence for such centres is increasing: Petras on the bay of Siteia seems to have been functional as a small palatial centre, while Monastiraki in the Amari valley was clearly involved in storage and redistribution of agricultural produce.

This does, of course beg the question of demarcation between what are sometimes called 'first order centres' (major palaces) and 'second order centres' (smaller-scale subordinate centres with palatial functions). If a strict hierarchy existed, these smaller centres presumably worked under the control, or at least influence, of one of the major palaces. Where, though, should the demarcation line be drawn?

Architecturally we can define palaces as complex, multi-functional buildings with rooms arranged around a large rectangular central court, usually on an approximately north–south axis, with a second important courtyard on the western side. The First Palaces at Knossos, Phaistos and Mallia almost certainly conformed to this plan. The smaller centres do not always have all these architectural elements. Their claim to be considered 'palatial' depends more on function: specifically, the centralized storage of agricultural wealth from a surrounding region, and sometimes the control of incomings and outgoings using a system of administration based on seals and writing.

Knossos, Phaistos and Mallia still stand out, on both definitions, for their architectural elaboration and for the scale of their operations. Each offers rather different sorts of evidence for the protopalatial period, depending on chance circumstances of preservation and opportunities for excavation. In surveying protopalatial Crete, then, we might begin with the major palaces and move on to consider smaller sites, thus roughly articulating them within a hierarchy of settlements.

The First Palaces and Their Towns

Because we cannot retrieve the entire layout of any of the First Palaces it is very tempting to extrapolate backwards, and to base conclusions on what the First Palaces were like on the evidence from the Second Palaces. This is sometimes justifiable, and can in places be supported by excavated evidence. We must, however, be on the alert for the possibility of differences, both between the palaces and between their two major phases. If the First Palaces were autonomous and independent, and perhaps at odds with each other for part of the time, this could encourage some physical differences between them (though not necessarily – factions among essentially closely related people need not be reflected in their architecture). The Second Palaces may have been part of a more unified pattern. They were apparently heavily influenced by Knossos, and their physical layout may have undergone some evolutionary change.

Knossos

The position of the palace at Knossos was predicated by the choice of the low hill in the Knossos valley for settlement in Neolithic times. This, known as the Kephala hill, lies in the valley bottom, to the west of the Kairatos river, and became the heart of the Minoan settlement. The natural advantages of

29 The palace of Knossos seen from the east.

the position are clear: it had supplies of water, ample wood and stone for building, and an agriculturally rich hinterland. The hill itself has been made higher by the 'tell' effect of layers of habitation debris, but both the palace and the town were always flanked by much higher ground to the west and east. Defensive considerations seem scarcely to have figured in the palace's position, though it was protected from direct sea-borne attack by being some 6 km (3¾ miles) inland. And the palace had, through its coastal harbours, the same advantageous position about half-way along Crete's northern coast that would make Herakleion commercial capital of the island so many centuries later. The relatively low hills south of Knossos also allowed access to the south of the island and the region of Phaistos.

Knossos, the largest and most complex palace, had an equally complicated architectural history. Walls, basements and foundations of the First Palace period are incorporated into the later phases of the building at various places throughout the site. Indeed, while the destruction at the end of MM II that signals the close of the First Palace period is a major horizon, many other destructions and rebuildings of various rooms and areas mark the palace's long history. We tend to characterize the First and Second Palaces at the major sites as though they were quite separate phenomena. The division is a useful one, but still we should keep in mind the fact that we are seeing continuous processes at work in these palaces as they developed over time.

30 Remains of the First Palace at Knossos are mostly hidden beneath later structures, but the rounded corner of the Throne Room complex may derive from the protopalatial period.

A further general point to consider is that the time taken to build the First Palaces, and that taken to reconstruct them as the Second Palaces, may have been considerable. Our chronology based on architectural phases cannot be over-precise: some buildings or rebuildings may have taken a generation or more to complete.

What, then, can we say about the First Palace at Knossos?[1] Certainly it was built around a Central Court, on a roughly north–south axis. Interestingly this lines up with the position of Mount Juktas and its important sanctuaries to the south. The palace had an imposing West Court, laid out in a second construction phase and covering earlier houses. The *koulouras*, or large circular storage pits, in this court may have been used for storing grain. Within the palace there was also extensive storage capacity: much of the west wing was given over to store-rooms, with agricultural produce and other goods probably kept both in pithoi (large pottery jars) and in storage pits. Some storage capacity also existed on the east side of the palace, and here too there is evidence for manufactured goods. The so-called 'Royal Pottery Stores' had high-quality ceramics, though these seem to have been stored rather than actually made there, while the presence of loom-weights is evidence for textile manufacture.

A predecessor to the Throne Room complex seems to indicate that places for ritual or ceremonial use were already an integral and important part of the palace on the west side of the Central Court. The rounded north-east corner of this complex was one of the features that led Evans to suggest that the First Palace was laid out in quasi-independent blocks which were later integrated into a whole. This is, though, difficult to demonstrate throughout the palace.

On the east of the Central Court, though major rebuilding to create the so-called 'Domestic Quarter' dramatically changed what had been there before, it is possible that certain gypsum column-bases indicate the existence of pillared halls in the area later taken up by the Grand Staircase, the Hall of the Double-Axes and adjacent rooms. The area called by Evans the 'Queen's Megaron' may have been a paved courtyard at this time. Sandy MacGillivray[2] ingeniously suggests that the provision via the drainage system of running water to this area could indicate processes connected with textile production – apparently central to the activities of the First Palace as to the Second. This east wing may also have had ritual or domestic functions, as it did in neo-palatial times.

The facades of the building seem not to have used the ashlar limestone masonry characteristic of the Second Palace, but instead to have been built from neatly cut gypsum blocks. Other construction materials used in the palace included limestone, wood, rubble, mud-brick and perhaps variegated stones for pavings and column-bases. The Minoan craftsmen were clearly becoming skilled in quarrying, cutting and transporting stones. Their engin-eering skills are also shown in the large-scale remains of the viaduct crossing the Vlychia stream to the south of the palace, which led to the great Stepped Portico – a monumental stepped way that led dramatically up to the palace from the south.

Other ways of access included the Royal Road, which approached the palace at the north-west corner, whence, presumably, the Central Court could be accessed from the north. It seems that no main entrance existed on the west side, and so from the West Court it was probably necessary to enter via the north or south. It is not clear whether there were entrances on the east. It does appear, though, that for all its impressive facades and grand approaches the First Palace, like the Second, did not offer easy access to the Central Court and the most important rooms. The security of the centre of power, perhaps too the secrecy of the centre of religion, seems to have been a consideration in palatial architecture and layout.

The foundation of the Minoan palaces gave the impetus for the use of writing, even if only among a specialist group of scribes. While archive rooms of protopalatial date do not survive, we have some evidence for the seal-based and tablet-based administration of the palace. The main script in use at protopalatial Knossos was the so-called Hieroglyphic script, though recently a scrap of a Linear A tablet of this date was found in an area just outside the palace. Seals and sealings (the impressions of seals on clay) also come from the palace and provide some insight into the system of administration.

Because of later rebuildings and confused stratigraphy on the site it is difficult to give a cogent account of the administrative system in the First Palace at Knossos. It is perhaps more helpful to discuss the evidence for writing from all of protopalatial Crete together, and this is done below. We might note here, though, that Hieroglyphic script seems to have been prevalent at Knossos, Mallia and Petras at a time when an early form of Linear A was used at Phaistos – another indication of regionalism in protopalatial Crete.

From its inception the palace seems to have had a number of different functions: providing storage for accumulated wealth, acting as a base for manufacturing processes and being a centre of administrative control. It also provided areas for ritual and probably – if elusively – living quarters for the ruling group or family. Some of these seem very appropriate for a 'palace', some for a 'temple', some for both. The First Palace thus instantly begs all the questions about whether the word 'palace' is truly adequate shorthand for so complex and multi-functional a building. We will return to the issue of characterizing the palaces when discussing the Second Palaces, but might perhaps briefly defend here the decision to retain the word 'palace' in this book. At the very least it has the advantage of maintaining consistency with all the archaeological literature. For many years – indeed since Evans' own time – it has been recognized as shorthand. The Minoan palaces are unique, and their particular combination of aspects is not found in buildings elsewhere. The term 'palace' may be inadequate, but we can perhaps reasonably claim that the expression 'Minoan palace' defines a specific phenomenon.

KNOSSOS TOWN

The settlement of Knossos grew in size at the beginning of the Middle Minoan period, and may have been as big during the time of the First Palace as it ever became. It extended on all sides of the palace. Scattered tests and excavations give some indications of its nature and extent, while the locations of cemetery areas also help to indicate the limits of the town.

To the west of the palace quite substantial traces of the protopalatial town have been found in the area of the hostel occupied by the British School at Athens and the nearby Stratigraphical Museum. This part of the Minoan city was reached by the Royal Road and its westerly extension, and spread over the lower slopes of the hill to the west that was the acropolis of the Classical city of Knossos. On the east the settlement seems to have extended across the Kairatos river, and there are some monumental structures – perhaps terrace walls, though of uncertain purpose – on the steep slopes of Ailias on this side.

David Hogarth excavated town houses to the south of the palace during the first season of work at Knossos. These were on Gypsadhes hill, and were probably near to the southern border of Knossos town. Although apparently neopalatial in date, they must have had protopalatial predecessors, as pottery described simply as 'Kamares Ware' was discovered beneath their floors. The remains of the houses did not survive, as Evans dryly remarks, because 'native marauders…carried off most of the gypsum remains within the buildings, to be used in pursuance of their barbarous methods of preserving wine. The process of destruction was as complete as its purpose was unheard of. Door-jambs, paving slabs, the broken-up fragments of sacred pillars, were dissolved, to be eventually drunk up.'[3]

Classical and Roman Knossos largely occupied the area north of the palace. The Minoan town certainly extended in this direction too, though it is difficult to determine at what point occupation petered out. Cemeteries, particularly with burials of the Final Palace period, were situated north of the palace. Protopalatial burials are known from the slopes of Ailias on the east, and occasionally elsewhere.

The estimation of extent and population of the town is not easy, since the evidence is so patchy. Estimates for the neopalatial population of the immediate area around the palace suggest about 12,000 inhabitants, and this may be of relevance to protopalatial houses too, since the town seems, so far as we can tell, to reach a size that was not exceeded later. A higher figure should be suggested to include the broader hinterland from which manpower could potentially be drawn. This might take the figure to something like 15,000–20,000 inhabitants. At the very least we must suggest a population large enough to support the major building projects in the palace and its environs.

PHAISTOS

Phaistos is poised on the very end of a long ridge, with commanding views of the immediate surroundings on three sides and breathtaking longer views of both the Mesara Plain to the east and, to the north, the twin peaks of Mount Ida. The Kamares cave, an important sanctuary on the side of Mount Ida, is visible from the palace site when the weather permits, so again, as at Knossos, the approximately north–south alignment of the Central Court lines up with a sacred mountain.

The position of Phaistos would seem reasonably defensible, though the ridge rises to yet higher ground on the palace's west side and no fortifications are apparent. Certainly wood and building stone would have been locally available, and the fresh water provided by the Ierpotamos river would have been an essential resource. Above all, the Mesara Plain, which sweeps away like a carpet from the foot of the ridge, provided Phaistos with a fertile hinterland. A nearby outlet to the sea existed at Kommos, while a fairly easy 56-km (35-mile) journey across the centre of Crete led to Knossos and the north coast.

The First Palace at Phaistos paid a high price for the precarious beauty of its position. It showed instability on its western side, leading the builders to shift the west facade eastwards to construct the Second Palace. Later the eastern side of the building began to collapse, so that now visitors can see that even the extreme south-east corner of the Central Court itself has been 'bitten away' and slipped down the slope of the hill. The importance of Ayia Triadha in the Second Palace period may partly have arisen from the fact that Phaistos as a building was just too unstable.

The First Palace at Phaistos, then, was bigger than the Second Palace and was clearly impressive. We know this because the shifting of the facade left a considerable part of the west side of the old palace not built over, and therefore recoverable by the archaeologists. In particular, the facades of both an upper and a lower west wing were recovered, along with some of the rooms behind them, and the paved courtyards on to which they faced.

The three paved courts on the western side of Phaistos, the Upper Court, the West Court proper and the Lower Court, all existed at the time of the First Palace. They tamed the slope of the hill, and allowed access to the palace at its different levels. It is not clear how the Upper Court and West Court originally communicated: the staircase now visible is a neopalatial feature. Another considerable drop in level exists between the West Court proper and the Lower Court, and indeed between the upper and lower west wings of the old palace. The west facades of the two wings are on the same alignment, so the difference in level is not apparent from the palace plan, but in fact the lower west wing is tucked into the side of the hill. It is partly for this reason, too, that while the rooms of the upper wing, which are now back-filled, survived only to a low height, the rooms of the lower wing were extraordinarily well preserved.

31 The palace of Phaistos lies on the east (left) end of this ridge. The western end is the site of the Royal Villa of Ayia Triadha.

The west facade of the first palace has at its base a row of orthostats – that is, a carefully set course of upright stones used for decorative effect, as well as to support what was above. The shallow recesses in the wall break up the facade with a play of light and shade: a refinement typical of Minoan palatial architecture. The West Court, with its raised processional causeways and the shallow steps of the so-called Theatral Area, protopalatial in their original conception, show that already there was provision for meetings of people at this important cusp between the First Palace and the town. Large-scale gatherings of people for all sorts of purposes could have taken place there. The presence of a small three-roomed shrine towards the north end of the west facade is indicative of ritual in this area. Paved causeways are found in

32 Remains of the First Palace at Phaistos lie on the western (right) side. The north wing was filled after excavation, and now appears as a platform, while the south lies at a lower level, protected by modern roofing.

33 Part of the west facade of the First Palace at Phaistos, showing the orthostats and the use of recesses that were among its architectural refinements.

34 The remarkably well-preserved remains of the west wing of the First Palace at Phaistos.

the West Courts of both Knossos and Phaistos, and the 'Sacred Grove and Dance' fresco from Knossos shows them as the background for ritual activity.

The rooms of the lower west wing are remarkably well preserved and give an evocative impression of stone, half-timbered and mud-brick construction on more than one level. The remains are confusing: it has been a matter for some controversy whether successive phases are represented in the different levels, or whether they represent the superimposed storeys of a single phase. In fact the discovery in some places of sherds from individual vessels on upper and lower levels probably indicates contemporary storeys, at least in places. When the First Palace was destroyed at the end of MM IIB a layer of cement-like material was poured over the ruins of this wing. This also appears at different levels and was presumably intended to consolidate the remains. They were not stable enough to be built over, though – hence the subsequent shift of the west facade eastwards – and the unique preservation of the First Palace remains. A wonderful array of Kamares pottery was found at Phaistos, while the huge archive of seal impressions, mentioned below, has been a rich source of information.

Phaistos Town

The First Palace at Phaistos has an interface with the surrounding town on its west side, via the West Court, in keeping with the situation at the other palaces. However, the position of the palace otherwise makes it seem rather more separate from the town, because of the steep slopes of the ridge that it occupies. An area of the neopalatial town has been excavated to the south east of the palace, and can be seen by the visitor looking down from the palace site itself. Traces of the protopalatial town have been found to the west and to the north. Protopalatial occupation may have been more extensive in these directions, though probably, as at Knossos and Mallia, there was some protopalatial occupation on all sides of the palace.

The town area of Ayia Fotini, on the north-east slope of the ridge, revealed houses of protopalatial date. Many examples of fine pottery from the earliest protopalatial phase were found there, in a style combining bright polychromy with extensive use of plastic decoration.

To the west of the palace a building now visible from the modern pedestrian approach-road proved on excavation to be long and narrow, with a series of rooms that suggested similarities with the so-called 'council chambers' in the hypostyle crypt of Mallia's 'political centre' – discussed below. The building at Phaistos was not so well preserved, however, and its function cannot be determined.

Mallia

The situation of the palace of Mallia is different from that of Knossos and Phaistos because it lies on a flat coastal plain, and indeed is only five minutes' walk from the sea. Perhaps these two factors encouraged the building of a town wall at Mallia, for which there is some evidence on the east of the palace, though the precise date and extent of the fortifications are not clear. The plain of Mallia, though not very distant from Knossos, has a different feel, partly because of the notably red earth of the region. The palace itself is built largely of a rusty red local sandstone. The low but noticeable hill of Profitis Ilias lies on the same axis as the palace to the south. It may well have been a peak sanctuary, though only a scattering of rather indeterminate material was found there. Beyond lie the impressive mountains of the Selena range that fringe the Lasithi plain.

The coastline near the palace, though probably somewhat different today as a result of the rise in sea-level, would always have been relatively accessible, and so local bays were presumably used as anchorages. The area of Knossos was accessible by land – it is some 30 km (18 miles) away – or sea. Journeys to the south of the island must have been more difficult, perhaps usually made by skirting the Lasithi massif and crossing the isthmus of

35 The coastal plain of Mallia from the hill of Profitis Ilias. The low-lying remains of the palace are scarcely visible, but it is situated just five minutes' walk from the sea.

Ierapetra. Water may have been from springs as well as streams, but no larger river runs near here. Wood and stone were locally available. Today the Mallia plain is very fertile, though quite small.

The First Palace at Mallia is known from soundings under the remains of the Second Palace: only in certain places could information about its nature be extricated. However, it seems there was certainly a central court and a west court. There were large state-rooms with plastered floors on the west side, from which came the two very fine bronze swords, one with a gold pommel bearing the figure of an acrobat. In the north-west of the palace were remains of storage magazines and a corridor and plastered court. The large pithos with corded decoration still visible in this area belongs to the protopalatial period. The area of the east magazines was also in use.

MALLIA TOWN

Excavations at Mallia have revealed more of the protopalatial town there than at Knossos or Phaistos, with results that are both fascinating and puzzling. The real surprise lies in the fact that 'palatial' activities were going on in important buildings in a part of the town known as Quartier (Area) Mu, which, though close to the palace, is clearly separate from it. Other structures contiguous to the palace perhaps had public functions, and it is with these that we should start our survey of Mallia town.

The conviction of the French excavators that the structures directly north-west of the palace had a public function is shown by their calling the area the 'Centre Politique'. The two elements of this 'political centre' are a

36 The so-called 'hypostyle crypt' at Mallia, mainly of mud-brick, with plastered benches in the rooms at each end.

semi-subterranean building described as a 'hypostyle crypt', adjoining an open square some 30 m (100 ft) from the palace's north entrance known, perhaps misleadingly, as the 'agora'.

The agora was an open square some 30 × 40 m (100 × 130 ft) in size, with a monumental border of dressed white standing stones. Reached by a wide entrance-way from the palace side, the agora gave on to a crossroads on its northern side with roads leading to the sea, other areas of the town and, presumably, the cemeteries lying to the north. On the east were town houses; on the west a connection was made with the hypostyle crypt via an area perhaps occupied by small shops. The square may well have been used for assemblies of the people. Whether they met for political purposes, as the excavators suggested, or for other reasons must remain a moot point. The square could have been used for ritual activities or for sport (or indeed for some combination of the two). Whatever its purpose, it seems to have gone out of use in the neopalatial period.

Partly because of its close connection with the agora, the hypostyle crypt was interpreted by the excavators as a council chamber, with a store-room attached. The crypt proper is a long, narrow structure, divided into five rooms. It was carefully constructed, mainly of mud-brick, and much of its internal plaster survives. Plastered benches run around the walls of the two end rooms. Its semi-basement level gives an impression of secrecy, but since no finds other than a large number pottery cups came from the crypt we have little real evidence for its original function. The adjoining store-room continued the alignment of the crypt. One large jar was found still in place. The system of collection channels for spilled liquids in the floor is common in Minoan store-rooms. The hypostyle crypt, like the agora, fell out of use at the end of the First Palace period, so if the suggested interpretation is correct there seems not to have been direct continuity with Crete in later times. As mentioned above, a further building arguably, but not certainly, of this type has been found at Phaistos.

QUARTIER MU

The town area of Mallia known as Quartier Mu, of protopalatial date, consists of two large buildings of some complexity and architectural pretension, along with associated workshops, courts and paths. The buildings were constructed largely of mud-brick at the beginning of MM II and were destroyed at the end of that period, at the same time as the destruction of the First Palaces at Mallia and elsewhere. Finds recovered in the excavations included much pottery and, interestingly, archive documents on clay. A workshop closely associated with the buildings of Quartier Mu contained evidence for the manufacture of seal-stones.

The grander of the two buildings in Quartier Mu, Building A, seems very irregular in plan because it had two main phases of construction. In fact the northern part was built first and is roughly rectangular and quite symmetrical. The southern rooms were then added and filled the space available. The two phases are visible in the west facade, which is the principal face of the

37 A view of Building A in Quartier Mu at Mallia.

38 The very large lustral basin in Building A, Quartier Mu, Mallia.

building and contains the main entrance. The northern part is built of dressed blocks of sandstone, the southern part continues in mud-brick.

The west facade of the building looks on to a small paved courtyard and paved causeways, and is thus reminiscent of the west facades of the palaces. Within the building, too, are echoes of palatial architecture, particularly in the principal rooms which occupy the western side of the northern part of the building. Here a spacious arrangement includes a light-well, an antechamber in which stood two columns of cypress wood and a further room in which there is a large lustral basin (discussed on page 102). It has been pointed out that this suite of rooms is analogous in arrangement to the Throne Room complex at Knossos. The lustral basin is 2 m (6½ ft) in depth, making it extraordinarily big for an installation of this type. A room directly to the west contained a hearth with a circular depression of a kind associated with sanctuaries.

Part of the south section of the house on the east side was of robust but roughly finished walls that had clearly supported an upper storey. The excavators suggest that the rooms here may have been used for animals. The presence of an office or archive on the upper floor is, though, indicated by the extensive finds of inscribed tablets and 'medallions', along with seal impressions, that had fallen into this area. Elsewhere in Building A there are staircases that led to the upper floors.

Building B of Quartier Mu lies to the north of Building A, and is reached by following the paved causeway through the small west court. At its heart lies a very large room on ground level, from which access was possible to the other parts of the building, including the upper storey and the basement level. The importance of the upper storey was again shown by clay documents that had fallen from it, and, as in Building A, parts of Building B were built strongly but roughly to support this storey.

Rooms at basement level in the south-west corner of Building B could be approached by a staircase from this central room and are remarkably well preserved, with walls nearly 2 m (6½ ft) high and therefore approaching their original height. These rooms include elements that rarely survive, such as remains of doors and windows, niches, cupboards and wooden beams. A large pillared room is of uncertain function, but was clearly important. The status of the area as a whole is underlined by the discovery of a fine bronze dagger with an openwork gold handle.

Adjoining Quartier Mu were found four houses of particular interest because the upper floors were used as workshops. In each case the house seems to have been occupied as a normal residence, presumably by the craftsman and his family. Other similar buildings have been identified in the immediate vicinity, but these have not been fully excavated. The four house-workshops that have been revealed, however, give a unique insight into the working life of the craftsmen of the First Palace period. They were destroyed at the end of MM II, at the same time as the First Palaces.

In one house-workshop seal-stones were made. Blocks of raw material – steatite and rock-crystal – were found, along with tools, waste and a number of seals in various stages of manufacture. These included blanks, and seals broken during working and therefore discarded. The workshop specialized in making steatite three-sided prisms, or at least was doing so at the time of its sudden destruction. The work room was about 3 × 3 m (10 × 10 ft) in size and therefore not big enough for more than two or three craftsmen. The style of the engraving on the seals is rather rough and ready. Many have animals and some have human figures, while motifs perhaps derived from plant forms are also common.

In the adjoining house-workshop pottery, much of it moulded, was made. Moulds for sea-shells and the horns of wild goats were found, and these would have made complete objects, probably used in cult. The workshop also made moulds for appliqués to be attached to pots, and pottery vessels of particular forms, notably portable braziers. Most seem to be 'special' items, rather than pottery for daily use. The discovery of potter's wheels underlined the identification as a ceramics workshop, though there was no evidence for a kiln and the products must have been fired elsewhere.

Similarly the house-workshop producing bronze items contained no evidence for a kiln or furnace, though the presence of raw materials and waste from the production process perhaps showed that the furnaces were somewhere nearby. Stone moulds for making chisels and double-axes were found.

Evidence for stone vase production came both from the potter's workshop and the south workshop. The latter was perhaps used for various processes. Near to it there was evidence for the primary working of bone.

These four house-workshops do not differ essentially from purely residential houses of the same period. They have storage areas and living rooms to support a household, and seem to have been family homes. The specialist workshop areas were usually somewhat separate from the living rooms, often with their own access, but still the craftsmen seem to have been working as part of a family unit. Even so, the concentration of the house-workshops in a particular part of Mallia town indicates a conscious grouping together of specialist activities. They are close to the important buildings of Quartier Mu, with which their activities must surely have been closely associated.

This whole area of protopalatial Mallia poses interesting questions about relationships: both the relationship of the house-workshops to Buildings A and B, and the relationship of A and B to the palace itself. Was Quartier Mu directly controlled by the palace, as a sort of out-station, or is it possible that an elite group within the Minoan social structure operated in some sense independently there? One suggestion is of a priesthood working in parallel with the royal household, though the evidence scarcely supports this, and such a separation is not apparent elsewhere. These two realms seem certainly to have been amalgamated in the Second Palaces. What, then, of the possibility of a rich merchant class? This might make sense: the activities in the buildings of Mu required records keeping track of the movements of materials and goods, and manufacturing processes took place in the same neighbourhood. Whether or not this could be truly 'private enterprise', it certainly represents a stage where activities parallel to those of the palace could be carried on outside in finely constructed, rich and important buildings in the immediate vicinity.

We seem, then, to be seeing here a stage of development in protopalatial Crete where there was less centralization, with activities that would later largely be concentrated within the palaces taking place elsewhere. No detailed comparisons can be made between the buildings of Quartier Mu and the First Palace at Mallia, because relatively few traces of the latter survive. Nonetheless the two complexes are close to each other, and the likelihood is that both were integrated into the workings of a single elite or ruling group at Mallia in the protopalatial period. In a sense the problems of interpretation of Quartier Mu are similar to those of interpreting the large and important houses in close proximity to the palace of Knossos in the neopalatial period. There, too, we must surmise that offshoots of the elite carried on privileged activities in tandem with those taking place in the palace itself. We cannot reconstruct their status – whether an aristocracy related by family to the rulers of the palaces, important religious or official figures or members of a merchant class. The buildings of Quartier Mu warn us not to underestimate the level of complexity and sophistication of Minoan society in the First Palace period.

ZAKROS AND PETRAS

The small palace recently excavated at Petras on the bay of Siteia had a canonical plan in the neopalatial period, and excavations have revealed that parts of the building certainly date from protopalatial times. The presence there of a Hieroglyphic archive, discussed below, supports the contention that the building was already functioning as a palace in this period.

No such certainty is possible for Zakros. Some scanty architectural remains hint at a predecessor to the Second Palace, but evidence for administrative functions is lacking. We may surmise that the advantages of the site (described below) were already apparent in protopalatial times: whether it really was the site of a palace then remains a moot point.

39 The small sheltered bay of Zakros, seen from the edge of the Minoan site.

Protopalatial 'States'

Can we, at the broadest level, separate the island into the main palace territories or states? Our evidence is far from complete, and it is not always obvious where the boundaries lay. Knossos may logically be felt to have dominated north-central Crete, Phaistos the south-central part of the island, Mallia an east-central state and perhaps Zakros an easternmost territory. Chania may always have been the dominant site in the far west of the island, though a west-central state might be posited, including Monastiraki, and perhaps based on that site, unless a bigger centre existed that has not yet been found. It is however possible that the Amari valley was in the territory of Phaistos.

Support for such groupings comes from the distribution of pottery and other artefact types, and certain natural geographical boundaries can be invoked to delineate the territories. Nonetheless, we cannot be too precise. It seems logical to suggest two separate states around Knossos and Phaistos, yet the areas are contiguous and communication between the two was easy. A single large central state should not be dismissed as a possibility, though a state containing two major palaces may be felt to be unlikely, particularly when those palaces were using different systems of administration.

Sites near the boundaries of territories can be difficult to place in terms of pottery styles. The many sites on the isthmus of Ierapetra are a case in point: do they belong to the east-central Mallia territory or the extreme east? It is not surprising that boundary sites should be problematical – perhaps their allegiance changed, or perhaps the patterns we can discern are not in any case a matter of tight political control. To add to the complexities, some sites that are geographically separated sometimes have similar pottery – Mallia and Petras might be cited as examples, or, more extremely, Knossos and Palaikastro. In both instances these sites should on a geographical basis be in different 'states': moreover, different types of pottery are found on other sites that intervene between these pairs. Special relationships based on sea-borne communication may be suggested, but these instances serve to underline that the situation is not clear-cut.

KNOSSOS 'STATE'

Evidence for a Knossos 'state' in the First Palace period has been collected by Gerald Cadogan.[4] Natural geographic boundaries for such a state are created by the Psiloriti massif to the west, the passes to the Mesara Plain to the south, and the Lasithi massif to the east. Northwards, of course, lies the sea. Cadogan argues that both pottery and perhaps some other cultural indicators, including multi-chambered or kidney-shaped tombs dug into hillsides, separate the Knossos region from the areas to the east and west. Relations with Phaistos and its area are, he acknowledges, much more difficult to pin down, though in fact the Mesara Plain does seem to have a different pottery tradition, continuing from the prepalatial period. The tholos tomb, too, continued to be characteristic of the area in the period of the First Palaces, and occurred much more rarely in the north.

PHAISTOS 'STATE'

The Mesara Plain can be considered the heartland of the probable Phaistos 'state', and the palace must certainly have included the harbour town of Kommos within its territory. The Ida massif to the north of the palace created a natural barrier, and only such special sites as the Kamares cave were situated in that direction. However, the sites in the Amari valley perhaps came under the influence of Phaistos. These included the palatial centre of Monastiraki and the settlement of Apodoulou. It seems that a road led from Phaistos to the north of the island through the Amari valley, linking these sites and ending at Chamalevri, some 10 km (6 miles) east of Rethymnon. This natural route probably acted as a conduit for the influence of Phaistos, which may have extended as far as the north coast, though as ever, the boundary between this 'state' and the influence of the next territory to the west – perhaps that of Chania – is hard to determine.

MALLIA 'STATE'

We must seek to define what sort of relationship the sites within these territories can reasonably be thought to have had, and light has been thrown on this question by Carl Knappett's detailed consideration of the protopalatial 'state' of Mallia.[5] If we characterize the First Palaces as centres for collection, processing, storage and distribution of goods, it is tempting to assume by extension that they exerted direct political and economic control over the whole of their territory. Yet the practicalities of such precise control over a wide area must be questioned, and the mechanisms have never truly been visible in the archaeological record. The First Palaces no doubt controlled their immediate regions tightly, and drew agricultural wealth from them, but could this have worked further afield?

Study of the Mallia state has produced interesting results. Its extent is suggested to have been from around the area of Gournia on the west to the isthmus of Ierapetra on the east and to have included the sites of Fournou Korifi and Myrtos-Pyrgos on the south coast. The Lasithi plain has in the past been felt to be in the area of Mallian influence, partly on the basis of pottery distribution and partly on the basis that it could have provided a rich agricultural hinterland from which the palace could draw its wealth. In fact, though, recent studies have suggested that the plain was not so fertile in antiquity as it later became after periods of alluviation. Moreover, some protopalatial-period fortifications in the plain perhaps suggest a defended independence at this time. Whether the Mallia state included Lasithi or skirted round it must therefore remain a moot point.

Very interestingly, fine pottery from Myrtos-Pyrgos is stylistically almost identical to that from Mallia, though the sites are really quite distant from each other, on opposite sides of the island. Analysis shows, however, that the pottery was made locally at each site. Moreover, though there is evidence for movement of pottery and other goods within the Mallia territory, direct links between the palace site and Myrtos-Pyrgos are few and far between. This makes it seem much less likely that Mallia was exerting direct political and economic control over sites at the periphery of its territory. Yet clearly Myrtos-Pyrgos comes within Mallia's area of influence. The nature of this influence is that of shared values – the use of the same type of fine table wares shows social and, if they were used ceremonially, perhaps religious alignment. This is a form of 'control', the palace's influence making a coherent whole of the Mallia territory. There may also have been some looser or less direct political or economic control, but it is perhaps safer, if vaguer, to character-ize broad areas of palatial influence in Crete as a whole, the palace 'states' proper possibly being more tightly drawn, and including the palace, the town and the neighbouring countryside.

Writing in Protopalatial Crete

While scattered examples of prepalatial writing have been found in Crete, it was the foundation of the palaces which really made the use of writing a necessity. From the beginning goods were moving in and out of the palace store-rooms and work areas on a scale that required systems for record-keeping and control.

A major tool for such control was the use of seals. Seals are known from prepalatial Crete, made in various materials including a variety of soft stones, ivory and bone. Such seals were used to make an impression on soft clay, and originally the lumps of clay perhaps sealed jars, boxes or doors in the homes of individuals, to safeguard the contents and to mark their personal property. The employment of seals to indicate the contents or origins of a container would have been a natural extension from this essentially personal seal use. We seem to see the beginnings of a wider function of seals, beyond the purely personal, at the very end of the prepalatial period. The existence of so-called 'noduli' is an example. These are lumps of clay impressed with seals just like any other sealing, but with no string-holes or evidence for any sort of

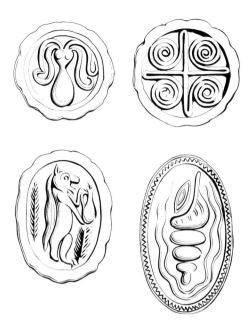

40 Seal impressions from protopalatial Phaistos.

attachment to anything. It is plausibly suggested that these acted as tokens which could be given to individuals, perhaps on the completion of certain work, and then exchanged for rations or some other form of payment, the nodulus carrying the authority of the owner of the seal.

While the beginnings of seal-based administration can be seen before the time of the palaces, there is no doubt that their foundation required more elaborate systems to deal with movements of goods and materials that were both more complex and on a larger scale. Goods in palace store-rooms could be controlled by seals on the doors or on containers, and there is evidence that broken sealings were kept and counted to keep basic records. Excellent evidence for this system comes from protopalatial Phaistos, where some six and a half thousand sealings were found, stamped by more than three hundred different seals. Store-room seal-ing systems of comparable type were used elsewhere in the ancient Near East.

At the most basic level, such systems do not require the use of writing. Nonetheless, if the information is to be recorded, writing must be used, and it may be that written records existed in the palaces from their inception. Two scripts are known from the First Palaces, Cretan Hieroglyphic (which, in spite of the name, is quite different from Egyptian Hieroglyphic) and Linear A. Both are Cretan inventions, though the idea of writing no doubt came from the Near East or Egypt, where writing was invented in about 3000BC.

Hieroglyphic seems to have been particularly at home in northern Crete, where it is found in the palaces of Knossos, Mallia and Petras, while Linear A was used in the First Palace of Phaistos. Both scripts remain undeciphered, and it is possible that two different languages or dialects are represented. On the other hand the scripts seem to have been used rather differently. Partic-ularly noticeable is the fact that Hieroglyphic was widely used on seal-stones, but Linear A, on the whole, was not. Nonetheless, the Hieroglyphic records of Knossos, Mallia and Petras seem to be comparable in function with the Linear A tablets from protopalatial Phaistos. The two scripts may have been

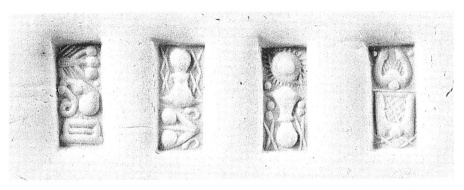

41 Impressions from a small four-sided seal-stone of green jasper, engraved on each side with signs from the Hieroglyphic script.

used in parallel for the same language, the choice of script being partly regional, partly based on the purpose for which it was used.

The early Linear A documents from Phaistos are clay tablets recording quantities of produce, using a decimal system of counting that can be understood. This, combined with the use of ideograms or small drawings of the commodities listed, means it is often possible to see what they record, and in what quantities. Linear A was also used in this way in the Second Palace period, when it became established on an island-wide basis and was used on a greater variety of objects, as we shall see. Only a single fragment of a Linear A tablet comes from Knossos in the First Palace period, from an area close to the palace itself.

Hieroglyphic, by contrast, is quite commonly found on seals and sealings. It also occurs written free-hand on clay tablets and clay tokens or labels of various shapes: bars, medallions and the like. The recently discovered hieroglyphic archive from Petras includes bars, medallions, crescents and nodules. This group of material is important because it had fallen from an upper room into an area near the north entrance of the protopalatial phase of the small palace at Petras. It clearly belongs together, and can be dated to the MM IIB period. Hieroglyphic signs are sometimes incised on pottery vases. The script seems to die out at the end of the First Palace period.

In spite of the fact that the scripts are undeciphered, philologists can work out that both are syllabic and each consists of some dozens of syllabograms – that is, signs representing certain syllables. Groups of syllabograms thus form words. Hieroglyphic and Linear A are between them the precursors and somehow the 'parents' of Linear B, though the precise relationship is disputed. Linear B was an adaptation of the native Cretan writing system or systems to represent Greek, and is discussed on page 183.

Archaeologists can also glean useful information about the protopalatial period from these undeciphered scripts. In the Phaistos Linear A archive, for example, we begin to see the concerns of the palace, with listings of men, vases, grain, wine and figs. A tablet from Quartier Mu at Mallia has been interpreted as listing 7,000 sheep, which would certainly represent a considerable accumulation of wealth. At no site, though, can we achieve anything like a complete picture, and indeed we must assume that only a very small proportion of the clay documents originally used has been retrieved. The usual vagaries of survival and excavation are compounded by the fact that the clay documents of both Linear A and Hieroglyphic, like the later Linear B tablets, are only preserved when baked accidentally in fires. In contrast to Near Eastern practice, Cretan documents were not fired, but simply sundried. They therefore represented only temporary records. Perhaps the clay was redampened and re-used when the information was no longer required. Whether the information was in fact transferred to more permanent records in a material such as parchment or papyrus that has not survived is disputed. It seems likely, but there is no evidence for this in the First Palace period, and indeed only indirect evidence in the time of the Second Palaces. The existence of neopalatial clay sealings that seem to bear the imprints of folded parchment is surely significant, while the fact that Linear A inscriptions were sometimes painted on pottery shows that clay tablets were not the only medium used for writing later in the Bronze Age.

Protopalatial Arts and Crafts

Gerald Cadogan rightly observes that a glance at the galleries in Herakleion museum shows quantities of pottery from the protopalatial period, but relatively few works in other media.[6] Nonetheless, among the surviving finds we have tantalizing glimpses of fine art and craftsmanship, some indicating achievements that may have been equalled but were not necessarily surpassed in the succeeding periods.

The pottery itself is noteworthy, and was clearly an important product. The fine wares of the First Palace period are often still grouped under the term Kamares pottery, named after the sacred cave near Phaistos where such pottery was first discovered. The term is useful, though pottery specialists point out that the picture is complicated by the production of Kamares pottery in some centres outside the palaces, and by contemporary production of simpler pottery styles. Indeed palatial Kamares Ware itself, which is characterized by the use of polychrome decoration on a dark background, actually includes examples of a variety of techniques. At its best it achieved thin-walled elegance and shows the highest level of technical achievement. The Cretan clay was well-levigated by the potters and was capable of producing a very fine fabric. The use of the potter's wheel, an innovation of

RIGHT
42 A particularly exuberant example of
Kamares pottery from Phaistos, this large
stemmed bowl has chequer-board and
other painted decoration and applied
white flowers.

BELOW
42 A simple cup from Knossos in the
⁀ ⁀ᵈ and white paint

the First Palace period, enabled the throwing of light, balanced shapes.
Orange, red, yellow and white paint was applied to a dark background in
richly swirling patterns that were mostly abstract, though often suggesting
plant motifs and making much use of spirals. Other techniques included the
decorative roughening of the surface of the clay to form a textured pattern
(barbotine decoration), the use of moulds into which the clay was pressed to
form decorative patterns in relief, and the addition of appliqués in various
forms. The most common vessel shapes were bridge-spouted jars, jugs and a
range of cups. Sometimes matching sets of jugs or jars and drinking cups have
been found.

The finest Kamares pottery was discovered in the palaces of Knossos and
Phaistos. As well as being used as table ware, it seems to have been used in
some religious rituals. Some was stored, either for palace use or to be sent
elsewhere in Crete or abroad. The pottery workshops may not actually have
been in the palaces: probably they were near to the sources of clay, which
occur quite widely in the region between Knossos and Phaistos. While
'provincial' production centres also existed, the most complex examples of
this inventive and accomplished type of pottery come from these two
palaces. They exported Kamares Ware to the Aegean area, to the Syro-
Palestinian coast and to Egypt, where the pottery was obviously admired so
much that local attempts to copy it were made, though it must be said rather
unsuccessfully.

Protopalatial pottery, then, is both plentiful and impressive. What of the other arts and crafts? We might start with a word about what does not survive. Evidence for wall-painting in the First Palace period is scanty. Fragments from Mallia town with geometric or floral patterns join fairly extensive, if rather scrappy, evidence for the use of plaster painted in single colours (usually red and blue) from both the palaces and elsewhere to suggest that a wall-painting tradition already existed in Crete at this time. Some simple borders and decorative patterns are known, though there is no evidence for pictorial compositions. The lack of survival may, though, largely be due to subsequent rebuildings.

The creation of large-scale stone sculptures seems not to have been a feature of Cretan craftsmanship at any period, in extreme contrast to practices in contemporary Egypt and the Near East. Nonetheless, Minoan skill in working stone is very apparent in two particular areas: the creation of stone vases and the carving of seal-stones.

Stone vases had a long tradition in Crete by the time of the First Palaces. They were established as a common feature in the palaces and houses of the protopalatial period, and shapes included cups, bowls, lamps and so on. So-called 'bird's nest' bowls, named because their incurving shape is like that of a nest, were particularly popular. A range of 'libation tables' was also made. These are rectangular in shape with a central circular bowl. The name is somewhat misleading as they are usually perfectly portable and are therefore rather small to be called 'tables'. Moreover the central bowl could have held many different things. They do, however, certainly seem to have had ritual use, as they have mainly been found in peak sanctuaries, sacred caves and shrines in palaces and houses. The type occurs in both the First and Second Palace periods. Some protopalatial examples are quite elaborately decorated. Neopalatial examples sometimes have Linear A inscriptions, presumably dedicatory, or at least connected with cult.

During the protopalatial period seal-stones started to be made from hard stones, and new techniques of engraving were adopted, using fast rotary drills and cutting wheels. The stones included red and green jasper, rock-crystal, amethyst, agate and carnelian. Most must have been imported from the Near East or Egypt. Animal-shaped seals were less common than they had been in the Early Minoan period, though a variety of elegant stamp-seals with stalks were produced, along with various shapes that enabled the user to grasp the back of the seal. Three- and four-sided prisms were used, and discoids with transverse string-holes were among the types that needed to be strung for use. Sealing surfaces began to be convex to allow a cleaner impression to be made on the clay sealing. Pictoral motifs, which had been rare in the Early Bronze Age, became common on protopalatial seals. Human figures appear, as do a wide range of animals, insects and birds. Sphinxes and griffins enter the repertoire, perhaps from Egypt, though they may have come to Crete via the Syro-Palestinian coast or Anatolia. The Egyptian hippopotamus goddess Taweret, rapidly transformed into the Minoan 'genius' (see page 100), seems to be a direct borrowing from Egypt. Most seals must have been worn attached to the neck or wrist; they therefore had a function as adornment or jewellery, and perhaps also as good luck charms, as well as their use for sealing purposes.

Jewellery of the First Palace period is rare, though the well-known bee-pendant from the Chrysolakkos funerary building at Mallia gives some insight into the technical and artistic achievements of the time. This piece uses the techniques of filigree and granulation – the addition of gold wire and fine granules of gold to decorate a golden surface. Its symmetrical design has abiding charm, as the numbers of modern replicas testify.

There is some evidence that the group of jewellery known as the Aigina treasure, now in the British Museum, may belong to the First Palace period. While almost certainly found on Aigina, and probably made there, it seems to be the work of Minoan craftsmen. Technically much of the treasure is of fairly simple repoussé work, with no granulation and little use of filigree, though some of the inlaid rings are of quite complex workmanship. The effect of the four large ornaments usually interpreted as earrings is, however, very dramatic. They look wonderful spread out in a museum display, yet if worn suspended from the ears the dangling elements would have hung together in some confusion. Perhaps they were intended for funerary use.

44 Two ornaments, probably earrings, from the Aigina treasure. They are of gold and carnelian. Dogs and monkeys at the centre are surrounded by pendant birds and discs.

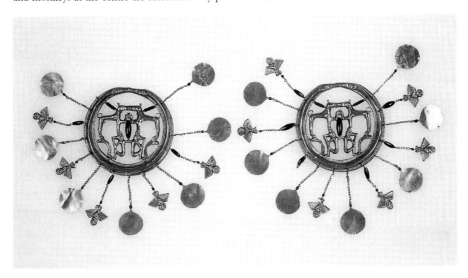

45 Gold pendant showing the 'Master of Animals' from the Aigina treasure.

The most famous element in the treasure is the 'Master of Animals' pendant showing a nature-god holding two birds, probably geese. He has a tall, feathered crown, a typically Minoan kilt with a tassel at the front, large earrings, and bracelets on his upper arms. He stands among lotus flowers, probably on a stylized papyrus boat, and is framed by curving elements derived from the shape of bull's horns. This piece is unique, and for many years could not be more closely paralleled than in a very general way by the Chrysolakkos pendant, which is similarly symmetrical in arrangement and has in common with the Aigina pendant the fact that it is backed by a plain sheet of gold. An even more closely comparable piece came to light in the early 1990s during excavations at Tel el-Dab'a (ancient Avaris) in the Nile delta. This shows confronted dogs, but has close stylistic similarities with the Aigina pendant and uses the same technique. It has plausibly been suggested that it is an import from Minoan Crete, and it was found in Egypt in a context dated to 1780–1740BC, thus within the Minoan protopalatial period. This suggests that the Aigina pendant could also be protopalatial.

Even more recently a third comparable pendant, this time in silver, has been recognized.[7] Brought back from Egypt by Flinders Petrie, and described by him as of XIIth dynasty date, the pendant belongs to the Petrie Museum in London. It was heavily corroded, but extensive conservation work has revealed two falcon-headed griffins, confronted in a symmetrical arrangement that brings this piece closely into line with the two gold

46 Silver pendant with confronted falcon-headed griffins, found in Egypt.

pendants. The technique of the silver pendant is exactly the same. While the iconography may at first glance look more Egyptian, the pendant is not closely paralleled in Egyptian jewellery. Sadly its provenance is unknown, but we may suggest, at least, that it is a third example of a piece of Minoan jewellery imported into Egypt, arguably, but not certainly, in the time of the First Palaces.

Foreign Relations

In the time of the First Palaces the influence of Crete began to be felt on the islands of the Aegean, the Greek mainland and the western coast of Turkey. Minoan pottery and other objects were exported, as Crete established connections of trade and exchange. At the same time Crete's influence began to appear in the lifestyles of her Aegean neighbours, in a pattern that would increase as the Bronze Age progressed. Presumably this was partly emulation of Minoan culture simply because it was seen to be desirable. In some cases, though, a Minoan presence abroad is certainly indicated. Such Minoan settlements are unlikely to have been colonies created because of population pressure at home, nor is there evidence of military or political control: it seems much more likely that they were a response to the establishment of trade routes, with groups of expatriates making a living that was essentially based on maintenance of exchanges between Crete and her neighbours.

In fact a pattern of three main Minoan trade routes has been suggested for palatial Crete as a whole, and it seems that these were already gaining importance in the First Palace period. The first follows what have been described as the 'western string' of islands, Thera, Melos and Kea, linking

Crete with the Greek mainland, and particularly the important area of the silver mines at Lavrion. Protopalatial pottery has been found at Akrotiri on Thera, Phylakopi on Melos and Ayia Irini on Kea.

Kastri on Kythera was clearly a Minoan settlement, as is indicated not only by the use of Minoan pottery and the type of burials made there but also by the presence of a Minoan peak sanctuary very like those on Crete itself. This island formed the natural route from the western end of Crete to the Peloponnese, perhaps specifically Ayios Stephanos in Lakonia, with the important site of Lerna in the Argolid as its ultimate goal.

From the east end of Crete the islands of Kasos and Karpathos, which both have protopalatial pottery, are natural stepping stones to the Dodecanese and the west coast of Turkey. The island of Rhodes perhaps already had a Minoan element in the population of the towns of Ialysos and Trianda, while Minoan settlement on the west coast of Turkey is indicated by finds from Miletos.

An intensification of contacts with the wider world had occurred in Crete before the foundation of the palaces, and was characteristic of the spirit of the age that presaged their creation, but the palaces themselves seem quickly to have become prime movers in long-distance trade and exchange, providing the incentive (driven by their need to obtain metals), the investment and the infrastructure required. This role was clearly established later in the Bronze Age: the evidence that it was also an integral part of the workings of the First Palaces is relatively slight in quantity, but nonetheless suggestive.

The primary evidence lies in the Minoan pottery and other objects found in Egypt and at sites along the Syro-Palestinian coast and in the foreign imports found in Crete. Some instances perhaps show high-value exchanges – particularly if a Minoan origin is accepted for the silver vessels of the Tod treasure, discussed below. Mutual iconographic or artistic influences are also indicative of reasonably intensive contacts at this time.

A single protopalatial Cretan vessel was found as far down the Nile as Qubbet el-Hawa, near Elephantine, but the largest body of Middle Minoan pottery found in Egypt comes from the town site of Lahun, on the edge of the Fayyum depression. This is the largest excavated Middle Kingdom town in Egypt. While digging in the houses in the town Flinders Petrie found fragments of vessels that he presciently described as 'Aegean' in origin: this was not only before the discovery of the palaces in Crete, but even before the finds in the Kamares cave would give a name to this brightly coloured pottery ware. The fragments from Lahun itself and from its associated cemetery at Haraga represent more than thirty Minoan vases.[8] The number is not large, but the presence of local, Egyptian copies of Kamares Ware implies not only that the Cretan pottery was admired, presumably for its fine clay and bright polychrome decoration, but also that enough was imported to make an impact on the local potters and to inspire them to copy it.

Kamares pottery has been found at Byblos, the handful of examples including two cups, three jars and a number of sherds. While local pottery does not seem to imitate Cretan wares, two silver hemispherical cups with relief spiral decoration seem to be either imported from Crete or made at Byblos in imitation of Minoan products. At Ugarit, too, a small number of imported Minoan vessels indicates exchanges with Crete, and local copies of Minoan wares are found. The earliest Minoan import to Cyprus is a vessel dating from the period directly before the foundation of the palaces. Fragments of Minoan pottery have also been found at Beirut, Qatna and Hazor.

The total number of pottery vessels from Crete found in Egypt and along the Syro-Palestinian coast is not large, but their distribution suggests Minoan input into the circular trading patterns of vessels travelling around the eastern Mediterranean. The details of the organization of this trade are not known. Naturally ships carrying Cretan goods need not all have been Cretan, but it does seem very likely that Minoan ships were being built, equipped and manned for long-distance voyages. Such enterprises were perhaps always undertaken at the behest of the palaces: merchants, captains and other specialists may well have operated, but it would seem scarcely likely that they could have done so in a manner independent of the support of the palaces and the concentration of wealth, power and influence that they represented.

The export of Minoan pottery for its own sake seems likely enough, and many examples found abroad are such things as cups and bridge-spouted jars, and therefore not shapes suitable for the transportation of contents. The pottery may, though, have been a fairly casual accompaniment to more substantial exchanges, either of perishable goods and commodities or even trade in metals. We may envisage that ships' captains, even if they were directly controlled by the palaces, could carry on casual exchanges of goods which might then end up in places such as the houses in an Egyptian town, while their more substantial cargoes were perhaps destined for rulers and courts.

The system of 'princely gift-exchange', known from written sources in the Late Bronze Age in Egypt and the Near East, saw gifts between rulers that could actually amount to very substantial exchanges of raw materials as well as of finished luxurious goods. The perishables offered by Crete may have included wood, textiles and agricultural produce such as grain, wine and oil – though vessels used for liquid exports might be expected to have survived in the archaeological record. It is possible, too, that silver from

47 Part of the Tod treasure in the Musée du Louvre, Paris.

Lavrion in Attica was exported via Crete, but direct evidence is lacking. The Tod treasure, however, may represent Aegean silver in Egypt, albeit in rather unusual form.

The Tod treasure was found in a deposit beneath the floor of a temple at Tod, near Luxor, in Egypt.[9] The treasure consisted of materials foreign to Egypt dedicated to the god Mont. Some were of Mesopotamian origin, but a large number of silver vessels may have come from Crete. Contemporary silver-work from the island scarcely survives, but the Tod vessels can be closely compared to Minoan pottery from the early part of the First Palace period. The treasure was found in boxes, two of which were labelled with the cartouche of Amenemhat II, who reigned from 1922 to 1878BC. The vessels, mostly cups, were squashed and folded and had clearly been deposited not as valuable articles but simply as valuable raw material. The likelihood of their being of Minoan origin is not accepted by all scholars, and analysis has proved inconclusive. The presence in the treasure of a silver pendant with designs that can be closely paralleled among Minoan seals does nonetheless support a Minoan connection.

The presence of possibly Aegean silver bullion in Egypt, although in this rather unusual scrap-metal form, is interesting when it comes to speculating about protopalatial trade. Exchanges may in fact have been minimal, but equally the sparse and intermittent evidence that is archaeologically preserved may only be the remains of small-scale exchanges essentially operating in parallel with a more substantial movement of goods.

48 Drawing of the silver pendant
from the Tod treasure.

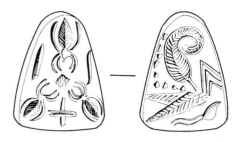

Arguments from silence are always dangerous, so we might end this brief account of long-distance protopalatial exchanges with rare evidence from written records of the time. From the palace at Mari on the Euphrates there exist documents dating to the eighteenth century BC – MM II in Cretan terms, and the height of the First Palace period. They mention goods coming from a place called Kaptara, and also a consignment of tin destined for a man from Kaptara who is resident at Ugarit. Kaptara, the Caphtor of the Bible, is usually identified as Crete. The goods include an inlaid metal weapon, a pair of leather shoes and textiles. These certainly sound both possible and appropriate as Cretan products: fine swords were made in the Crete of the First Palaces, and there is every likelihood that the palatial textile workshops were producing luxury goods, some of which would have found their way abroad.

The products may sound rather slight – just a handful of luxury goods – but the tablets list them as Kaptaran gifts that the king of Mari was sending to Hammurabi of Babylon. This, then, is the world of 'princely' or 'palatial' gift-exchange, where luxuries, including desirable foreign exotica, were presented between rulers. Sometimes this was in tandem with much larger consignments of important raw materials. We know from the Mari tablets that tin was distributed through Mari from points further east to places westwards, including Ugarit. There is no indication of direct trade between Mari and Crete, which presumably always took place through intermediaries, but the presence of a Cretan in Ugarit receiving tin is a sign that Crete was engaged in well-planned and purposeful exchanges. In fact, though, for the eastern peoples the homeland of the Kaptarans may have seemed very remote – so much so that the god of handicrafts was said to come from Caphtor, in a tradition that would seem to be connected with the fine products of Minoan Crete.

There is only one Egyptian reference to Crete of Middle Kingdom date, and that is in the 'Admonitions of Ipuwer', a text apparently composed in late Middle Kingdom times but preserved only in a single late New Kingdom manuscript. There the description, which is not necessarily to be taken literally, of an impoverished Egypt includes the lament that cedar is no longer obtained from Byblos, depriving the inhabitants of the embalming materials used as far as Keftiu. This remark is tantalizing, since embalming was not a Minoan practice, though it is of course possible that materials used by the Egyptians for the purpose came from Crete.

Foreign imports into Crete in the time of the First Palaces must complete this picture of eastern Mediterranean interconnections. Raw materials coming from Egypt, perhaps sometimes via Levantine ports, no doubt included gold, ivory and precious stones. Copper or bronze, as well as tin, probably also arrived from eastern sources, though perhaps not exclusively. Finished products imported to the island continued to include scarabs. The lower part of a statuette of a Middle Kingdom Egyptian official named User was found at Knossos. The context is not precisely dateable, but the statuette may have been a gift that marked a visit of User to Crete.

Some Minoan influence on Egyptian art has been noted in this period, and there is clear evidence for a reciprocal Egyptian effect on Minoan iconography. Judith Weingarten[10] has charted the fascinating case-study of the way in which the Egyptian hippopotamus goddess Taweret is turned into the Minoan 'genius' – a type of figure frequent in Minoan ritual scenes, usually shown carrying water or sprinkling it on to vegetation or sacred stones. The borrowing process certainly began in the time of the First Palaces. It is not clear whether Taweret originally brought some of her Egyptian significance with her, but the figures based on her seem subsequently to become purely Minoan in context and meaning.

Pottery with appliqué decoration from Quartier Mu at Mallia also indicates foreign influence. An appliqué in the form of an elegant sphinx was originally felt to show Egyptian influence, though recent research has revealed that it is close to an Anatolian sphinx in style. A cat from another vessel probably does show the influence of Egypt, though both appliqués were presumably made locally.

Long-distance interconnections, then, indicate that after the foundation of the palaces Crete became an international player as never before, confidently taking a place in a wider nexus of contacts, exchanges and influences, and becoming a major presence on the eastern Mediterranean stage.

Protopalatial Religion

Already in protopalatial Crete areas used for religious observance – shrines and sanctuaries – divide between those in the countryside and those in the towns. The former are usually either peak sanctuaries or sacred caves, the latter may in rare instances be free-standing buildings, but more usually are rooms or areas within the palaces or houses. The criteria for the identification of such areas are discussed in the section on neopalatial religion, as are religious symbolism and the possible nature of the deity or deities worshipped. The Second Palace period offers a wider range of evidence, both of actual cult paraphernalia and in iconography, though many elements of religious observance can be traced back to protopalatial origins.

The peak sanctuaries, founded before the palaces, flourished particularly in the First Palace period. Rutkowski[11] lists thirty-seven such sites, of which about twenty are securely identified, though no doubt originally there were more. Specific links seem to have been established between each palace and its nearest peak sanctuary, such as between Knossos and Juktas, Zakros and Traostalos, perhaps Mallia and Profitis Ilias, and so on. Finds at these sanctuaries often seem to be of palatial origin. Clay figurines still predominate and pottery is found in quantity relatively rarely. Bronzes and stone vessels are also found.

The palace of Phaistos is slightly unusual as it seems to have had a special relationship not with a peak sanctuary but with the Kamares cave. As we have seen, the caves of Crete had been used as dwelling places from earliest times, and some were burial sites in the Early Minoan period. It is very possible that certain caves had long been thought to be sacred places, but clear evidence for cult in sacred caves really begins in the protopalatial period. Some caves continued to be considered sacred throughout Minoan times, and indeed into later antiquity, though continuity of cult does not of course necessarily imply continuity of the same belief system. About thirty-five Minoan sacred caves have been recognized.

The Kamares cave, mentioned above because it gave its name to the characteristic pottery of the Cretan First Palaces, contained quantities of such pottery, much of it presumably dedicated by people from Phaistos. Some of the fine pottery may well have been dedicated for its own sake, though storage jars found there contained evidence for offerings of grain. Other vessels may have been used in rituals in the cave. Pottery is in general more frequently found in caves than at peak sanctuaries, showing some difference in the nature of the observances carried on at each type of site.

The existence of palace shrines in the protopalatial period is usually inferred from the presence of cult material and a certain amount of extrapolation backwards from the neopalatial situation. An exception is the First Palace period tripartite shrine in the West Court at Phaistos that adjoins the protopalatial facade towards its northern end. The three rooms recall the tripartite shrines known in later Minoan art. One room had benches with cavities and a drain in one corner, and may have been used for animal sacrifices; another room contained a stone mortar, perhaps for grain used in offerings, while the third contained a triton shell and an 'offering table' decorated with impressed bulls' heads.

The type of room that Evans called a 'lustral basin' is known in the protopalatial period from several examples, including the unusually large one excavated in Quartier Mu at Mallia. These sunken rooms, reached by right-angled steps leading down to a floor that is often carefully plastered or paved, may have had some function in ceremonies of ritual cleansing. In spite of their somewhat cistern-like appearance they did not contain standing water. It may, though, be significant that they led down into the earth. The Greek word *adyton* is sometimes used for such emplacements.

Other rooms in both palaces and houses have been identified as sanctuaries, usually on the basis of finds made within them. The use of open courts for large-scale rituals has been suggested above, and may have applied both to the courtyards belonging to the palaces and to open spaces in the towns. Town shrines that stand as independent buildings are most unusual in Minoan Crete, though a single protopalatial example is known from Mallia. The shrine was a small building, some 11 × 5 m (36 × 16½ ft), of which only the ground plan was preserved. It had three rooms. A vestibule gave access to the main cult room, distinguished by the presence of a large rectangular altar with a central depression. The third room was a store-room.

ANEMOSPILIA: HUMAN SACRIFICE IN A MINOAN SHRINE AND THE END OF PROTOPALATIAL CRETE

On the north slopes of Mount Juktas, looking down over the Knossos valley towards the sea, an extraordinary building of the protopalatial period has been excavated. It was a free-standing structure, of which three main rooms and an ante-room survive, and the contents clearly show that it was a shrine. By a remarkable chance – and this makes the building unique – the earthquake destruction of the shrine was so sudden that it caught within the collapse not only the cult equipment and the building's fixtures and fittings, but also, and very dramatically, the participants in the last Minoan rites to take place there. Skeletons identified as those of a priest, a priestess and the young male victim of a human sacrifice were found among the remains. This interpretation, suggested by the excavators Yannis and Efi Sakellarakis and backed up by the team of experts that they consulted, shocked many commentators, who were unwilling to accept that so barbarous a rite could have been practised by the Minoans. Nonetheless, it is difficult to find alternative explanations for their discoveries.

The Anemospilia shrine consists of three rooms that open on to a corridor-like ante-chamber to the north, which runs the entire width of the building. Three corresponding rooms seem to have existed on the north side of the corridor, but these are badly eroded and indicated only by scanty remains. The building is small, at less than 15 m (50 ft) wide, and its symmetrical plan

49 The shrine at Anemospilia, looking to the north. The modern emplacement in the west room covers the 'altar' on which the skeleton of the apparent victim lay.

is very unusual. The tripartite arrangement, though, instantly brings to mind representations of shrines in Minoan art, perhaps particularly that of the sanctuary among mountain scenery carved on the chlorite rhyton (sprinkler vessel) from Zakros (see fig. 86, page 158).

The corridor or ante-chamber contained more than a hundred and fifty pottery vessels. These included a number of large pithoi that must have held agricultural products dedicated at the shrine. Cooking pots and pestles were perhaps used to process these products to make specific mixtures for offerings. A pile of animal bones in the western part of the corridor came from pigs, goats and bulls. These may have been sacrificial victims. All three are shown as such in later representations of Minoan or Mycenaean sacrifices. The best-known example is on the Ayia Triadha sarcophagus, which shows the sacrifice of a bull trussed on an altar. The blood from the sacrifice is being collected in a vessel positioned below the neck of the bull.

The excavators suggested that the westernmost of the three rooms of the shrine was used for blood sacrifices and the eastern room for bloodless sacrifice. The identity of the central room as the 'holy of holies' was supported by the presence of a deep stone basin in the corridor adjacent to its door, probably for ritual cleansing of those entering. Traces of a wooden double door were found.

Inside the central room a rough bench created from the natural rock along the back (south) wall may have been occupied by a cult figure made of wood. This is suggested by the large pair of terracotta feet found there, which could have supported such a statue. (The existence of wooden statues in Minoan Crete is discussed on page 153.) The floor of the room was densely covered with vases, large and small. These presumably held the offerings made to the deity.

The suggestion is that the central room saw the final offering to the deity of the results of rituals in the two adjoining rooms. The east room, perhaps the scene of preparation of the bloodless or non-animal offerings, contained a stepped altar. Such altars are shown in representations, and known from an actual example in the Central Court of Phaistos. In the room a large variety of small jugs could have been used to contain a range of liquid offerings, while large basket-shaped vases would have been suitable for such things as loaves and fruit. Storage jars were also found there.

The west room may have been reserved for blood sacrifice, and it is suggested that the ritual involved cutting the throat of the victim, collecting the blood and dedicating it in the central room of the shrine. A very fine, large, painted vase with an appliqué decoration of a bull was found outside the door of the central room of the shrine. This was clearly a special receptacle, and was perhaps normally used for the blood of bulls, though it may have held human blood when it was broken and buried on the last occasion of its use. The west room contained few finds, but some pottery came to light there, including a vase fragment that had fallen from an upper storey – the only such evidence from Anemospilia, though the existence of an upper storey was indicated by the remains of a staircase in the ante-chamber. The three skeletons from this room, however, provided telling evidence for events there at the time of the shrine's collapse.

One was the skeleton of a young man, about eighteen years of age. He was lying on his side on a low rectangular structure made of stones and clay which was presumably an altar. The position of the bones suggested that the body was tied up. A rare type of bronze lance-head was placed across the skeleton. The weapon is 40 cm (15¾ in) long and decorated on each side with a boar's head motif. It seems beyond doubt that this man was a sacrificial victim, and that he had already been sacrificed when the moment of destruction came. The other two occupants of the room, though, were victims of the destruction, and were overwhelmed by it. The skeleton of a female about twenty-eight years of age and 1.45 m (4 ft 9 in) in height was found, her head towards the south-west corner of the room. She was sprawled face-downwards, her skeleton evocative of helplessness even after more than three and a half millennia. Next to the altar, face-upwards, lay a man estimated to have been about forty-seven years old. He was tall, at 1.78 m (5 ft 10 in), and, like the other two skeletons, was said by experts to have enjoyed good health before he died. He was wearing a very unusual ring, made of silver and iron, on the little finger of his left hand. This is the earliest example of the use of naturally occurring iron in the Aegean. It must have been a rare and precious material. The ring is unique, too, because it is the only Minoan or Mycenaean ring that has been found in position on the owner's finger. An extraordinarily fine agate seal-stone, showing a figure in a boat, was also found where it had been worn, on the left wrist of the man, to which it must have been tied. These ornaments suggest the special status of the man. He was perhaps the priest who conducted the sacrifice.

Poorly preserved remains of a fourth human skeleton were found in the ante-chamber or corridor area. They were not sufficient to indicate sex or age. This individual may have been trying to escape, or was perhaps going from the west room to the central room of the shrine.

The evidence from Anemospilia seems clearly to indicate a human sacrifice, and modern unwillingness to suggest such practices must be left to one side. There is no archaeological evidence for the practice being widespread or common in Minoan Crete. It can be argued that accounts of human sacrifice in Greek mythology provide a background against which such rites would not be impossible. It is also true that in the ancient world particular circumstances prompted these rites, such as the sacrificial killing of enemies captured in war. In Crete, though, only one other excavation has produced evidence that may indicate human sacrifice: this, the house in the Late Minoan town of Knossos containing children's bones, is discussed on page 138. The remains at Anemospilia may be from an unusual event, enacted in a desperate attempt to avert the disastrous earthquake, perhaps presaged by tremors, that caused the building to collapse.

Was this earthquake part of the devastating events that destroyed the First Palaces and many other sites in Crete, bringing the protopalatial period to an end? Canonically this destruction has been placed at the end of MM IIB. It has been attributed to the effect of earthquakes, particularly in central Crete, though it is recognized that a single seismic event island-wide would be unusual, and other factors may have played a part.

The excavators of Anemospilia felt that the sacrifice there was carried out to avert this natural disaster, though in fact they classify the pottery as MM IIB–IIIA. This potentially confuses the issue, as there is also an MM IIIA destruction at Knossos that has been attributed to earthquake damage. The two sites are near to each other, and would certainly be likely to have suffered the same seismic events. While we cannot discount the possibility of the later link, MacGillivray, in his recent study of the pottery from protopalatial Knossos,[12] agrees with the excavators that the destruction horizon at Anemospilia is that which saw the end of the First Palaces. The human sacrifice would therefore have been an attempt to ward off a disaster of truly great proportions that caused extensive damage to Minoan Crete.

The People

The physical appearance of Minoans in the First Palace period can to some extent be reconstructed, partly from skeletal evidence, partly from representations in art. Although we lack the fresco painting that adds colour to the picture in the Second Palace period, the figurines dedicated at peak sanctuaries, which provide our best protopalatial evidence, are arguably more likely to represent the ordinary populace.

Evidence from the study of bones and teeth shows that throughout the Minoan period the average height of men was 1.67 m (5 ft 5¾ in), that of women 1.55 m (5 ft 1 in). First Palace period skeletons from the Ailias cemetery east of Knossos and from burials at Zakros have been studied. The level of nutrition seems to have been reasonable, with no evidence of major malnutrition, though the life-expectancy of individuals seems to have been short, at about thirty-five years for men and thirty for women. There are frequent indications of anaemia, which could have been congenital and caused by Mediterranean thalassaemia, a condition that is found in malarial areas. Alternatively anaemia could have been acquired and would therefore constitute evidence of a poor diet. Rudimentary medical knowledge is shown in, for instance, the setting of bones and extraction of teeth, but disease, in an age before understanding of hygiene and antibiotics, must have contributed to a short average life-span. A hard physical life-style must also have taken its toll. The skeletons show some adaptations to intensive walking in rough country.

Cranial reconstruction using techniques developed in forensic science has been carried out on the well-preserved skulls from the Anemospilia shrine, giving back faces to both the 'priest' and 'priestess' engaged in the last ritual there at the end of MM II. (The skull of the sacrificial victim was not sufficiently well-preserved.) The technique has been proved to give reliable and recognizable results in the case of unidentified victims of modern crime, so we need not doubt that the faces are close to the originals. The colouring, facial hair and hairstyles of the individuals remain a matter of surmise, based largely on representations in art.

The most common representations of human figures in the First Palace period are the small clay models of men and women left in sanctuaries and probably representing the continuing presence of the person making the offering. These figures are generally shown in formalized attitudes of prayer. Their clothing is indicated either by modelling or with paint.

The male figures often wear a simple garment which Paul Rehak[13] has called a 'breechcloth': a rectangular piece of material passing between the legs and anchored by a belt at front and back. (He admits that the term lacks elegance, but points out that it is more accurate than 'loincloth', which suggests a cloth around the hips.) The ends of the Minoan breechcloth could extend over the belt at the back or the front to create a flap of material. The garment itself would have been of wool or linen. It could be pulled tight to form a sort of codpiece, but the rigid codpieces shown on some representations must have been separately made. They were presumably of harder material such as leather, and worn either inside or outside the breechcloth itself. The emphasis of a narrow waist by means of a belt appears in the First Palace period and is a continuing feature in Minoan male dress. The belts may sometimes have been of leather, though they later often look as though they were made of rolled cloth. The figurines sometimes wear a large dagger tucked into their belt at the front.

The Minoan kilt, frequently shown in Second Palace period representations, was also worn in the period of the First Palaces. This was similarly a rectangular piece of cloth, but in this instance it was wrapped around the waist. Some terracotta figurines wear a simple, short kilt. In more elaborate representations, such as that of the 'Master of Animals' pendant of the Aigina treasure and the acrobat on the hilt of a gold sword from Mallia, a tassel is shown down the front of the kilt.

The footwear of the figurines is sometimes indicated in paint and appears to be either boots or possibly some sort of socks or leggings worn with sandals.

Figurines of women show that already they were wearing the large skirts and open bodices that are better known from Second Palace period representations. The skirts are often bell-shaped, and do not seem to be flounced – though this may be partly due to schematization in these clay figures. The breasts are bare, and the bodice sometimes curves into a high collar behind the neck. These women often wear high head-dresses or hats.

In conclusion we can say of the protopalatial period that it represented the first great flowering of Minoan culture. Much that was to remain characteristic of Minoan Crete was established or evolved during this period of some two hundred and fifty years, from the palaces themselves to the various arts and crafts practised in the island's workshops. Our glimpses of the protopalatial world within the palaces are partial and piecemeal because of the later developments at these sites, though elsewhere – in the town of Mallia, for example, or in the shrine at Anemospilia – our window on protopalatial Crete is more fully opened. Some works of art stand out, too, clearly representing a much larger repertoire, and showing that works in all media were already being made. Few innovations can be attributed to the succeeding, neopalatial period, though many more fine examples of neopalatial art have survived.

The political structures implied by the foundation of the palaces and the settlement hierarchy around them no doubt evolved through the period, as the centres of power established themselves and their relations with each other and with the rest of the island. The process may not always have been peaceful. Indeed it is suggested by some scholars that the destructions at the end of the First Palace period may be attributable to the hand of man, and represent internal dissent as the powerful elites abrogated to themselves more and more control.

In fact, though, the effects of extensive earthquake damage emerge as a more probable cause. Both the severity and the apparent simultaneity of the destructions are better explained by a natural disaster, particularly in view of the fact that no apparent change in Minoan society appears in their aftermath. Rebuilding and re-establishment began straight away. Things were not exactly the same as before, but essentially the Minoan culture, after this setback, continued to flourish. The protopalatial period had established firm roots for the neopalatial period in Crete.

Chapter Four

NEOPALATIAL CRETE

IN THE PERIOD of the Second Palaces the island of Crete was home to a remarkable civilization. Characterized by flourishing palaces, urbanization on a scale not seen elsewhere in the Aegean, country houses and important shrines, the era also witnessed the production of some of the finest works of Minoan artists and craftsmen to have survived. Whether neopalatial Crete truly eclipsed the First Palace period in grandeur and importance cannot now be known, but the era is widely seen as the apogee of Minoan civilization. Quite which part of the period from MM III to LM IB saw the really greatest Minoan flowering is also arguable: MM III represents a century of regrouping; LM IA is thought by some to include the best of times; in LM IB, it has been argued, the island showed signs of stress in the aftermath of the Thera eruption – though it is to this last phase that some of the finest works of art can be attributed. The picture in fact is not static within this long period: the fortunes of individual sites ebb and flow.

During the period known as MM III (about 1700–1600BC), the Minoans engaged in large-scale construction projects to repair the damage from the destructions, probably caused by earthquakes, which brought the First Palace period to a close and devastated most standing buildings. At the palace sites much remained that could be incorporated into, or used as a basis for, the new versions of the buildings. At Knossos this phenomenon was very marked, and extensive protopalatial remains underlie later structures. At Phaistos a radical repositioning of the west facade of the palace took place, and the Second Palace was smaller than the first. Mallia too saw First Palace constructions incorporated into the new, though here again there is a sense of refocusing: Quartier Mu, which in the First Palace period had had many apparently 'palatial' functions (or at least functions which overlapped those of the First Palace) was not rebuilt, and the palace in its new incarnation seems to have taken over these functions in a thoroughly centralized way.

The MM III period also witnessed the inauguration of the so-called 'villas' or country houses which became characteristic of the Cretan countryside in the Second Palace period. These may be an indication of more peaceful times in Crete: although many are not as isolated as was at first thought, they are not fortified and presumably did not feel vulnerable to attack. They are administratively linked to the Second Palaces, the links sometimes underlined by the finding of the same seal-impression at more than one site. The country houses copy the fashions of Knossos in art and architecture, and thus form part of the picture of a truly island-wide Knossian dominance at this time.

The transition from MM III to LM IA was a time of expansion and new building at many sites. The palace at Knossos was extensively remodelled after a serious destruction, perhaps caused by earthquake, and new town houses were built: the Royal Villa at Ayia Triadha was constructed over an earlier protopalatial building; a new monumental structure was erected at Kommos, and so on.

The eruption of Thera can be shown to have occurred late within the LM IA period. The extent of its effect on Crete has been much debated. Once it became clear that Thera could not have caused the extensive destructions of LM IB that brought an end to neopalatial Crete, the tendency was to down-play any destructive effect on the island. Clearly the theories of huge sea waves flooding and damaging the northern coastal sites had to be abandoned, nor did the ash-fall on the island's eastern end apparently amount to much. Nonetheless, destructions are apparent on Cretan sites in LM IA that may have been related to the Thera explosion. The very exposed position of the Villa of the Lilies on the north coast at Amnisos no doubt meant that it really did bear the brunt of the effect. The newly discovered palace at Galatas also went out of use at this time. In other places, such as Palaikastro and Kommos, extensive remodelling took place, presumably after destructive episodes. Interestingly, pumice is found at some sites in rebuildings after these destructions, perhaps ritually positioned. At Petras pumice in conical cups was placed on the steps of an important staircase; pumice was also found at Pseira, and in association with a shrine in the 'villa' at Nirou Khani. The material does have practical uses, however, so a ritual association cannot be assumed. There is no evidence for devastating quantities of pumice or ash falling on to Crete, though it is recognized that ash may have fallen in sufficient quantities to damage crops in the eastern part of the island, and to disrupt agriculture there, if only for a year or two.

The noise of the Thera explosion and the darkened sky would certainly have been alarming. It would be surprising if so large-scale an event in such close proximity had no effect on Cretan morale, at the very least. Driessen

50 The Villa of the Lilies at Amnisos on Crete's north coast, perhaps destroyed in LM IA by the effects of the Thera eruption. The name derives from the fine frescoes of lilies discovered there.

and MacDonald[1] have argued that life on Crete was seriously undermined or destabilized by the eruption, and this perhaps ultimately led to civil unrest or even attacks from outside a generation or so later, in LM IB. Yet the immediate impact of the eruption is far from clear and there are many indications that Crete took the explosion of Thera in its stride.

In LM IB, then, life went on in Crete's palaces, country houses and towns. We might stand back now from precise chronological divisions to consider neopalatial Crete as a whole, discussing each of these types of sites.

Knossos in the Second Palace period is the largest of the four main palaces – it measures about 135 × 135 m (443 × 443 ft), excluding the West Court, and the Central Court is roughly 50 × 25 m (164 × 82 ft). The whole complex is more the size of a small village than of a single building. Phaistos probably achieved its greatest extent, of about 120 × 120 m (394 × 394 ft), in the First Palace period, and was slightly smaller subsequently, though at 48 × 22 m (157 × 72 ft) the Central Court is of a similar size to that at Knossos. Mallia is smaller than both, at about 115 × 87 m (377 × 285 ft), though again its Central Court is of commensurate size at about 46 × 22 m (151 × 72 ft). That of Zakros is only just over 30 × 12 m (98 × 39 ft), but the palace itself, at about 80 × 80 m (262 × 262 ft), is small. Continuing excavations at the newly discovered palace of Galatas in central Crete have revealed a Central Court of 32 × 16 m (105 × 52 ft). The well-preserved east wing of the building measures 70 × 60 m (230 × 197 ft), but it does not seem to have had a west court. The Central Court of the palatial building at Petras is tiny by comparison, at only 13 × 6 m (43 × 20 ft).

While these new discoveries underline the fact that we must be more inclusive in our definition of Minoan palaces, Knossos, Phaistos and Mallia still stand out for scale and complexity, and Knossos remains pre-eminent. It feels different to the modern visitor. This is a product of size and elaboration, certainly, but also derives from the impression of a richly decorated interior. The painted schemes of the walls date from the palace's final phase, but there is good reason to think that there was extensive frescoed decoration earlier. This, combined with the use of various coloured and variegated stones for pavings and column-bases, must have given a rich – perhaps even oppressive – opulence to the palace's interiors.

Phaistos, Mallia and Zakros seem simpler partly because they lack the sort of extensive restoration that Evans put in place at Knossos. There is no doubt, though, that we are perceiving a real difference. All the palaces must have been richly decorated and appointed, all must have had cushions, hangings and draperies, fine objects and beautiful furniture, but surely for a Minoan visitor, too, the experience of Knossos must have been awe-inspiring and special.

The sheer size of the palace at Knossos is matched by its complexity, and the nature of the architecture, with its characteristic asymmetries, could, one imagines, easily have led to a feeling of overwhelmed confusion. Here was a great centre of power – the greatest any Minoan could experience – and presumably the power wielded was absolute, so that individuals effectively owed to the palace not only their livelihood but in principle also their lives. Already this notional visit incorporates all the anxieties that in the modern world might accompany a visit to palace, parliament, tax office and law court. When we consider that the palace was also a holy place – perhaps the most holy – we can perhaps begin to perceive how awe-inspiring it must have been.

In considering Crete in the Second Palace period, then, we cannot do better than to start with Knossos and the other palaces and their surrounding towns. This will lead naturally to a consideration of the large town houses of the neopalatial period that are particularly characteristic of Knossos. Looking outwards, we will find other large houses of the period that are perhaps not so easy to divide logically. The large building at the heart of the town of Gournia is sometimes called a 'palace', though it is not of canonical form. Other imposing houses, such as the examples at Tylissos, were perhaps the homes of individuals who dominated their local settlements. Some of the large houses traditionally described as 'villas' or 'country houses' also actually fall into this category, since none seems to have stood in total isolation, though the nature of the surroundings is often not well known. The settlement hierarchy in neopalatial Crete is complex and fascinating; the picture is one of richness and diversity. Other sites such as shrines and sanctuaries must also be included. Discussions of art, religion and a consideration of the real life experience of Minoans and others in one of their 'outposts' – the town of Akrotiri on Thera – complete the chapter.

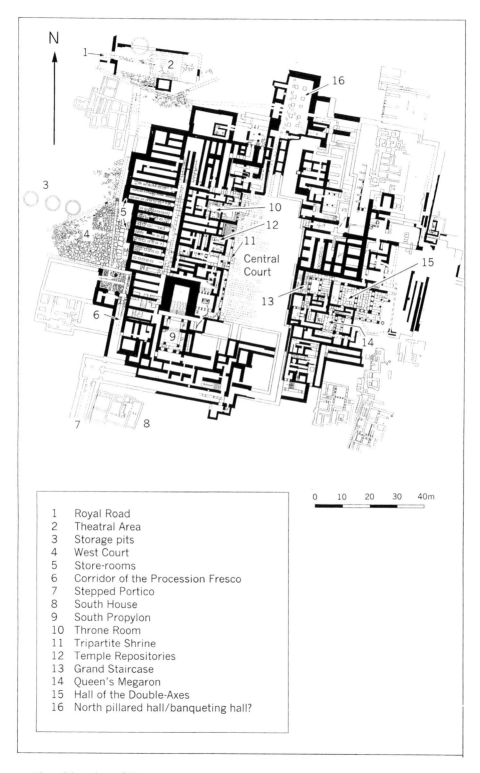

N

1
2
16
3
5
10
12
11
4
Central
Court
15
6
13
9
14
7
8

| | 0 | 10 | 20 | 30 | 40m |

1 Royal Road
2 Theatral Area
3 Storage pits
4 West Court
5 Store-rooms
6 Corridor of the Procession Fresco
7 Stepped Portico
8 South House
9 South Propylon
10 Throne Room
11 Tripartite Shrine
12 Temple Repositories
13 Grand Staircase
14 Queen's Megaron
15 Hall of the Double-Axes
16 North pillared hall/banqueting hall?

51 Plan of the palace of Knossos.

52 Copy of a miniature fresco from Knossos known as the 'Sacred Grove and Dance'. A large crowd
of spectators watches women dancing. Raised causeways, such as those seen in the west courts of
the palaces, are clearly shown.

The Second Palaces

The palaces are characterized by a rectangular Central Court on a roughly
north–south orientation and an important West Court. They have an imposing west facade, which, like some other areas of the buildings, used ashlar
masonry, and other rooms or groups of rooms of considerable architectural
elaboration, with light-wells, columns and multiple doors. Extensive store-
rooms, many with rows of pithoi (giant pottery jars), are typical, as are
workshops for various craft activities and archive-rooms where written
records were kept. Many areas seem to have been used for ritual or for the
storage of cult paraphernalia. It is often impossible to determine the precise
function of particular rooms: factors that make this difficult include remodelling, levelling, re-use, plundering and the lack of finds *in situ*. The palaces
certainly had more than one storey, but the surviving remains are generally
at basement or ground level, so storage or service areas are better preserved
than the doubtless more spacious apartments of the upper floors, which can
only be understood in broadest outline.

Let us take a generalized tour round the palaces of Knossos, Phaistos and
Mallia, proceeding anti-clockwise from the west. The important west facade

is one of the defining architectural elements of a Minoan palace. Characteristically of ashlar masonry, with a high course of smoothly dressed stones at
the base, the west facade at Knossos, Phaistos and Mallia has decorative shallow recesses, a feature inherited from the protopalatial period and perhaps
designed to break the monotony of a large wall surface. It adjoins the West
Court – a large paved area with slightly raised stone paths crossing it. Such
causeways or processional ways can plausibly be thought to have had ceremonial uses, as the fresco from Knossos known as the 'Sacred Grove and
Dance' seems to indicate.

The West Court served, both physically and functionally, as an interface
between the palace and its surrounding town. Assemblies of the people may
have met there, perhaps at times to view ceremonies that, it has been
suggested, may have been made visible to the populace through windows on
the west facade. At both Knossos and Phaistos there is also what Evans dubbed
a 'Theatral Area' on the west side of the palace: that is, a series of low steps on
which an audience could perhaps stand, rather than sit, to watch ceremonies.
The structures are slightly different at each site: at Knossos the Theatral Area
occupies the north–west palace angle, the steps form a right-angle and the
paved area viewed continues into the Royal Road. At Phaistos the very broad
steps of the Theatral Area cross the West Court at its northern end. Mallia and
Zakros seem to have no real equivalent of this type of structure.

Perhaps nowhere can the scale and quality of the Minoan architectural
achievement be better appreciated than in the West Court of the palace at
Phaistos. Here the visitor has an impression both of monumentality and of
grace. The grand staircase leading up to the palace, its broad and shallow steps
flanked by neatly squared ashlar blocks of great size, is itself a wonder. From
its junction with the steps from the Upper Court the eye receives an extraordinary impression of the breadth and spaciousness of this Minoan built

53 The West Court at Phaistos, where the steps of the Theatral Area and the steps of the
monumental staircase meet.

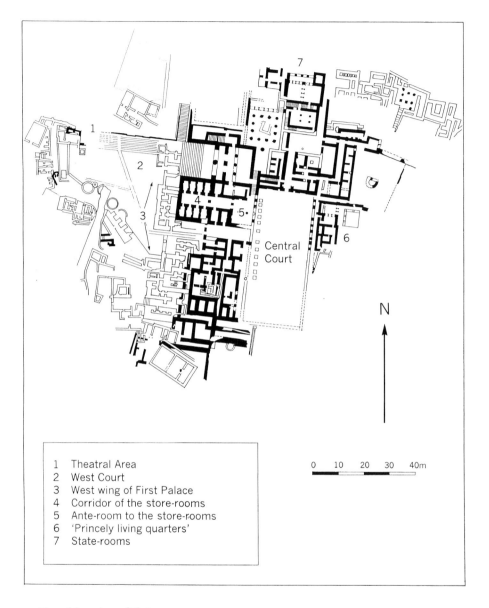

1 Theatral Area
2 West Court
3 West wing of First Palace
4 Corridor of the store-rooms
5 Ante-room to the store-rooms
6 'Princely living quarters'
7 State-rooms

54 Plan of the palace of Phaistos.

environment. Steps abound – the north end of the court has the broad sweep of the steps of the so-called Theatral Area. Behind them are fine ashlar blocks; in front the grey paving of the open courtyard, with its main raised causeway striking a boldly diagonal note.

The Central Court of each palace may also have been the site of certain festivals. The 'Grandstand Fresco' from Knossos has convincingly been suggested to show the west side of the Central Court at that palace, with crowds watching some spectacle in the court itself. The suggestion that bull-games took place in them is not very plausible – they are large areas, but scarcely large enough. We may suppose that special ceremonies were held there, but presumably at other times they were busy with people going about their everyday business.

The west wings of all four palaces have extensive storage areas. The serried rows of long, narrow store-rooms (known as 'magazines') at Knossos, with their lines of pithoi, are one of the characteristic sights of the palace. The

55 Copy of the miniature 'Grandstand Fresco' from Knossos. Crowds of spectators stand in a building that includes columns and a tripartite shrine, perhaps a representation of the west wing of the palace, from which they watch a ceremony in the Central Court.

56 The 'West Magazines' or store-rooms at Knossos. Storage in jars was supplemented by the use of rectangular spaces in the floors.

57 The west side of the Central Court of Knossos. The four doorways lead to the Throne
Room complex.

floors of these rooms also had rectangular, stone-lined cavities or cists for
further storage. The store-rooms of the west wing at Mallia are in an exactly
similar position, and are of the same shape. At Phaistos the equivalent store-
rooms are orientated differently (they run in rows from west to east rather
than from north to south) and they are rather broader rooms, though they
similarly contain large clay pithoi. Some protopalatial predecessors are also
visible here. The storage areas in the west wing of the palace at Zakros are
not arranged in rows, though clearly the west wing had extensive storage
capacity.

At Knossos the Throne Room complex, with its *adyton* or lustral basin,
occupied the part of the west wing that adjoined the Central Court towards
its northern end. Directly south of this a monumental staircase gave access
to the upper floor, and south again was a shrine area. Here a tripartite shrine,
perhaps illustrated on the 'Grandstand Fresco', faced on to the Central
Court, and in the vicinity were the so-called 'Temple Repositories': storage
places for ritual equipment that included the famous faience 'snake-
goddesses'. There is a sense here of the holiest part of the palace. The Throne
Room, in particular, seems secret and tucked away, accessible only through an
ante-room, and only from the Central Court, which lay at the palace's heart.

The equivalent position at Mallia seems equally to have been a cult area,
but rather differently arranged. Four steps from the west side of the Central
Court towards its northern end led into a large, beautifully paved room
known as the Loggia. Two stone bases here were perhaps for altars or libation
tables. The room is not itself secret – quite the reverse, as it was largely open
to the Central Court, its raised position perhaps designed to allow a view
from the court of whatever ceremonies were performed there. However,

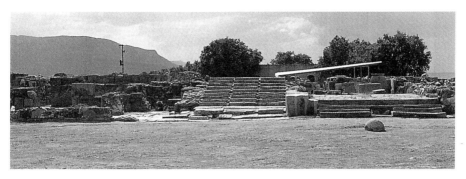

58 The Central Court of Mallia, with the Loggia and monumental staircase on the west side.

59 The 'ante-room to the store-rooms' at Phaistos.

behind the Loggia a series of small, secret rooms perhaps held the cult para-phernalia. To the south, as at Knossos, a monumental staircase led to the palace's upper floor.

In the southern part of the west wing at Mallia a long room with a row of central column-bases has been interpreted as a Great Hall. It was perhaps two storeys high internally, as the wall separating it from the Central Court does not seem to have been strong enough to support an upper floor. This room finds an equivalent at Zakros, but not at Knossos or Phaistos: it may be a rather provincial feature in the two palaces that were not so large and rich. Equivalents at the two bigger palaces may have occupied parts of the upper storey.

An imposing room towards the north end of the west side of the Central Court at Phaistos has rather prosaically been identified as an 'ante-room to the store-rooms'. This certainly describes its position, as behind it extends a broad corridor with store-rooms on each side. It is, though, a large room with a beautifully made floor and bases for three columns running across its

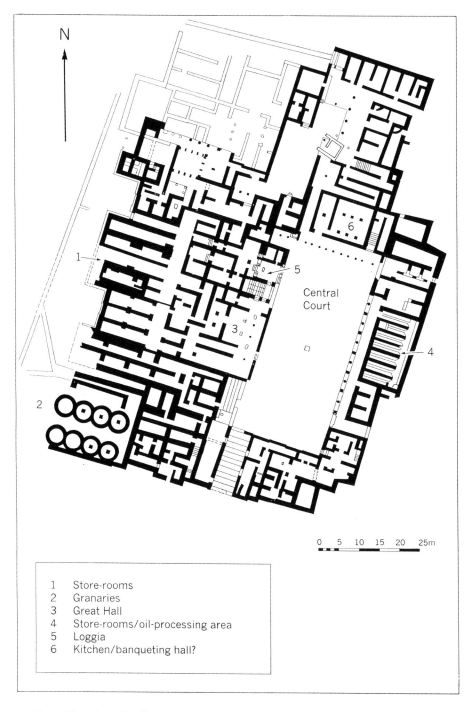

N

1
5

Central
Court

6

3

4

2

0   5   10   15   20   25m

1   Store-rooms
2   Granaries
3   Great Hall
4   Store-rooms/oil-processing area
5   Loggia
6   Kitchen/banqueting hall?

60 Plan of the palace of Mallia.

61 The South Propylon at Knossos, with copies of the processional frescoes found in the area placed on the walls.

centre. It is open to the Central Court and may therefore be some sort of equivalent of the Mallia Loggia, though no finds were made within it to help identification.

At Phaistos there are entrances to the palace on the west side. Surprisingly the great stairway leads to a blank-walled light-well from which there are only narrow exits: perhaps an indication that the stairs, like those of the Theatral Area, were used mainly for assemblies of people. The other entrance from the west is via the corridor to which the processional way on the West Court leads. At Knossos a main entrance was positioned on the south end of the west facade, and a perhaps even more impressive way in to the palace was from the north. At Mallia the west entrance is rather self-effacing: the north and particularly the south entrances were on a grander scale. Minoan palace entrances are interesting – even the grandest of them are somewhat indirect, and often the visitor picking a way through the existing ruins will not see clearly where the entrances were.

The southern sections of the palaces can quickly be described, partly because of poor preservation. Indeed, at Phaistos the area directly south and south-east of the Central Court does not survive at all: it has been destroyed by erosion on the steep slope of the ridge.

At Knossos the restored south entrance dominates the southern part of the palace. The modern visitor reaches this by a short cut not available before the south-west corner of the building was destroyed. Originally the south-west entrance from the West Court led into a long corridor, the Corridor of the

62 The bottom of the Grand Staircase in the east wing at Knossos.

Procession Fresco. Here, accompanied by painted processional figures on the corridor walls, the visitor had to walk to the south, to the east and to the north again before approaching the symmetrical South Propylon or entranceway. This was a grand entrance giving access to a stairway leading up to the main rooms on the palace's west side. As was his frequent custom, Evans restored only one side of the propylon (the west), leaving the other in its state as found. The modern visitor should therefore mentally restore the mirror-image of the existing restoration in the mind's eye. Evans also placed copies of some of the processional figures on his restored wall: the Cup-bearer was the best-preserved figure from this composition.

The rooms on the south side of the palace are not well preserved, and the tumbled basements are rather confusing. It is interesting to see here, though, the Knossian town houses that approached the palace quite closely on its southern side.

The east wing of the palace at Knossos preserves some of the most extraordinary suites of rooms in the whole palace. The Grand Staircase, which originally led both to the upper storey and to the lower levels from the

63 The 'Queen's Megaron' at Knossos. The balustrade on the left shelters a small part of the room perhaps used for bathing: fragments of a bath-tub were found in the doorway.

Central Court, now gives access downwards to rooms built into the side of the hill. These are a triumph of Minoan architecture, and a triumph, too, of excavation and preservation. Evans was justly proud of the restoration of the Grand Staircase. It is not currently possible for visitors to use it – too many thousands of feet take their toll – but a view can still be obtained by leaning over the balustrade from the Central Court.

At the bottom of the Grand Staircase, two floors below the Central Court, is the Hall of the Colonnades, from which a corridor leads to the Hall of the Double-Axes. An indirect route leads from here to the so-called Queen's Megaron. All of these evocative names were Evans' invention, and reflect his views of the functions of various parts of the palace. Indeed, he called this group of rooms the Domestic Quarter, interpreting the Hall of the Double-Axes as the king's apartment, used for some royal functions but essentially private in nature. The Queen's Megaron was also seen by him as having a primarily residential purpose. The adjoining bathroom, and the nearby 'flushing toilet', supported his arguments.

Since Evans' day it has been increasingly apparent that a king and queen at Knossos are conjectural beings, and that in any case it is ambitious to attempt to see their living quarters within the palace with any degree of certainty. Two things can reasonably be said. First, these rooms are of very considerable architectural elaboration – they incorporate *par excellence* all the features that we recognize as 'elite' architecture, both in the other palaces and

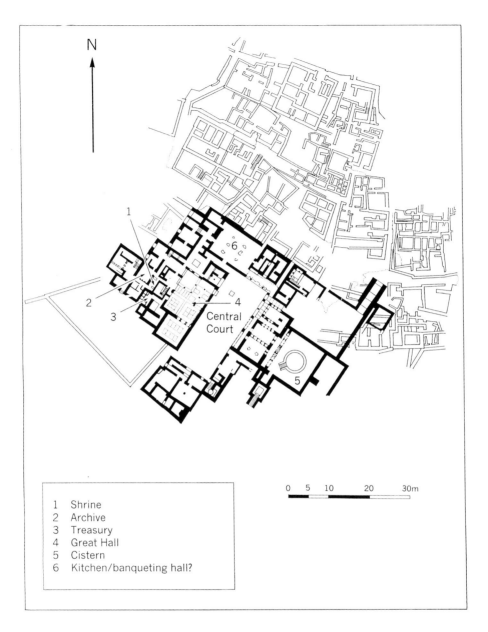

64 Plan of the palace of Zakros.

in the Minoan villas. A princely or kingly interpretation is appropriate in this broad sense. Second, they are positioned in a private part of the palace complex in the literal sense that they are not easy of access – though at the same time they have a fine view over the Knossos valley. Certainly it would be possible to live in these rooms very comfortably. Nonetheless, a residential function is not easy – it might truly be said not possible – to prove.

The rooms could have been used for state or ritual purposes. (Indeed, the residential quarters of a 'royal family' could also have had state or ritual functions.) The inhabitants or users of the rooms could have been priests or priestesses rather than kings and queens.

The Hall of the Double-Axes – named after the double-axe-shaped masons' marks that appear on some of its stones – has an external portico, a *polythyron*, an inner room and a light-well. The *polythyron* (the Greek word means 'many doors') is a room of which three sides are formed of pier and door partitions – the accomplished Minoan way of dealing with the Cretan climate. Each wall could essentially disappear if the 'doors' or shutters were opened and fitted into the recesses on the sides of the square piers, allowing maximum circulation of air in the hot summer. In winter the doors could be closed, and additional heat presumably provided by portable braziers: fixed hearths are not common in the Minoan palaces.

The light-well is similarly a typical feature of elaborate Minoan architecture. As the name implies, light-wells were open to the sky, and allowed light to penetrate to internal parts of the building that would otherwise have been very gloomy. Evidence for light-wells comes, too, from the 'Town Mosaic' from Knossos, a series of decorative faience plaques showing town houses. These have roofs with a raised central part, perhaps indicating that light-wells were covered at a higher level as a protection against rain. They must also have helped considerably with the circulation of air.

The northern part of the east wing at Knossos reverts to more utilitarian purposes, with storage areas and rooms that were probably craft workshops.

At Phaistos the main rooms that seem most closely equivalent to those just described at Knossos were in the northern part of the palace, and are described below. However, in the rather poorly preserved area of the palace directly east of the Central Court a suite described as 'princely living quarters' shows considerable refinements. Here a *polythyron* was accessible from the Central Court, through the portico with alternating pillars and columns along its east side and up four stairs. The room itself had a small separate area that might have been for sleeping, and adjoined a small ante-room leading to an *adyton* or lustral basin. To the east side a further portico gave access to an area that might have had gardens and looked out over the Mesara Plain. A well here, first used in protopalatial times, is a reminder of the practical needs of the palace, while a rock-cut drain led from a small room adjoining the *adyton* that was perhaps a lavatory.

This suite of rooms could certainly have provided comfortable living quarters, but the rich finds from the *adyton* remind us of the clearly ritual nature of some such installations. They included small double-axes and 'horns of consecration', as well as fine pottery, including rhytons or ritual sprinklers.

65 The rooms in the east wing at Mallia apparently used for processing and storage of oil. They have drainage channels and collection points in the floors.

Interestingly, at Mallia the whole of the east side of the Central Court as preserved consists of an area apparently dedicated to the processing, storage and distribution of oil. Large pithoi were stored in magazines with collecting channels in the floor to control spillages, and tubs may have been used in the oil extraction process.

The state-rooms lying to the north of the Central Court at Phaistos are among the most elegant apartments in Minoan architecture. Somewhat smaller in scale than their equivalent at Knossos, they show very clearly the Minoan use of *polythyra*, or rooms with many openings, in a suite of rooms that also incorporates light-wells and porticoes. Minoan control of light and space can be seen here at its most sophisticated. There were few solid walls, but receding views of circular columns and square piers, with light filtering down from high above, must have given an effect rather like a painting of the Florentine renaissance.

Where solid walls existed in this suite of rooms they were not painted, but rather were veneered in thin slabs of gypsum, creating cool, smooth surfaces of faintly mottled pale grey. The distribution of figured frescoes within Minoan Crete is particularly centred on Knossos. None has come from Phaistos, though fine examples were found at neighbouring Ayia Triadha. Painted plasters in washes of plain colour were, though, used at Phaistos from the protopalatial period onwards. Usually blue or red, these decorated both walls and floors. Traces of a decorative zigzag pattern in red paint can be seen in the two niches that flank the broad way from the north side of the Central Court that leads to this suite of rooms.

66 An elegant room in the north part of Phaistos, where gypsum veneers have been used to decorate the walls.

67 At the north end of the Central Court at Phaistos attached half-columns flanked by niches marked the entrance to the corridor leading towards the state-rooms.

It has been suggested that there were banqueting halls at first-floor level on the north sides of the Central Courts of all four main palaces. The evidence is only circumstantial, but the idea is plausible enough where the ground floor has walls and pillars of sufficient strength to support a large upper room, along with staircases for access and areas suitable for the storage and preparation of food. At Knossos the banqueting hall is postulated above the north pillared hall called by Evans the Custom's House. At Phaistos a suitable room occupied a north-eastern situation, the ground floor having cupboards with pottery and a nearby possible service area, while at Mallia, too, a room in the analogous north-east position seems a suitable candidate. The absence of hearths in Minoan palaces makes the identification of cooking areas difficult, and is in fact rather a surprise. Only in the newly discovered MM III–LM I palace at Galatas has a fixed hearth been found.

68 A general view of the palace of Zakros from the north.

Elsewhere portable braziers were no doubt used, but while they might have been adequate for the heating of rooms in a climate where winter temperatures were not usually severe, they would surely have made large-scale catering difficult. At Zakros a possible 'banqueting hall' at the north-west corner of the Central Court had service rooms beneath, and in one a cooking pot was recorded as found still standing in the ashes of a fire.

We might pause here to say a little more about Zakros, which only certainly functioned as a palace in the neopalatial period. Zakros lies close to the sea on a bay at the extreme eastern end of Crete, and though it has a small fertile hinterland this position seems largely to have been chosen for reasons of maritime trade. The palace was not completely plundered at the time of its destruction, so the finds made there provide a unique insight into the original contents and, sometimes, the functions of various rooms.

Imported raw materials included bronze ingots and elephant tusks, found together in the west wing, where they had fallen from an upper storey. Other finds from the west wing included very fine pottery in Floral and Marine Style, and a range of elaborate stone vessels. Many of these came from the shrine complex: a series of rooms in a position analogous to that of the shrine at Knossos. Others came from the so-called 'Hall of Ceremonies'.

Vases in precious metal were not found, and had perhaps been removed by the inhabitants before the destruction, but the stone vessels included the elegant rock-crystal rhyton and the 'peak-sanctuary' rhyton, as well as a small but beautifully carved bull's-head rhyton akin to that from the Little Palace

69 Raw materials imported to Zakros included bronze ingots and ivory tusks.

70 A room in the storage area of the west wing of Zakros, which has carefully constructed internal compartments, known as the 'treasury' because rich finds were made there.

at Knossos. An Early Dynastic Egyptian vessel, dating from about 3000BC, shows signs of a chequered history. It was probably already an antique when it was imported to Crete, where a Minoan craftsman has converted it into a typical bridge-spouted jar by adding a spout and, originally, handles – a procedure that perhaps showed more ingenuity than taste (fig. 12, page 27).

The storage capacity of the west side of the palace was represented by the usual store-rooms with pithoi, though at Zakros these rooms were relatively scattered, and were not arranged in serried ranks. An archive room was identified near to the shrine. This contained remains of carbonized wood that the excavators felt came from shelves or boxes, though perhaps surprisingly only thirteen Linear A tablets came to light there.

Architectural elaborations included the decorated floors of the 'Hall of Ceremonies' and 'Banqueting Hall'. Squares created by raised strips of red-painted stucco must have contained some material now lost. The 'Banqueting Hall' also had an impressive plaster frieze with spirals in relief.

On the east side of the palace fine rooms were designated the 'royal apartments'. On this side, too, are the prominent and carefully constructed water

LEFT
71 The circular
cistern, reached by
steps, on the east
side of the palace
at Zakros.

BELOW
72 A general view
of Petras, on the bay
of Siteia.

features, filled by springs, that are such a special feature of Zakros. As well as being decorative these no doubt had a practical purpose as a source of water, and they may also have been a focus of cult. They are essentially unique to this low-lying palace, where the immediate presence of springs made them possible. Similarities exist, though, with the building known as the 'Caravanserai' at Knossos, which also had a spring chamber with a pool.

The town at Zakros flourished in both protopalatial and neopalatial times, and its remains seem at first glance to continue seamlessly from those of the palace itself. We do not know what stood on the palace site in the protopalatial period, but the palace seems to have occupied a space perhaps predetermined by the layout of the town.

The palatial building at Petras, also in eastern Crete, and the palace at Galatas in the centre of the island can now be compared to Zakros, which for a long time was the smallest palace known. Petras, which probably had palatial functions in both the First and Second Palace periods, is tiny by comparison. Galatas, 30 km (18½ miles) south of Herakleion, is closer in size. As at Zakros there is no evidence that the First Palace period remains there constituted a palace. The palace proper seems to have been built in the MM III period. It is unusual because it declined and went out of use by the end of LM IA.

OTHER PALACES

Sometimes we can postulate the presence of a palace even when complete investigation is not possible. This is the case at Chania. Excavations have been limited in scale because of the overlying modern city, but extensive areas of the Minoan settlement have been found on the Kastelli hill in the city, while in the Splanzia district a narrow excavation, limited by the width of the modern street, has revealed parts of an extensive building complex. It is of some elaboration, and includes a fine *adyton* with fresco decoration, a large courtyard with a stone exedra (platform or base), remains of a pyre where animals were slaughtered and a series of underground rooms. The complex is clearly a shrine, and may well have been part of a palace. If a central court existed, as presumably it did, it was probably in this area.

The Kastelli quarter has yielded an extensive array of administrative documents, including Linear A tablets, roundels and sealings. All indications, then, support the existence of a palace at Chania. West Crete had important Minoan settlements in the neopalatial period, and it seems likely that Chania served as the administrative centre for this part of the island. The buildings there suffered destructions at the end of LM IB, though Chania was also a major centre in LM II–III and seems to have been the Kydonia of the Linear B tablets.

In Archanes, also a flourishing modern town, a similar situation obtains in that the excavation of part of an important building has led to the suggestion that there was a palace there. While the overlying modern town hampers investigation as to whether this building had a central court, the part preserved is clearly of considerable scale and architectural refinement, and had fresco decoration. There is also evidence for administrative functions and the existence of craft workshops.

Arthur Evans knew of a large Minoan building at Archanes, and viewed it as the 'summer palace' of Knossos. He described the relationship of Phaistos and Ayia Triadha in similar terms. In neither case, though, is the interpretation convincing. Instead it has become clear that Crete had a greater range of buildings filling the spectrum between palace and ordinary residence than had previously been thought. Archanes was no doubt an

73 The Royal Villa of Ayia Triadha occupies the western end of the same ridge as the palace of Phaistos.

important regional centre and the same is true of Ayia Triadha. This site lies just some 3 km (1¾ miles) from Phaistos, and in fact is situated on the western end of the same ridge. Two tholos tombs give evidence for early occupation of the site, and a protopalatial building complex and further tombs show that the site was inhabited in the time of the First Palaces. The Royal Villa was built at the beginning of the Late Minoan period. The remains are complicated, and its preservation incomplete. The presence of the foundations of a large megaron of the Mycenaean period on top of the Royal Villa further complicates the picture. Nonetheless, the visitor can see two very fine groups of important rooms, one at the eastern end of the building and one at the west. The western rooms had wonderful views towards the sea.

Living, working and storage areas make up the rest of the villa, and in many places there are clear traces of the severe fire that destroyed it in about 1450BC. Gypsum pavings are burnt black, their surfaces appearing vitrified in some places, perhaps because oil was stored nearby.

Figured frescoes were found at Ayia Triadha. Their presence is one of the respects in which Ayia Triadha differs from Phaistos, and together with the many other rich finds made there they suggest a very important centre. These finds included not only fine pottery and stone vases but also a number of bronzes. Some were figurines and votive double-axes, but others were tools, including two huge saws. A group of nineteen copper ingots also came from one store-room.

74 An elegant room at the western end of the Royal Villa of Ayia Triadha, with gypsum benches and gypsum veneers on the walls. The spaces left by wooden elements can be seen.

Ayia Triadha had wealth and luxury, then, at least to rival a Minoan palace, if not canonically to be one. Perhaps most significantly of all, there is ample evidence for administration in the form of 146 Linear A tablets and about a thousand clay sealings. Most of these seem to have fallen from an upper floor.

The relationship of the palace at Phaistos and the Royal Villa at Ayia Triadha may never be precisely known. Their proximity suggests that they must have worked in tandem. Some scholars suggest Ayia Triadha essentially took over from Phaistos as the most important centre in south-central Crete in the neopalatial period. This view rests, reasonably enough, on the rich finds from Ayia Triadha as compared with the relative paucity of finds from Phaistos, though we must remember that, unlike Phaistos, Ayia Triadha was never plundered. The architectural refinements of Phaistos warn us against dismissing its significance too lightly. Perhaps, then, the safest conclusion to be drawn from comparison of the two sites is that in neopalatial Crete, as in the preceding period, the demarcation between palaces and 'buildings with palatial functions' cannot be too tightly drawn.

What Happened in the Palaces?

The palaces were centres of power, both sacred and secular, with wealth based on the stores of agricultural produce from the fertile hinterland that they controlled. What happened within them? Presumably they were busy places.

The receipt, recording and storage of goods brought in from the surrounding countryside must have been a major job, particularly at those times of year when the corn was harvested, the olives ripe or the wine newly made. Administration of the goods and commodities leaving the store-rooms for consumption in the palace, for use in the workshops or for wider distribution must have taken place throughout the year. We may imagine the storage areas as busy by day, and probably carefully guarded at night.

The craftsmen creating precious works in such materials as gold, ivory and semi-precious stones may well have been full-time craft specialists, totally dependent on the palaces and working constantly within them, their products in demand both for immediate use and possibly for exchange quite far afield. Their raw materials were part of palatial wealth, and must have been kept under strict control. Similarly bronze-workers, whose raw material would have been carefully recorded, no doubt worked close by. Pottery workshops seem to have been further afield, situated near to the clay-beds and fuel for the kilns rather than within palace confines, though their products could still have been largely or totally under palace control.

The production of textiles figures importantly in the Linear B records for the last period at Knossos, and was probably always an important palace-based activity, though we do not know in precisely which rooms spinning and weaving took place.

Some 'revisionist' interpretations of the palace of Knossos have questioned whether people lived within it to any great extent. We must face squarely the fact, implicit in the above account, that unequivocal evidence for human residence, as opposed to human use, is hard to find. Nonetheless, it seems overwhelmingly probable that all the palaces were lived in by some, if not all, of the people engaged in the many activities for which they show evidence. Many non-specific rooms could have been lived in by various dependants – craftsmen, guards, textile-workers, servant or slaves. This remains true even if we follow those interpretations that would prefer 'temple' to 'palace' as the buildings' prime identification.

In fact, the choice of 'temple' rather than 'palace' is a change of emphasis rather than a change of interpretation. From Evans onwards the ingrained and embedded religious nature of the palaces has been accepted, as has the fact that 'palace' is inadequate shorthand for the buildings' complexities. There are, though, good reasons not to change wholesale to 'temple', which in truth is similarly inadequate. The most obvious problem with such a change is the fact that, while a society based on large palaces with no temples has always been recognized as anomalous in the ancient world, large-scale temples with no palaces would be equally so. Unless there is a truly huge gap in our excavated evidence – possible, but as time goes on increasingly unlikely – these complex buildings are all we have. The most logical conclusion remains that they fulfilled the two sets of functions simultaneously. Accurate terminology that did not privilege one function over another would require the coinage of a portmanteau term such as palace-temple or temple-palace, but this seems an undesirable deviation from terminology that is long-established, whatever its shortcomings.

What, though, of the ruling elite, whether priests, kings or both? Is there evidence that the palaces housed a 'royal family', as Evans proposed? Was Knossos really the palace 'of Minos', or of a Minos?

The attempt to see 'royal apartments' throws into high relief not only the difficulty of identifying precisely the function of a room from its form, but also the fact that we really do not know who, in Minoan society, held the reins of power. The tradition of Minos indicates a king, and it remains perfectly possible that Minoan Crete was ruled by a king – yet power may have been wielded by a priest, or by a priest-king, combining functions that we would divide into sacred and secular. Nonetheless, it still seems overwhelmingly likely that the ruling elite lived in the palaces, or perhaps in both the palaces and the important houses in their immediate vicinity.

Knossos Town

While all the Second Palaces were surrounded by the buildings of their respective towns, Knossos stands out for the number of substantial houses in its immediate vicinity. Presumably the homes of the ruling elite, these reinforce the impression that Knossos was the largest and most important centre of the Minoan world, with a very considerable concentration of wealth and power. Some houses were contemporary with the rebuilding of the palace at the beginning of MM III, but many followed in the wake of the 'great destruction' at the end of MM IIIB, and were part of a real LM IA building boom.

Extensive remains of a series of houses that approached the palace closely on its south side can be seen by visitors today, and the most impressive of these is the South House, which lies close to the south-west palace corner. The house was built after the MM IIIB earthquake, and partly encroached on the area previously occupied by the stepped portico: the monumental entrance that had led up to the palace from the south. Because the South House was constructed in a deep cutting it was remarkably well preserved, and parts of a basement level, a ground floor and an upper floor could be restored, giving a good impression of the scale and architectural elaboration of the building.

A pillar crypt and an *adyton* represent areas used for religious ritual within the house, while elegant living apartments looked out over the valley of the

75 The South House at Knossos.

Vlychia stream. Bronze tools from a store-room at basement level were part of the house's wealth. Fine art was owned and used by the inhabitants: a small group of silver vessels was found there, as was a fragment of an ivory relief showing a griffin and a bull. Fresco fragments indicated that the walls were painted with scenes including natural landscapes and birds.

To the south of the Vlychia stream lies the building called by Evans the 'Caravanserai', an elegant construction with a large porch-like room, a foot-bath and a Spring Chamber. The water from natural springs was perhaps used here by travellers to refresh themselves before approaching the palace from the south. Towards the end of the Minoan era the Caravanserai was a focus of cult activity.

Leaving the palace from its north-east corner gives access, in a short distance, to the Royal Villa, another impressive structure of LM I date that has been extensively restored. The main room of the villa has a balustrade and columns on its west side that separate off a narrow area that presumably had some special significance. A ceremonial seat may have stood there, perhaps used by a priestess in the guise of a goddess in a so-called 'enacted epiphany', lit from above by a narrow light-well. In the adjoining pillar crypt, which is a characteristic feature of Knossian town houses, the very solid square central pillar is surrounded by square cists (pits) in the floor into which channels run – a demonstration of the fact that blood sacrifices or other liquid offerings were made there.

The traveller using the finely paved Royal Road to leave the palace at Knossos would soon arrive at a junction where he could turn either right, towards the sea, or left, to travel towards Juktas, Archanes, central Crete or indeed all the way to Phaistos and the south coast. A third possibility, though, would be to visit the houses flanking the Royal Road and then the Little Palace, just across the road in Knossos town.

Buildings constructed in MM III and LM IA flank the Royal Road, and include some important workshop areas, though these were perhaps combined with residential functions too. On the north side of the road an ivory workshop has been identified, while on the south is the House of the Frescoes, so named by Evans because it was richly decorated with frescoes showing birds and monkeys in elaborate natural settings.

The Little Palace was built in LM IA into a cutting on the west side of the Knossos valley, over which it must have had fine views. The main suite of rooms on ground-floor level was spacious and elegant, comprising a double *polythyron* and a peristyle hall. A verandah is partly preserved on the east side of these rooms and must have looked out over the valley. On their west side is an *adyton* which, after the destruction of Knossos in about 1375–1350BC, was converted into a rather different form by walls blocking the spaces between the columns on the parapet. The impressions of the wooden columns survived in the clay and mud mixture used for this. They were fluted, and this was probably unusual. Our knowledge of Minoan wooden columns is based only on representations, but they are quite frequent in art, and flutings are rare.

Arthur Evans called this room the Fetish Shrine, and in a misleading piece of tidying-up reality for the sake of a photograph put the roughly shaped stones ('fetishes') on to the balustrade as though he had found them in this position. In fact he did not: they were found scattered on the floor and probably fell from the storey above.

The south side of the Little Palace had no fewer than three pillar basements. The two to the east contain typical combinations of square pillars and cists in the floor. The pillars may have been a focus for offerings or sacrifices, and the cists receptacles for them. The rich nature of the cult practised in the Little Palace was clearly indicated by the extraordinary finds from a shaft next to the south-west pillar basement. Here was discovered, among other pieces of cult paraphernalia, the steatite bull's head rhyton (ritual sprinkler) that is one of the most often reproduced pieces of Minoan art – as well, perhaps, as one of the most misleading: half the head is restored and the horns are, of course, entirely reproduction, as they were originally of gilded wood.

Adjoining the Little Palace is the building still known as the Unexplored Mansion, in spite of the fact that it has been fully excavated and is the subject of a detailed publication. The name arose because Evans found the fine ashlar east facade of the mansion while excavating the Little Palace. Although the two are on different alignments, they were joined by a bridge. It seems that the Little Palace was built first, and the Unexplored Mansion constructed shortly afterwards. It can hardly be described as an 'annexe', being a large and important building in its own right, but the two buildings were physically connected, and perhaps intended to have complementary functions. They were part of the urban regeneration at Knossos that was a feature of the early LM IA period.

The Unexplored Mansion had an elegant central hall with four pillars, and traces of frescoes from an upper storey show that a fine building was planned and partly finished, but the excavators discovered that the building work was not completed. Instead, after about fifty years, when the ground floor remained unfinished and unoccupied, the fortunes of the building took a turn for the worse, as we shall see below.

Further west, an interesting area of the Minoan town was revealed in excavations behind the Stratigraphical Museum (which houses sherd material from British excavations in Crete.) Here the direct continuation of the Royal Road was flanked by houses, and three lime kilns were found, presumably used to make powdered lime for fine lime plaster.

In one of the houses in this part of the town of Knossos the bones of two young children, aged about eight and twelve years, were found. The bones were very fragmentary and scattered, and knife marks showed that the flesh had been removed from them. The finding of some of the bones in a cooking pot with remains of edible snails led the excavator, Peter Warren, to the grisly conclusion that parts of the children had been cooked and eaten, in an act of ritual cannibalism.

While the earlier Anemospilia shrine, described above, indicates human sacrifice in Minoan Crete, the evidence in this instance seems less compelling. Part of Minoan funerary ritual seems sometimes to have included the removal of flesh from bones, and this may be relevant here. The finds remain anomalous within what appears otherwise to be an ordinary town house, though, and it must be admitted that no certain alternative interpretation can be offered.

Destructions by fire occurred in many areas of Knossos town in LM IB. These included the buildings behind the Stratigraphical Museum and the building with the ivory workshop north of the Royal Road. These destructions are roughly contemporary with those that destroyed the other palaces and sites of Crete. Knossos is unusual in Minoan Crete as a whole because no destruction seems to have taken place in the palace at this time. This is explicable if the agents of destruction were Mycenaeans from the Greek mainland, who might have chosen to retain Knossos as a 'going concern', taking it over as the centre of their own domination of the island. However, civil disorder within Crete might also explain the phenomenon.

The destruction of the palace itself, the Little Palace, the Unexplored Mansion and many areas of Knossos town is traditionally dated to LM IIIA. The reasons for these destructions are again unclear, though it has been suggested that the Minoans may have rebelled against Mycenaean presence.

Knossos is unique in having buildings of such size and elaboration as the MM III–LM I structures described above in its immediate vicinity, and their presence is one reason for suggesting the pre-eminence of the site as in some sense the capital of Minoan Crete at this time.

Phaistos Town

At Phaistos few important contemporary structures have come to light in the immediate vicinity of the palace, and there are no buildings equivalent in size or elaboration to those at Knossos unless the villa at Ayia Triadha is brought into the equation. Structures of some substance that are probably to be interpreted as town houses have been found in the Chalara area of the town, lying at the bottom of the ridge to the south-east of the palace, and other remains survived in the Ayia Photini area to the north.

Mallia Town

Much excavation has been possible in the area of the town around the palace of Mallia, and important neopalatial structures have been discovered. Indeed arguably Mallia gives us our clearest impression of the range of types of dwelling in a palatial town. The largest building, House E, lies to the south of the palace. Measuring some 50 m (164 ft) long and 28 m (92 ft) wide, it had spacious rooms with fresco decoration, storage areas and workshops, and can perhaps be seen as the Malliot equivalent of the Knossos Little Palace. House E as it now appears is mainly of neopalatial date, though it was built on an area already occupied in the First Palace period. Interestingly, and rarely for the houses at Mallia, it also shows signs of occupation in postpalatial times. Overlying the badly preserved remains of the east side of the house were traces of rebuilding and occupation dating from LM IIIB.

East of the palace an interesting area of houses has been explored, and called by the excavators Area Zeta. Here three substantial houses largely date to the Second Palace period, but it is clear that they were built on to earlier streets – the alignments of the buildings and the streets, of protopalatial date, do not always match exactly. In this area, too, are interesting traces of a protopalatial town wall.

North-west of the palace, the road leading to the sea passes through an area of Minoan habitation called by the excavators Quartier Delta. Here remains of houses of both First and Second palace date were found, including House Delta A. This is a carefully constructed neopalatial house, the exterior walls of which have been restored. Although not large – about 15 × 14 m (49 × 46 ft) – it has many refinements, and the excavators suggest it can be taken as a model of a well-to-do residence.

As well as this evidence for habitation areas, the town of Mallia contained both shrines and cemeteries. There is some slight evidence for a peak sanctuary on the hill of Profitis Ilias, the small but noticeable hill lying to the south of the palace, though because of the distance this cannot be viewed as part of the town. However, Mallia is unusual in that there are two separate buildings within the town – one protopalatial, one neopalatial – that have been identified as sanctuaries. This contrasts with the apparently more normal situation where shrines are found within palaces or houses. The neopalatial 'Sanctuaire aux Cornes' is a rectangular building of long, thin shape. The name derives from the series of plaster 'horns of consecration' that decorate its parapets.

The site of Mallia, then, perhaps gives us our best evidence for the arrangement of a neopalatial period town around a palace. The generalities must have been much the same in all the palace towns: the palace itself was at the centre, an evolved street plan surrounded it serving various parts of the town, with large and small buildings, and the cemetery areas lay outside the town. Excavation in various places has revealed a range of neopalatial houses and town areas, from the large and richly appointed to the smaller and simpler. The impression given is that life for some people in the town must have been very pleasant: the larger houses are well designed for the comfort of the inhabitants, particularly with their careful arrangements to ensure coolness in summer and warmth in winter. Simpler living quarters certainly also existed. Mallia therefore shows a quite and coherent picture of a town dominated by a palace but also supporting a well-to-do population, who made a living, if not independently, at least in parallel with the palace and its activities. A larger group of inhabitants had a simpler lifestyle.

Nonpalatial Towns and 'Country Houses'

Beyond the palaces and their surrounding settlements the island of Crete presented a diversely settled landscape in the neopalatial period. Extensive remains of Minoan towns have been excavated in various parts of the island, some, though not all, with obviously dominant buildings where local governors may have lived. While most are in areas of good agricultural land, some

76 A street and houses in the town of Gournia.

seem to be port towns, situated to take advantage of natural harbours. So-called 'villas' or 'country houses' have also been found throughout the island.

Examples of Minoan towns include the settlement on the island of Pseira, off the north coast of Crete towards its eastern end, and the town of Palaikastro at the extreme eastern end of the island. Both seem to have been flourishing places, but in neither case has excavation revealed an equivalent to a palace or an obviously dominant building. Excavation continues at Palaikastro, however, and the site, which has substantial blocks of Minoan houses, is not completely revealed. At both Pseira and Palaikastro rich finds have been made. Relief frescoes of female figures, perhaps goddesses, adorned a building at Pseira that may have been a shrine. They have affinities with Knossian palatial art. The ivory statuette of a youth found at Palaikastro is equally of the finest Minoan workmanship.

Both these sites no doubt prospered at least in part because of their coastal locations. Pseira is in a position similar to that of Mochlos, which continued to flourish at this time. On the south coast of Crete, Kommos has remains of a rich and extensive settlement, and was clearly a very important and flourishing port. It was in a key position at the western end of the Mesara Plain, at the only point where this large fertile area finds an outlet to the sea.

The best impression of a Minoan town can still, though, best be gained from a visit to Gournia where the remains of houses and streets spread out like a net over a low hill remain evocative and impressive. The town had a long life, from EM II to reoccupation in LM III, but it flourished particularly

ABOVE
77 The courtyard
where the 'Governor's
House' at Gournia
articulates with the
town.

LEFT
78 The large altar-
like slab in the corner
of the court at
Gournia, with the
collecting vessel in
place beneath it.

in LM I. At this period an impressive building, sometimes called the 'Governor's House', sometimes referred to as a small palace, was built at the heart of the town on top of the ridge, the houses and streets clustering round it. Gournia thus gives the most coherent picture that we have of a neopalatial settlement – a sense of busy liveliness can still be felt by the visitor, even though it is more than three millennia since Minoan voices shouted in the streets and Minoan donkeys' hooves clattered along the paved alleyways. The sense of intimacy with the distant past perhaps derives from the feeling of familiarity of the place: the buildings survive only at basement or ground-floor level, but the small houses and paved streets are much like those of modern villages in Crete or the islands. The town is small: about 185 m (202 yds) north to south, about 135 m (148 yds) east to west, though there may have been further building in the valley to the west, which was perhaps also used for agriculture. Food, water – from springs in the valley, wells and cisterns – and building materials would have been plentiful. At the same time Gournia probably profited from its coastal position. Fishing was possible, connections with the sea routes along the north of Crete may have been important, and the town's position near to the north end of the narrow isthmus of Ierapetra was advantageous for communications within the island.

The Governor's House is large – about 50 × 37 m (164 × 121 ft). Some scholars choose to refer to it as a palace, though it is not as large as the four main palaces that we know. Certainly it has features in common with the palaces, including evidence for important rooms, storage areas and areas for cult or ritual. Architectural elaborations included a fine west facade, with ashlar masonry and a system of recesses, looking out on to a west court.

In spite of such palatial features, the building did not have a canonical central court. It faces south, though, on to a courtyard dominating the town, the so-called Town Court, and is closely connected with this. In fact a stepped area at the north-west corner of the court constitutes the south-west corner of the Governor's House. It may be a verandah or a shrine, and marks a seamless articulation between the court and house. The possible identification as a shrine is supported by the presence of a large stone slab with a hole drilled at one corner which stands to one side of the stairs leading to the Governor's House: this has been associated with blood sacrifice, the blood perhaps passing through the hole to be collected in the stone receptacle that originally lay beneath it. The excavations revealed a scattering of sealings and 'noduli' as evidence for administrative functions, and we may surmise that this building was a centre of government for the town and its surrounding area.

The houses of Gournia vary in size and elaboration, though most are quite small. Basement areas may have been mainly for storage, but staircases from the street in several places indicate the existence of upper floors. Stone construction was supplemented by the use of timber and mud-brick for upper storeys, and some houses were decorated with painted plaster. Details such as cupboards let into the walls of houses and stone vessels strategically placed on the floors, for use by the household or perhaps by animals, give us intimate glimpses into the lives of the inhabitants. Finds made within the rooms included a range of tools, evidence for various craft activities, fish-hooks, balance-weights, loom-weights and potters' turntables.

'Country houses' or 'villas' have been discovered throughout neopalatial Crete. Archaeologists have not found it easy to settle

79 Potter's turntable from Gournia.

80 The sophisticated architecture of House A at Tylissos.

on a single inclusive term to describe these buildings, and this difficulty reflects the fact that their diverse nature has increasingly become apparent as excavations have progressed. They have in common size and architectural elaboration, their architecture often plainly influenced by the palace centres, perhaps particularly by Knossos. Their functions included storage of agricultural produce and other raw materials, and they often have evidence for administrative activities. Cult areas and paraphernalia are also characteristic of buildings of this type.

Many have been categorized as 'second-order centres', taking a place in the hierarchy of Cretan sites that makes them secondary to the palaces, but important as centres of regional control. A strict hierarchy or 'ranking' cannot be drawn up: as we have seen, large urban buildings such as the Royal Villa at Ayia Triadha or the Governor's House at Gournia come close to being palaces, while villas such as those at Tylissos and Nirou Khani in central Crete, or Myrtos-Pyrgos in the south east were perhaps more obviously secondary in rank. Simpler 'country houses' such as Vathypetro in central Crete, Nerokourou in the west and the group discovered in eastern Crete in the Siteia valley may come lower down the order, their concerns perhaps more closely bound up with agricultural pursuits.

Difficulties of classification or terminology should not obscure the fact that we can recognize in the Minoan villas and country houses the life-blood of Crete in the Second Palace period. Seeking out the villa sites is well worthwhile: it is a remarkable experience to visit a remote part of the Cretan countryside with little modern habitation and suddenly to come across remains of a house that was clearly a small gem in its day. Ashlar masonry, pillar crypts, light-wells, lustral basins and elaborate pavings all bear witness to a wealth of provincial architecture in Minoan Crete that has not been surpassed in later periods. Modern visitors feel they are visiting the Minoan 'gentry' in their homes.

Who were these 'gentry', and how did they relate to the people in the palaces whose lifestyle they emulated? It seems clear that we are seeing the homes of local elite groups, who in some way governed or administered their immediate areas. They may have been wealthy families who owed allegiance, tax or dues to the palace centres. It is even possible that the inhabitants were administrators or functionaries installed directly by the palaces, perhaps specifically by Knossos.

We cannot know in detail how the system worked, but we can perhaps observe that it seems to have worked well. The sense of 'gracious living' that we get from the villa sites is sometimes accompanied by evidence for very real wealth. This is not just based on agriculture, though storage capacity for agricultural products is a main feature. A well-preserved store-room can be seen at Vathypetro, near Archanes, in a villa that also has a wonderfully well-preserved grape-pressing installation (see fig. 8, page 21). Non-agricultural wealth can be observed in the huge double-axes of sheet bronze from Nirou Khani on the north coast east of Herakleion, perhaps manufactured locally and stored for wider distribution. It has been suggested that the villa at Sklavokambos, west of Tylissos, was positioned to facilitate the transportation of serpentine from local quarries. The newly discovered, large-scale and very impressively built building at Zominthos, on the way to the Idaean plateau and cave, may have been a resting-place for travellers journeying up to the mountains, though its ground plan is not yet fully revealed.

The 'villas' and 'country houses', then, in all their fascinating diversity, are part of a picture of an island that was flourishing in the neopalatial period. We have extensive evidence for the land of the living, but what of the cemeteries and burial customs of this time?

Burial Customs

It is surprising how few burials are known that can definitely be dated to the neopalatial period. This lack is so marked that some scholars have even speculated about whether some burial custom was adopted that left no mark on the archaeological record, such as exposure of bodies to the elements or burial at sea. In view of the fact that we have burials from both the preceding and following periods, though, an extreme change in burial practice seems unlikely. Moreover, the picture is not a total blank.

In the Knossos area some of the fairly undistinguished tombs established earlier may have continued to receive the burials of the ordinary populace at this time. Elite burials perhaps took place in two extraordinary structures: the Temple Tomb, and the Royal Tomb at Isopata. Both were elaborate structures built in the Second Palace period, though it must be admitted that the burials found within them date from LM II–III. Their neopalatial use is therefore a matter for speculation.

Elsewhere in Crete some tombs established earlier also continued to be used: these include some of the house-tombs at Mochlos, for example. Nearby, at Pachyammos, a large cemetery of burials in pithoi, or large storage jars, was found, but grave goods were few. However, by far the best insight into burials of this time is offered by the neopalatial tombs found during Greek rescue excavations in Poros, a suburb of Herakleion. Here a cemetery came to light that presumably served a densely populated area of the Minoan harbour town. A number of large tombs have been excavated, their sprawling underground chambers approached by short *dromoi* or entrance passageways. The chambers are of rather irregular form, and it seems the tombs were enlarged as necessary to receive new burials. In fact these communal tombs were also used for successive burials throughout the neopalatial period. The cemetery has not yet been completely explored, but hundreds of burials must have been made there.

Because of repeated use the tomb contents were never undisturbed. Nonetheless, the tombs contained many hundreds of fine pottery vases, and a range of seal-stones and jewellery. Bronze objects were relatively few, and the excavators suggest that they may have been systematically removed by plunderers in antiquity. Fragments of attachments for bronze vessels and weapons show that the tombs originally contained such objects. Interestingly, tusks from one or two boar's-tusk helmets were found. This is an early occurrence in Crete of an item thought to be a Mycenaean invention. The Poros tombs presage the 'warrior graves' and 'burials with bronzes' of the succeeding period in a number of ways. Their relatively recent discovery holds out hope that further burials of this period may yet be found elsewhere in the island.

Arts and Crafts of the Second Palace Period

Many of the finest surviving products of Minoan artists and craftsmen can be dated to the Second Palace period, which was artistically very rich. The palaces themselves were centres for artistic production and used fine products, both native and imported. It is from them, as you would expect, that some of the finest preserved works come. The important houses of Crete copied palace life in many ways, from architectural forms to other aspects of material culture, and so they, too, have sometimes been the source of rich finds. Tombs add to the picture, while sanctuary sites, particularly sacred caves, have also yielded fine objects of various kinds.

It is perhaps necessary to point out that the two terms 'arts' and 'crafts' are used here jointly and inclusively to describe Minoan production in a variety of media. The motivation behind the various works is not always clear to us. It is generally held that the concept of 'art for art's sake' is anachronistic for the ancient world, and it is clear that the 'purpose' of much Minoan art was religious expression. However, no demarcation line can usefully be drawn between the art overtly addressing religious themes and the creativity that led to the shaping and decoration of many different types of objects. Scholars have argued, for example, over whether all of the Thera frescoes have religious or ritual significance. Some clearly do, but are others purely decorative in intent? It is impossible to say. All we can really do is to see the products of Minoan creativity as a continuum, and to try to understand them in their cultural context.

Art historians have equally grappled with the underlying aesthetics of Minoan art, and those characteristics that make it distinct. It is certainly true that a sense of fluidity of movement is a general characteristic, observable from the large-scale art of the frescoes right through to the miniature compass of the seal-stones and signet-rings. A love of shapes based on springy, spiraliform patterns may partly underlie this. Certainly, too, a unity exists in the themes chosen for treatment. The popularity of bull-sports, for example, is very obvious. This is just one of several themes that occur throughout Minoan art, reinforcing the sense of a specific Minoan identity across the full range of works preserved to us.

Minoan Frescoes

The use of painted plaster to decorate walls in Crete is known from the end of the Neolithic period onwards. Red was most common throughout the Early Bronze Age, though by the time of the First Palaces a greater range of colours was used, including red, blue, yellow, grey and white. In addition to plain washes, early compositions were geometric and perhaps sometimes floral. Knossos seems from the beginning to have been the centre of the art of wall-painting in Crete, with the largest number of examples, though from the First Palace period these are very fragmentary. Figured frescoes are not known before MM III, and the earliest surviving example seems to be the 'Saffron-gatherer' from Knossos, a representation of a blue monkey that was famously wrongly restored as the figure of a boy when it was first discovered.

The largest groups of wall-paintings of the Second Palace period were found in Knossos itself and in Akrotiri on Thera. The Final Palace at Knossos was also richly decorated, mainly with processional figures, at the time of its destruction. The frescoes from Akrotiri are discussed further below, but we might pause here to note that we would not have known of them had it not been for the extraordinary natural accident that preserved them. It is therefore difficult to evaluate how unusual they were in the Bronze Age world – they are probably an indication that a wealth of similar material has been lost.

Minoan frescoes were painted on to lime plaster, made from the island's limestone, which gave a fine, smooth, white surface. Technically this distinguishes Minoan paintings from those of Egypt, where lime plaster was not used. Typically a Minoan wall, usually of rubble construction, would be coated with a coarse layer of mud and straw. Over this a layer of lime plaster about 1.5 cm (½ in) thick was laid. Subsequently one or more even thinner layers of lime plaster were applied to receive the pigments of the fresco.

The pigments were of mineral origin, and the artists worked with a limited range of colours. Red came from ferrous earths and haematite, yellow from yellow ochre and black from carbon. Blue was sometimes glaucophane, sometimes so-called 'Egyptian blue' – an artificial compound of silicon, copper oxide and calcium oxide. The technique for making this pigment was learned from Egypt, as the name implies. Azurite had been employed as a blue pigment in the Cyclades from the Early Bronze Age, but its use in frescoes has not yet been analytically proved. White was the natural colour of the lime plaster, and lime wash could be mixed with the other colours to achieve various shades. Other mixtures were used to achieve colours such as grey, brown and pink. Green was used in Crete, but is absent from the Thera paintings.

Certain conventions arose in the use of colours from this limited palette. Male figures were painted in a deep reddish brown, while white was used to represent female flesh tones. Intermediate shades sometimes indicate youthful male figures. Some apparent anomalies need explanation: the musculature of the torso and leg of the 'Priest-King', for example, makes it certain that the fragments are from a male figure or figures. In this case the relatively pale skin tone is perhaps simply due to poor preservation of the original colour. Perhaps anomalous, too, are the white-skinned bull-jumpers of the miniature frescoes, whom Evans assumed to be women dressed in male costume. Could they be youthful men? Nothing other than their white skin identifies them as female, and the convention may not be so clear-cut as has sometimes been supposed.

The use of blue to represent the green of plants is very noticeable on the Thera frescoes, and on Cretan examples too, even though green was available there. Green may have been a late addition to the colour range, and perhaps tended to be fugitive. Blue was also used to represent certain shades of grey. The fur of the blue monkeys depicted at both Knossos and Thera must have been grey, the rhyton carried by the 'Cup-bearer' is shown in blue but was almost certainly silver, and the blue scalps of the figures on the Thera frescoes seem to represent shaved areas that would have been a greyish colour in life.

The pigments seem sometimes to have been painted on to damp plaster in a 'true fresco' technique, where the damp surface absorbed the colour and fixed it in place. Sometimes, though, colour was applied using an organic fixative, possibly egg-white. Guidelines for the straight lines of borders were created by stretching a taught string across the damp plaster and thus making a faint impressed line.

A group of fragments from the LM IA 'House of the Frescoes' at Knossos can be restored as a scene of monkeys and birds in a flower-filled landscape through which streams of water flow. The sense of living plants and animals shown in this and other similar compositions has often been described as 'naturalism' in Minoan art, though it has equally frequently been pointed out that the flora and fauna are not depicted with true botanical or zoological accuracy. Indeed the more static and, on the face of it, less 'naturalistic' paintings of contemporary Egypt display more detailed observation drawn from life. Minoan artists, though, created fluid compositions imbued with a sense of vitality and movement. These are dream landscapes – sometimes simply populated by animals, though sometimes figures who may be deities or worshippers appear.

Remains of other comparable compositions were found in the 'House of the Frescoes', and the same painter may have worked both there and in the contemporary South House at Knossos, where some fragments of frescoes were preserved. Compositions based on idealized landscapes were found, too, on the island of Thera (see below). According to Sara Immerwahr,[2] however, 'what may have been the finest of all Minoan nature frescoes' was that which decorated the three walls of a small room in the Royal Villa at Ayia Triadha. The colours were badly damaged by the fires that swept through the building in LM IB, though the frescoes themselves date from the LM IA period. The composition included frequently reproduced details such as the cat stalking a pheasant or the deer leaping on rocky ground, though at least two life-sized female figures appeared in the decorative scheme as a whole. One was seated at an altar or shrine, the other was picking crocuses.

This painting was typical of Minoan frescoes in that it swept continuously around the three walls that it decorated in a unitary composition. This disregard for a single boundary is one aspect of the sense of fluidity in Minoan art. Because of the fragmentary preservation of such compositions, however,

LEFT
81 Copy of a detail
of a fresco from
Ayia Triadha – a
cat stalking a bird.

RIGHT
82 Drawing of
W-D. Niemeier's
suggested
reconstruction of
the 'Priest-King'.

it is rarely possible to attempt a complete restoration. Instead, well-preserved areas of such paintings have been restored, and these are frequently reproduced. Our perception of Minoan fresco painting can be badly skewed by our resulting familiarity with what are in fact only excerpts from larger works. It has increasingly been recognized that the interpretation of frescoes depends on bearing in mind the whole of the broader scheme in any particular part of a building.

A second factor that should be borne in mind when studying the Minoan frescoes discovered in early excavations is that many have been heavily restored. Some of the restorations may mislead by confusing ancient and modern work, while others are probably inaccurate. An example is the so-called 'Priest-King' from Knossos, which belongs to the group of relief frescoes made during the LM I period and found mainly at that site. The use of plaster to build figures in low relief created an effect that was as near to monumentality as Minoan art ever got, though the figures of humans or animals treated in this way rarely exceed life-size.

The 'Priest-King' has become an iconic figure, striding to his right in his tall, plumed crown. However, he is made up of non-joining fragments, and an alternative reconstruction suggested by W-D. Niemeier[3] attributes the three main parts of the composition – head-dress, torso and thigh – to three different figures. The torso becomes part of a commanding figure holding a staff and facing to the viewer's right, thus reversing the direction of the original reconstruction. The thigh is attributed to an approaching figure, and the head-dress is given to a sphinx, with whom such elaborate head-dresses are more commonly associated in Minoan art.

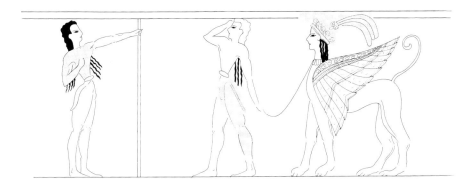

Frescoes using Minoan techniques and with Minoan themes have been found outside Crete. The most remarkable examples are certainly those from Tel el-Dab'a, ancient Avaris, in the Nile delta. Here the subject matter includes scenes of bull-jumping, which in Crete are particularly associated with Knossos. At Avaris, though, combinations such as that of a front-facing bull, an acrobat and a maze-pattern in the background create something almost more Minoan-looking than anything found in Crete.

These paintings are dated to the Hyksos period or the early XVIIIth dynasty, which on the traditional chronology adopted here would make them close in time both to the paintings from the 'House of the Frescoes' and to the Thera frescoes, with which they have much in common. Themes paralleled in Thera, and the same Minoan techniques, are also found among the frescoes from Tel Kabri in Israel. There seems every possibility that Minoan craftsmen travelled abroad to execute these works.

Iconographic influences from abroad are certainly recognizable in the frescoes from Thera and Crete, and it is possible that foreign inspiration lay behind the inclusion of life-size figures. Incomplete evidence hampers firm conclusions. We know that Cretan painting had a long history by the time of the Second Palaces, but we can scarcely surmise what pictures decorated the walls of their predecessors. The chance element of preservation particularly affects these uniquely fragile works.

Sculpture and Figurines

The body of Minoan art preserved to us is dominated by works on a small or even a miniature scale. Is this simply an accident of survival, or is it a real phenomenon, dependent on the circumstances and attitudes surrounding artistic production? The question is interesting, because on the face of it Minoan art contrasts strongly with that of Egypt and the Near East in the same period. In those cultures art was often monumental and grandiose, with large stone statues and reliefs glorifying both gods and men. This approach seems to have been foreign to Minoan temperament. Extraordinarily we have no single example of a large-scale representation of a Minoan deity, nor of a Minoan ruler.

The reasons cannot be sought in lack of technical skill. Minoan architecture involved sophisticated use of a range of stones. Moreover, the carving of stone vases and seal-stones required mastery of the medium. The techniques used for the latter are perhaps scarcely comparable, but the techniques employed in the making of the larger stone vases could certainly have been transferred to the carving of sculptures, if the motivation had been there.

What, though, of the stones themselves? It has been argued that the stones of Crete were unsuitable for large sculptures. Certainly the island has only a little marble, and it is not of high quality. Some of the stones used in architecture could, however, have been used for sculpture. Indeed we may have an example of the Minoan use of gypsum for carving. It has convincingly been suggested that the two gypsum fragments carved in relief with parts of bulls which were said to have been found in the Treasury of Atreus at Mycenae are Minoan works, imported from Crete. The stone is certainly suitable for carving, although the colour is rather dull. The bulls are shown on a relatively small scale.

While the statues of the Greek and Roman periods found on Crete are generally of imported marble, it is interesting to note that in the Archaic period, before marble was imported, sculptures from the seventh-century-BC temples at Prinias and Gortyn were carved from local limestone.

It does not seem, then, that lack of suitable stone can have been the whole story. If it was a factor inhibiting production of large-scale sculpture, alternative materials would have been sought. Terracotta is an obvious possibility, and terracotta statues of women in Minoan style, either deities or worshippers, have come to light in the Late Bronze Age shrine on the island of Kea. These approach life size, and are thus much bigger than the LM II–III Minoan female statues with wheel-made bases that are usually interpreted as goddesses, and are the nearest equivalent from Crete.

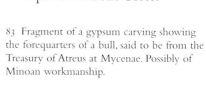

83 Fragment of a gypsum carving showing the forequarters of a bull, said to be from the Treasury of Atreus at Mycenae. Possibly of Minoan workmanship.

While evidence for terracotta statues might be expected to have survived, wooden sculpture would certainly have perished, and we must consider the possibility that an extensive repertoire of Minoan statues in wood has been lost. One example may have existed in the Anemospilia shrine, discussed above, where a pair of life-size terracotta feet was found. They are very heavy, being made of coarse clay, and are shaped above the shin in a way that would have enabled them to be fitted into a wooden trunk or 'body' for a statue. Other terracotta feet are known from Minoan Crete in later contexts. Some have traditionally been interpreted as votive offerings, but the possibility of their use as part of composite statues largely made of wood remains. It is clear from later Greek sources that in certain Greek shrines and sanctuaries there was a *xoanon,* or wooden statue of a deity, usually supposed to be of great antiquity. These were often draped in real textiles. Some could be so-called acrolithic statues (literally, statues with stone extremities). In these cases a body, usually of wood, was hidden by the drapery, but extremities such as the head, hands and feet were of stone or indeed other materials.

Further scraps of evidence supporting the original existence of composite statues includes a stone wig from Knossos, somewhat less than life-size, and curls of bronze that Evans found at Knossos and interpreted as being from a wooden statue of about life size. An alternative interpretation, though, suggests that each curl formed the complete hairstyle of a series of smaller figures.

The ivory figure of a youth from Palaikastro, which was discovered in fragments between 1987 and 1990, instantly took its place as one of the most remarkable surviving figures in Minoan art. Standing some 50 cm (19½ in) high, it is large for an ivory sculpture, and it is a composite work. The body, with its remarkably fine and detailed carving, is in ivory, but the hair is an added piece of carved serpentine. The figure also originally had attachments in gold.

In conclusion it may be stated both that there were some practical reasons for the lack of large-scale stone sculpture in Minoan Crete, and that there may have been large sculptures in wood. Nonetheless, this does not seem to be the whole story. In those arts such as fresco painting, for which we have good surviving evidence and in which presumably the artists had a choice, they seem not to have chosen a grandiose scale, as was common in contemporary Egypt. Figures in Minoan frescoes rarely exceeded life size and were often smaller or even miniature in scale. Though there may have been large sculptures of wood, the evidence is relatively slight.

The apparent lack of grandiose ruler-portraiture or monumental representations of deities tell us something about Minoan psychology and society. It seems that ritual is consistently emphasized, whether in the form of bull-sports, ceremonial processions, the harvesting of saffron, or the sports and games of young men. The people were constantly surrounded by representations of the ritual actions that bound them to their gods, and thus defined their place in the universe. This would seem to make sense in a theocratic society, where priest-kings held power.

The excellence of works in miniature is clearly shown by a range of statuettes and figurines, reliefs, vessels and particularly finely carved seal-stones, where a small compass was used to great effect. Of course seal-stones are relatively indestructible, and thus more likely to survive. Nonetheless, even allowing for accidents of preservation, it seems that there is evidence for an intrinsic choice of a smaller scale in much Minoan art.

SMALL-SCALE SCULPTURES IN IVORY, BRONZE AND FAIENCE

The Palaikastro figurine mentioned above brings us into the realm of small-scale figures in neopalatial art, and their interpretation. It has been suggested by MacGillivray, Driessen and Sackett that the youth is a god, and specifically 'Diktaian Zeus, associated with Egyptian Osiris and immortalized as Orion'.[4] The reader is referred to their thorough publication for the complex reasoning behind this interpretation. It must be said, though, that while he is unusually large and elaborate, the youth does not differ in dress and pose from many Minoan statuettes in both terracotta and bronze that are usually identified as worshippers.

Parts of several ivory figurines were found at Knossos. The finished pieces must, like the Palaikastro figure, have been made from several sections held together with dowels or pins. Sinclair Hood[5] suggests that one figure of a man may originally have been some 40 cm (15¾ in) high, though only part of the chest and the bent forearm survive. The best-known of these figures is the acrobat, who could be restored, and is 30 cm (12 in) long. Carved in the taut, stretched-out position of an athlete perhaps springing over a bull, he is anatomically well observed, and where the surface of the ivory is preserved it can be seen that the craftsman added fine details such as the veins and the fingernails on the hand. The same fine carving is also a feature of the Palaikastro figure.

A fine series of bronzes of the neopalatial period seems also almost exclusively to represent figures of worshippers or, in rare cases such as the group of bull and acrobat in the British Museum, ritual actions. These bronzes are solid cast using the 'lost wax' method, and have a characteristically rough and bubbly surface, probably because the alloy was poor in tin and did not flow well into the mould. The missing lower legs of the acrobat were probably lost as the result of a casting fault, though the upper arms were perhaps consciously modelled as abbreviated stumps. The craftsman has been ingenious in attaching the acrobat to the bull by means of his flowing locks of hair.

LEFT
84 Bronze group showing
an acrobat vaulting
over the back of a bull.

BELOW
85 Bronze figure of a
worshipper of unusually
stocky proportions.

Worshippers, both men and women, are shown in stylized attitudes of prayer. A common gesture is the raising of one hand to the forehead. The women wear the layered skirts and open bodices of Minoan formal dress, the men usually wear breechcloths and cod-pieces. Most male figures conform to the Minoan aesthetic that demanded sinewy bodies and very thin waists, but one or two figures are more corpulent and are perhaps intended to represent older men.

Most – indeed probably all – of these bronzes were made for dedication in sanctuaries: many have been found in sacred caves. As well as human figures, bronzes of animals were dedicated. These included bulls and Cretan wild goats.

Faience is an artificial compound, consisting of crushed quartz crystals covered with a vitreous glaze. It was made in Mesopotamia and Egypt at an early date, and the technology was probably introduced to Crete by the late prepalatial period. Faience beads were found in some of the tholos tombs of the Mesara region. Protopalatial faience included the so-called 'Town Mosaic', mentioned above. We might add here that the plaques depicting town-houses were in fact part of a larger composition showing a town by the sea, armed men and men swimming. The whole scene may have been analogous to parts of the 'Fresco of the Fleet' from Thera, discussed below.

Neopalatial faience is represented particularly by the contents of the 'Temple Repositories' at Knossos, where the so-called 'snake-goddesses' were found. These were the two best-preserved of three such statuettes. Their identification is discussed below in the section on religion. Their workmanship is very fine: they are delicately modelled and carefully coloured. With them were found other works in faience, including votive girdles and dresses, models of shells, and plaques of flying fish. Relief plaques also showed animals, including goats and cows suckling their young. These presumably originally decorated such things as furniture, boxes or chests. Faience vases also came from the 'Temple Repositories', including tall one-handled cups with painted leafy sprays.

In all, this is a remarkable group of objects, showing that the craftsmen making faience at Knossos had achieved a high level of technical perfection. The pieces no doubt originally came from a shrine, and seem to have been buried in the two stone-lined cists in a room to the west of the Central Court at Knossos after the destruction, probably caused by earthquake, at the end of the MM III period. Faience objects that probably originated in the workshops of Knossos where also found in the Shaft Graves of Mycenae.

Metalwork

Bronze figurines have been mentioned above, but of course the main use of bronze was for an extensive range of tools and weapons. The sheer size of some of the practical tools, such as saws, makes them impressive. The huge sheet-bronze double-axes that seem to have been used as standards are also remarkable for their dramatic scale. Bronze swords and daggers, some with elaborately decorated pommels of gold, must be counted among the finest products of Cretan craftsmen.

Bronze vessels, some of great size and others with neatly accomplished decoration, give a good indication of the bronze-workers' skill. A series of huge cauldrons from Tylissos includes one that weighs 52 kg (115 lb). The amount of bronze that we can see to have been in use certainly shows the wealth of neopalatial Crete, particularly since the survival of such artefacts is greatly compromised by the fact that metals could be melted and re-used.

The same consideration applies even more acutely to vessels in precious metal. A tradition of such vessels, perhaps particularly in silver, has been suggested for the First Palace period because the pottery vases, notably the shiny-surfaced, crisply shaped, palatial Kamares Wares, often seem to copy metal characteristics. Actual survival of protopalatial silver vessels is limited, though, to only one or two examples, unless indeed the Tod treasure is included in the total. A number of silver vases dating to the neopalatial period are known, including the group from the South House at Knossos mentioned above. Survival of gold and silver vessels in neopalatial Crete is no doubt affected by the fact that we lack the rich burials in which they might be expected. However, a number of silver vessels from the Mycenae Shaft Graves may be of Cretan manufacture. These include the silver 'siege rhyton' with an elaborate relief scene of the siege of a city, and the silver rhyton in the shape of a bull's head. Some of the gold vessels from the Shaft Graves may show Cretan influence, though the majority seem to be of mainland manufacture.

Two fine gold cups from the tholos tomb at Vapheio near Sparta may be of Minoan workmanship. Ellen Davis[6] has suggested that the cup with the 'quieter' and more elegantly planned scene of the capture of bulls was made by a Minoan craftsman, and the one with the livelier scene with more action, more filling ornament but perhaps rather less grace was made by a Mycenaean to form a matching pair. Comparisons are hampered, though, by the lack of gold vessels from Crete. It is possible that the Minoans did not produce a large number of vessels in gold, preferring perhaps to gild their relief stone vases – a practice for which we have good evidence. The gold cup in the Aigina treasure may, though, be the work of a Minoan craftsman.

The survival of neopalatial jewellery has similarly been compromised by the re-use of materials and the lack of rich tombs. However, the burials at Poros have produced a good range of jewellery of this period, including necklaces, pendants and ornaments of gold, semi-precious stones, faience and glass. An interesting group of earrings was made in gold, silver and lead, and the tombs contained gold, silver and bronze pins. In addition, gold and silver rings included two very fine gold signet-rings with cult scenes.

Such signet-rings have also been found elsewhere in Crete, including at Knossos and Archanes. Jewellery was among the dedications made in sacred caves, and the cave at Archalochori in central Crete produced a remarkable series of miniature gold double-axes with incised decoration. Some of the gold jewellery of the Mycenae Shaft Graves seems Minoan, although much belongs to the mainland tradition. Representations of elaborate jewellery worn by figures and frescoes, particularly those from Thera, complete our picture of a sophisticated craft.

Stone Vases

Stone vases of many types were produced in neopalatial Crete, some of considerable elegance, others bearing elaborate scenes in relief. They were part of the furnishings of palaces and country houses, and were also dedicated at shrines and sanctuaries. A particularly fine series was found at Zakros, while remarkable relief vases came from the Royal Villa at Ayia Triadha. A range of stones was used, including local steatites, serpentines, chlorite and banded limestones, and some harder stones that were imported. Occasionally very precious stones were used: the small rock-crystal rhyton from Zakros is a fine example.

The chlorite rhyton with a relief depiction of a peak sanctuary from Zakros has been much discussed as a source of information about the nature of these mountain-top shrines. This is an example of a vessel originally covered in gold foil. The three relief vases from Ayia Triadha are similarly well-known, and each has subject matter apparently connected with ritual. All are made from black steatite. The Harvester Vase, an ovoid rhyton, depicts a procession of muscular youths bearing winnowing fans, led by a priestly figure with a sistrum, mentioned above. The Boxer Vase is a conical rhyton, with relief scenes in four registers. Three show athletic contests between men, one a scene of bull-jumping. It has plausibly been suggested that these are rites of passage of young men. The Chieftain Cup may also fall into this category: it portrays a young man approaching an imposing older figure with outstretched staff. The relative ages of the two are made explicit by their carefully delineated hairstyles.

Animal-head rhytons, in the form of bulls or lions, have a sculptural quality and were fine products, often very sensitively carved. Remarkable, too, are the stone rhytons shaped like triton shells. An example in serpentine from the palace at Mallia not only captures the elegant shape of the shell, but also bears relief and incised decoration. Two Minoan 'genii' are shown, one of them holding a jug.

These rhytons of elaborate shape share with the more common types the fact that they are pierced. Animals have pierced muzzles and holes at the back of the neck so that liquid could be poured in and would emerge through the piercing. Liquid would, in fact, run from rhytons of all forms unless a finger was used by the bearer to stop the hole.

86 Chlorite rhyton or sprinkler vessel from Zakros with a depiction in relief of a peak sanctuary.

The uses of these ritual vessels are therefore difficult to reconstruct. Some shapes, notably the conical examples, could have been used as fillers to pour liquid into smaller vessels. Others may have been used for sprinkling, in rituals like those sometimes seen on gold signet-rings.

Pottery

The pottery of the Second Palace period shows a new interest in naturalism, and the pictorialized abstract motifs that had character-ized Classical Kamares pottery were replaced by motifs that were truly pictorial. The transition from the light-on-dark painting of the First Palace period to the dark-on-light style that dominated neo-palatial production was achieved gradually, and the new style

87 The Harvester Vase from Ayia Triadha.

gave the opportunity for varied decorative schemes, mainly inspired by plants, flowers and the marine world. Spirals of various forms were also popular.

The post-Kamares tradition of MM III saw white motifs, such as dots, spirals, net patterns, horizontal bands, oblique lines and floral patterns, painted on a brown or black background. This was joined by the popular 'tortoiseshell ripple' decoration of wavy dark lines on a light ground.

In general MM III seems to show a falling-off in the making of pottery after the achievements of the First Palace period, with rather routine produc-tion – perhaps a reflection of a general retrenchment in Minoan society at this time. Recovery came quickly, however, and some fine vases were produced in this period. Naturalistic motifs were not only painted on vases but occasionally added in relief: leaping dolphins on a vase stand from Phaistos are an example.

LM IA saw a new Floral Style, in which spirals, rosettes and foliate bands were joined by reed patterns and groups of plants and flowers, often shown in a very naturalistic way and full of movement, as if blown by the wind.

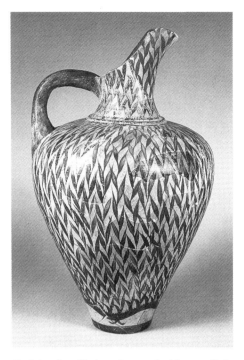

88 A jug from Phaistos decorated with naturalistic reeds in the Floral Style.

These were now consistently painted in dark-on-light style, using lustrous dark paint. This decorative scheme would continue until the end of the Bronze Age.

In LM IB the Floral Style was joined by other fine pottery styles particularly characteristic of palatial production, and sometimes described together as the 'special palace tradition'. These included Marine Style, Abstract and Geometric Style and Alternating Style. Marine Style, as the name suggests, drew inspiration from sea-creatures, sea-weed, rocks and shells with particularly engaging results. The octopus was often chosen as a main motif with its tentacles writhing sinuously around the surface of the vessel. The other marine elements, too, give a sense of wavy underwater movement. The Minoan love of fluid decoration that observes no boundaries is well exemplified by vases in this style.

The Abstract and Geometric Style used repeated motifs drawn from a wide spectrum of the Minoan repertory to cover the surface of the vase, while the Alternating Style sees such motifs used in a strictly alternating arrangement. The motifs were still sometimes plant-derived, though they also included religious symbols such as double-axes, so-called 'sacred knots', figure-of-eight shields and bulls' heads.

Considerable overlaps exist between the four styles recognized by experts, and together they form a fine body of pottery typical of the best palatial workshops. Other production at the time was more routine, with potters turning out quantities of vases that were not so carefully made or painted. As well as the decorated pottery a range of functional kitchen wares and cooking pots was made. As in the First Palace period, the export of Minoan vessels abroad shows that the pottery was widely appreciated by contemporary societies in the Late Bronze Age world of the eastern Mediterranean and Egypt. It stands out as an entirely characteristic Minoan product when it is found outside Crete.

PLATE I

RIGHT Steep, narrow gorges, like this one at Arvi in the south east, are characteristic of the limestone landscape of Crete.

BELOW Crete is agriculturally very rich and products that would have been familiar to the Minoans, such as wine, oil, olives, figs, honey, nuts and herbs, are still sold in the markets.

PLATE 2

PLATE 3

LEFT Mochlos is now an island
but was a peninsula in the
Minoan period.

LEFT BELOW The North
Entrance of the palace at
Knossos. The original blocks
can clearly be distinguished
from the portico restored
by Evans.

RIGHT The Royal Road
leading away from the Theatral
Area in the north-west corner
of the palace at Knossos.

BELOW A general view of
the palace of Phaistos from the
north west.

PLATE 4

RIGHT A corded pithos (storage jar) stands at the north side of the palace of Mallia.

BELOW The palace of Zakros from the north west, with part of the Minoan town.

PLATE 5

RIGHT The caldera at Thera, tranquil in the evening light, is the centre of an active volcano.

BELOW At Akrotiri on Thera modern visitors stroll in a square of the Minoan town, past the West House.

PLATE 6

PLATE 7

LEFT ABOVE The 'Town Mosaic': faience plaques showing typical houses of a Minoan town. MM III (1700–1600BC).

FAR LEFT CENTRE Gold bee-pendant from the Chrysolakkos cemetery at Mallia. MM II (1850–1700BC).

FAR LEFT BELOW A neopalatial Marine Style flask from Palaikastro decorated with a lively octopus. LM IB (1500–1450BC).

LEFT BELOW Faience 'snake-goddess' from the 'Temple Repositories' at Knossos. MM III (1700–1600BC).

BELOW The 'Priest-King' from Knossos: a familiar figure, though this restoration of the surviving fragments has been questioned. LM I (1600–1450BC).

RIGHT A group of seal-stones.

A Cushion seal of banded agate: on one side a goat and a dog, on the other signs from the Hieroglyphic script. MM II–III (1850–1600BC).

B Green jasper stamp seal with an elegant shaft and a bull's head motif. MM II–III (1850–1600BC).

C Amygdaloid (almond-shaped) carnelian seal with a representation of a boat. LM I (1600–1450BC).

D Three-sided prism of green jasper: a goat, a deer and a cat with a crab. MM III (1700–1600BC).

E Amygdaloid carnelian seal with a chariot drawn by two horses. From Knossos, LM II–IIIA (1450–1300BC).

F Amygdaloid haematite seal with a man holding a fish. LM I–II (1500–1400BC).

G Lentoid (lens-shaped) haematite seal showing bull sports: an acrobat leaps over the back of the bull while another stands apparently holding one horn. LM II–IIIA (1450–1300BC).

H Lentoid lapis lacedaemonius seal with a hybrid creature resembling a minotaur, though the legs of a man are combined with the upper parts of both a bull and and a goat. LM II–IIIA (1450–1300BC).

PLATE 8

One side of the 'Ayia Triadha Sarcophagus' showing offerings brought to a figure probably representing the dead occupant of the coffin. LM II–IIIA (1450–1300BC).

The best-preserved of the fresco panels from the Final Palace at Knossos showing bull-jumping. The figures are about one quarter life-size. LM II–IIIA (1450–1300BC).

Seal-stones and Signet-rings

The use of hard semi-precious stones for seals that had begun in the First Palace period continued in neopalatial Crete, and encouraged the predominance of shapes with convex surfaces. These allowed the craftsman, to see and control the point of contact made by the rotary drill. They also made clearer impressions. The most common shapes were lentoids, amygdaloids and cushions – respectively lens-shaped, almond-shaped and rectangular seals.

The designs on the seals include both human figures and animals, and the standard of carving can be very high indeed. Human figures are sometimes engaged in warfare, hunting or ritual actions such as bull-jumping, while animal studies include bulls, lions, goats and deer, individually or in group compositions. The fine gold signet-rings of the period often bear elaborate ritual scenes.

The use of seals had been known on the Greek mainland in the Early Bronze Age but had subsequently lapsed. Seals were re-introduced from Crete at the beginning of the Late Bronze Age, the earliest examples coming from the Mycenae Shaft Graves. While some seals found on the mainland were imports from Crete, others were made locally. Distinguishing Minoan and mainland fine seals is often impossible: the style remains essentially Minoan, but Cretan craftsmen no doubt travelled, and taught their skills to mainland practitioners.

Alongside hard stones, soft local stones such as serpentine and steatite were also used for Cretan seals. On these we find a similar range of motifs, but the carving is not so fine. Seal ownership was probably quite widespread in neopalatial Crete, but presumably gold signets and fine seals of hard stone belonged to members of the ruling elite. Seals may also have been worn as ornaments or amulets. The so-called 'talismanic' class, often in jasper or carnelian with stylized motifs, rarely appears in seal impressions.

Writing and Administration in Neopalatial Crete

The use of Hieroglyphic script died out early in the neopalatial period, and Linear A was essentially the script of the Cretan Second Palaces. The language represented remains unknown, in spite of various suggestions from a large specialist literature. A connection with Luvian, a branch of Hittite from south-west Anatolia, would seem an attractive possibility as this appears to have been the region from which some early settlers came to Crete, but other scholars see similarities with Semitic languages, while some maintain that the language of Linear A is not only Indo-European but also has connections with Greek. The problem is a complex one: its solution perhaps

89 Drawing of two clay page-shaped tablets with inscriptions in the Linear A script.

requires a greater number of inscriptions of longer length than the current corpus provides.

The distribution of Linear A is quite wide, finds from many sites in Crete being joined by a scattering from the Aegean islands that show the extent of Minoan influence. The script is also found on a number of different types of objects. The administrators of the palaces and country houses used rectangular clay tablets inscribed with Linear A script. They also used 'roundels', which are roughly circular clay discs with seal impressions around the edge. These are often, but not always, also inscribed with Linear A. Nodules, which are lumps of clay fashioned around string or used on folded parchment, and 'noduli', which are lumps of clay with no signs of attachment, both bear seal impressions, but are only additionally inscribed with Linear A in special circumstances.

Apart from administrative uses, Linear A also occurs on a wide variety of other objects. It was sometimes painted on to pottery vessels – there are some thirty-seven examples of this – but more often it was inscribed. The objects with inscriptions include pottery vessels, stone vessels, particularly 'libation tables', bronzes, jewellery and so on. Many were dedications in sanctuaries. The inscriptions sometimes consist of only one or two signs, but a longer 'libation formula' has been recognized. This repeated pattern of words probably included the name of a deity and perhaps a place name which was the location of the shrine or sanctuary.

Linear A tablets come from the palaces and 'country houses' of Crete.

90 A bronze axe inscribed with two signs in the Linear A script.

Knossos, Mallia and Zakros have yielded examples, and while only four tablets were found at neopalatial Phaistos, Ayia Triadha yielded an archive of some 146 tablets. Tablets have also come from Chania, Myrtos-Pyrgos and Tylissos. Their wider distribution includes examples from Thera and a single tablet from Kea. The tablets were mostly page-shaped, and were inscribed in lines of script from left to right. As noted above, the script is syllabic: each sign represents a syllable. The lists are of personnel and commodities, and the contents can partly be understood because of the use of ideograms – symbols that are essentially small drawings of the things listed. The system used to record numbers can also be understood.

The tablets were of unbaked clay and therefore survive only if accidentally burned. There is no evidence that they were ever fired on purpose. If the records were kept in any other, more permanent form we have no evidence for it. The Cretan conditions would not allow the preservation of materials such as parchment or papyrus. It has been argued that the existence of painted Linear A inside pottery vases shows that it was a reasonably fluent script that could have been written on 'paper' equivalents. This is supported by imprints of folded parchment left behind on the undersides of certain clay sealings. Since the pieces of parchment seem to have been very small, it is probable that the messages were short. They are much more likely to have been simple records of shipment and delivery than any sort of 'diplomatic correspondence', as is sometimes suggested. It remains possible that the uses of writing in Minoan Crete were always limited, even at the height of the neopalatial period, and that the surviving evidence is fairly representative, even if incomplete.

We do not know whether the seal-based control and accounting systems ran in parallel with the use of Linear A, or whether the two were fully integrated. Attempts have been made to distinguish between 'living' or active archives, 'discarded archives', which are more or less complete collections of broken sealings discarded after recording was completed, and material that was more randomly deposited. Since tablets and sealings are preserved by chance fires, however, such distinctions remain uncertain. Patterns of seal use are also difficult to unravel: some sealings may have accompanied goods arriving from outlying areas, others perhaps represent internal mechanisms of control.

Minoans Abroad in the Period of the Second Palaces

The Second Palace period saw Crete building on the patterns of trade and exchange established in the First. Evidence for contact with Egypt intensifies: Minoan pottery is found there, a number of XVIIIth-dynasty texts refer to 'Keftiu', and paintings in Egyptian tombs show Aegean peoples bringing gifts that are readily identifiable with high-quality Minoan products. The maintenance of good relations with Egypt no doubt reflected the need to continue trading links both with Egypt herself and with the Syro-Palestinian coast, where Egyptian influence was considerable. The presence in Crete of pottery from this region, including the standard Canaanite amphorae and pottery from Cyprus, is matched by a relatively small but significant amount of Minoan pottery along the eastern Mediterranean shore. Metals and other precious raw materials were no doubt still the prime focus of exchanges that also saw luxury goods moving between Crete, Egypt and the Near East.

Links with Anatolia were a part of this pattern too. Evidence for Minoan presence in the Dodecanese and the north Aegean islands shows the various stepping stones that could be used to approach the west coast of Turkey, and is joined by increasing evidence from sites such as Miletos, where there was a thriving Minoan settlement at this time.

The Second Palace period also witnessed an intensification of Minoan influence on the islands of the Aegean and on the Greek mainland. The rising power of Mycenae is amply illustrated by the rich finds from the Shaft Graves there. These aristocratic burials were being made in the two grave circles at Mycenae between about 1650 and 1500BC, and their extraordinarily rich contents included much Minoan material, produced either in Crete or perhaps in some cases on the mainland by Minoan craftsmen. This assimilation of Minoan arts and crafts would continue to be a feature of Mycenaean Greece, reciprocal influences on Crete creating a situation where a distinction between Minoan and Mycenaean products can sometimes scarcely be drawn.

Crete, then, can be seen as a lynch-pin at this period, broadly connecting the lands of the Near East and Egypt to the Greek mainland, which itself was beginning to be in contact with the rest of Europe. Closer to home, the islands of the Aegean became very 'Minoanized' at this time. Excavations on Melos, Kea and Thera, in particular, have revealed extensive towns that owe much to Crete in their lifestyle and material culture. We will turn to just one of these, the island of Thera, where the astonishing site of Akrotiri perhaps gives us more insight into the nature of life in a Minoan town than anything on Crete itself.

THERA

At Akrotiri on the island of Thera the visitor can enjoy a stroll through the streets of a Late Minoan town. The preservation of the remains under the ash from the great volcanic explosion has created here a sort of Aegean Pompeii. Excavations have so far revealed houses grouped around a main street and square, and, although affected by earthquake damage, their state of preservation is quite remarkable. It is possible to walk into the square and be surrounded by Minoan-style houses with facades two storeys high – a truly extraordinary and very evocative experience.[7]

Strictly speaking, of course, this is a Cycladic town, with a long history stretching back into the Early Bronze Age. By the time of the eruption, however, the inhabitants were very much influenced by Minoan Crete. Their buildings, their possessions and their lifestyle were clearly thoroughly Minoanized. Minoan weights and measures had been adopted, and the Linear A script was used.

The extent to which Akrotiri should be seen as a Minoan 'colony', and what precisely is implied by the term, has been much discussed. It seems likely that the town was important as a centre through which Minoan trade passed, and from which such trade was perhaps organized by a resident population of Minoan merchants. Cycladic, as well as Minoan, ships may have been used: the islanders had a long tradition as seafarers and 'middle-men'. A Minoan element in the population seems certain, though what proportion of those living there had originally come from Crete remains a matter for debate. We can quite clearly discern an island legacy in the art of Akrotiri. Less than 10 per cent of the pottery, for example, was imported from Crete. The rest was produced locally, and retains some Cycladic traits, though Minoan influence is more than apparent. The same pattern can be argued for the rest of the material culture. We should therefore see the site as important in its own terms, and enjoy the glimpses it provides of life lived in a Minoanized Cycladic town, as well as appreciating the insight it gives us as to what life must have been like on its bigger neighbour, Crete.

The island of Thera is the southernmost of the Cyclades, separated from Crete by only some 96 km (60 miles) of open sea. It is sometimes called Santorini, a name deriving from the period of Venetian occupation. The island was, and is, an active volcano, and it erupted with such force in the Late Bronze Age that the entire configuration of the land-mass was changed.

The characteristic shape of the island now, with its deep internal caldera, or sea-filled crater, is the legacy of the Bronze Age eruption. Previously the island had at least one, and probably two, smaller calderas: remnants of earlier episodes of volcanic activity. The Late Bronze Age eruption was of the explosive or paroxysmal type. Vast quantities of volcanic matter were ejected

91 The effects of earthquake can clearly be seen at Akrotiri, and the way this staircase has been crushed is an example.

under great pressure, much of it emerging in the form of fine ash. The ejection of matter emptied the magma chamber of the volcano, and its unsupported surface then collapsed downwards, leaving the steep sides of the caldera that are visible today. Much of the ash fell back on to the island, though some fell into the sea and on to nearby islands, including Crete.

The eruption occurred at a time when LM IA pottery had reached a mature stage, both on Crete and on Thera. The date relative to the archaeological sequence is therefore not in doubt, nor can it any longer be suggested that the eruption directly and immediately destroyed the Minoan civilization of Crete. The major destruction there occurred some fifty years later, at the end of LM IB, when most Minoan sites throughout the island were destroyed. Views about the effect of the Thera eruption on Crete vary, some scholars agreeing with Rehak and Younger that it probably amounted to little more than 'a loud bang and a light coating of pumice on the north-eastern part of the island that might even have been beneficial to agriculture', others, such as Driessen and MacDonald, believing that it seriously weakened Crete and made the island vulnerable.[8]

The effect on Thera cannot be doubted. The inhabitants of the Bronze Age town were used to earthquakes. Their houses had been damaged and repaired after an earthquake earlier in the Late Cycladic I period. When, later in the same period, an earthquake began the geological event that would destroy their town and change their island for ever, they at first reacted resiliently. They began to salvage possessions, to clear rubble and to rebuild the town. The houses were severely damaged and it seems more than likely that there were human casualties of the earthquake too. Nonetheless there was obviously every intention to rebuild at Akrotiri and carry on living there.

It is not clear exactly how much time elapsed after the earthquake and before the eruption, but it was probably a matter of months. Then, when the island quite literally exploded, the inhabitants of Akrotiri were defeated by the huge geological forces that faced them. They fled as their world violently collapsed, their island changed under their feet and vast quantities of volcanic matter rained down to obliterate their town. All escaped from the excavated part of Akrotiri town, though whether they escaped from the island altogether is not known. We can only hope that they had enough warning to take to their ships and sail away.

As at Pompeii, a disaster for the inhabitants has, centuries later, provided unparalleled opportunities for archaeology. The Thera ash became a good medium for protecting the Bronze Age remains. The residents seem to have taken their most precious possessions with them when they fled, but the site, unsurprisingly, is rich in pottery and other non-perishable finds. Where the ash has really helped, though, is in the preservation of evidence for perishable objects, such as basketry and wood. Beds, tables, baskets and so on were preserved 'in negative' as spaces in the ash into which plaster could be poured to obtain a cast of the original furniture. The wall-paintings, too, although mostly found in fragments that had been shaken from the walls, were preserved in glowing colours, and in positions where there original location could precisely be known.

So much for the way in which the town was destroyed and preserved. What was the Bronze Age settlement of Akrotiri like, and how did its inhabitants live? The town lay on the southern side of Thera, near to the sea and facing Crete. Though the pre-eruption state of the island is not easy to reconstruct, it seems that its south side offered less rugged terrain than the north, and the Akrotiri peninsula would have provided a reasonable amount of fertile land to feed the inhabitants. Plant remains and representations show that grain crops, olives, pulses, grapes, nuts and figs were grown, as well as a range of herbs and spices, including saffron. Some exotic, non-Aegean plant remains have come to light. These underline the second and ultimately more significant aspect of the position of Akrotiri. It was in the perfect place for sea-borne activities, and particularly for contact by sea with Minoan Crete.

Excavation here was made easier than elsewhere on the island because erosion had reduced the depth of ash over the remains. Nonetheless other Bronze Age sites have been found on Thera, and it is clear that by the Late Bronze Age Akrotiri was the single main town of the island. Elsewhere in the Cyclades, Phylakopi on Melos and Ayia Irini on Kea are excavated examples of sites that, like Akrotiri, had become the dominant town on their respective islands at this time. Akrotiri stands out from these on sheer size alone: the settlement is thought to have covered some 20 ha (50 acres), making it at least ten times larger than the other two sites. It also stands out for the size and elaboration of its buildings. The excavation has revealed the existence of five fine ashlar-built houses, though these have not all been completely uncovered. There are also a number of other substantial houses, and some town areas with rather more closely packed remains, no doubt representing simpler dwellings. The excavated area is only a small part of the town, which certainly holds exciting prospects for future exploration.

The buildings so far revealed are grouped around a main street which leads into a triangular square. Their pattern is irregular, and the effect very like that of modern island villages, where the clustering of houses around narrow and winding paved streets affords protection from winter winds and rain, and shady corners in the heat of summer. Ancient Akrotiri had paved streets and alleyways and an efficient drainage system beneath them.

Ashlar masonry was used in the most spacious houses, though timber-framed rubble and clay construction was common as well. The houses still stand some two or three storeys high, their external facades covered in straw-tempered clay. An external course of masonry at the level of the internal storeys gives a characteristic appearance also seen on the small faience plaques representing houses in the 'Town Mosaic' from Knossos. Doorways, sometimes with ashlar masonry surrounds, survive at ground level, and windows at this level were usually small. Rooms at basement and ground level seem often to have been kitchen, working and storage areas – generally the most utilitarian part of the houses. Mill installations were found in various houses, showing that the final stages of the processing of agricultural produce from outlying farms and fields took place there. Upper storeys, by contrast, had larger windows, and the interior walls of upstairs rooms were often coated with fine plaster and decorated with paintings. These were spacious living rooms. Some may have functioned as areas for domestic cult.

At least one building, known as Xeste 3 (the Greek word refers to an ashlar structure), was particularly large and elaborate. It seems to have had an important cult area and probably had a public function. Features borrowed from fine Minoan architecture – *polythyra*, rooms with benches, and in particular an *adyton* or lustral basin – make this building stand out from the others in the town, and the wall-paintings have very marked ritual content, even thought their precise interpretation is a matter for discussion. They include women gathering crocus flowers around a figure who is almost certainly a goddess, male figures engaged in what is perhaps the ritual presentation of a garment, and a representation of the door of a shrine decorated with 'horns of consecration' from which blood, presumably from a sacrifice, is dripping. Near to this are three women, one sitting on a rock holding an injured foot from which blood also drips.

Although these paintings were not all mutually intervisible, and occurred at different levels within the building, it has plausibly been suggested that they have themes in common. In particular, it is clear that the age of the male and female figures is differentiated by their dress, the maturity of their bodies and their hairstyles. Perhaps, then, initiation ceremonies connected with the transition from childhood to adulthood were celebrated in the *adyton* and the nearby rooms.

92 This female figure from Xeste 3 at Akrotiri is almost certainly a goddess. She has a snake on her head, elaborate earrings and necklaces with beads shaped like ducks and dragonflies.

This building stands out for its size and elaboration and apparently public function, but it is not the equivalent of a 'palace' or 'governor's house' and no building in the excavated section of Akrotiri seems to have had such status. It is, though, very possible that such a building will be found in the future.

The other houses of the town seem, in many cases, to have been well-to-do private residences. The West House, which fronts on to the Triangular Square, can be taken as an example. It is free-standing, and has a facade over 15 m (50 ft) long. The house was extensively remodelled after the earthquake that damaged Akrotiri early in LC I, and at the time of the eruption that buried it the building had two storeys in its western part and three in the east.

As usual, the ground floor was given over to practical functions. There were storage areas for food which, as in Crete, was generally kept in big storage jars or pithoi, and a room with a hearth which was presumably a kitchen. A room identified as a workshop may have been used for some process connected with metallurgy. The presence of workshops in residential houses is something we have seen in Crete. In Akrotiri, too, some of the workshops may have had more than just a domestic purpose, creating goods for wider distribution. Indeed it has been suggested that some of the buildings there may have been shops.

On the upper floor of the West House a large, well-lit room was used for weaving. More than four hundred and fifty loom-weights were found, and it

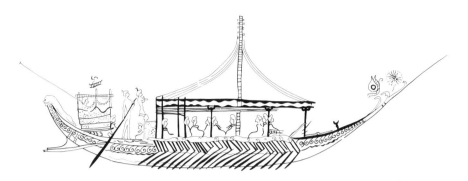

93 Drawing of a detail of the miniature fresco from the West House at Akrotiri.

has been estimated that the room was big enough for four or five looms, though these have not survived. Here too this potential for production perhaps implies a centralization of a specialist craft with a broader scope than household self-sufficiency. Concentrations of loom-weights have been discovered elsewhere at Akrotiri, but these are not distributed evenly throughout the houses, supporting the idea of concentration and specialization. Wool and flax would have been woven, and there is evidence too for the production of silk.

Another spacious room on the upper floor of the West House can be identified as a living room, though in view of its architecture and its rich fresco decoration some commentators have seen it as a shrine. The room is at first glance an unlikely candidate for wall-paintings as two of its walls, on the north and west, are broken up by windows, and the other two are interrupted by doorways and niches. Only a narrow band above the level of these interrupted surfaces and below the ceiling was available to be painted, but it was precisely this narrow band that contained the most remarkable miniature frescoes so far found at Akrotiri.

Only a few fragments of the composition from the west wall survive, showing parts of a town. The frieze from the north wall is better preserved, and is packed with incident, with another town, a scene that may be a ship-wreck, armed warriors and more peaceful figures apparently meeting on a hill. This richly detailed composition offers much scope for interpretation, though a precise narrative may now never be told. On the east wall the frieze depicts a river running through a landscape filled with exotic plants including palms and papyrus, and equally exotic, indeed sometimes mythical, animals – water birds, a jackal-like creature, a wild cat and even a griffin. The Egyptian influence is clear, and the frieze is usually described as a Nilotic landscape. The south wall was painted with a wonderful depiction of a fleet of ships, propelled by rows of paddlers, bearing important figures, perhaps warriors and/or dignitaries, and all richly decorated as if for some festival or triumphant procession. The ships sail from one town towards another, and the arrival town is thought by many commentators to be Akrotiri itself.

Interpretation of these compositions is difficult but fascinating, and much of interest has been written by scholars attempting detailed analysis of the scenes. They probably should be 'read' together as a pictorial programme, and most experts would agree that they have in common the theme of the sea, ships, journeys and other lands. The impression is reinforced by frescoes in the north-east and south-west corners of the same room that show two nude figures of fishermen, each about two-thirds life-size and carrying strings of fish. The link between the inhabitants of the West House and the sea is also underlined by the decoration of the adjoining room, where large-scale representations of the stern cabins shown on the miniature ships adorned the walls. The figure of a young priestess was painted in the doorway between the two rooms: perhaps she performed ceremonies on the sterns of the ships to bring them good fortune or to thank the gods for their successes.

Adjoining this room was a well-preserved lavatory, made of two stone benches separated by a slit and connected via a clay pipe to a pit outside the house and thence to the drainage system of the town. Washing and bathing may also have taken place in this room.

It seems perfectly possible to interpret the West House as the fine residence of a wealthy family. It is tempting indeed to suggest that a sea-captain lived there, or a merchant or trader, someone for whom the theme of the frescoes was particularly appropriate. Whether we must conclude that a religious function is indicated for the upstairs room with the miniature frescoes is a matter for debate. Probably we should simply accept that the two are not mutually exclusive. This busy house and household could have been a family home, the scene of various types of domestic production, and also the setting for ritual in an upper room that could nonetheless have been a fully integrated part of the living accommodation in the house.

Akrotiri, then, presents a bustling picture of a thriving town, with all the vitality of a sea-port and a place where different peoples met. We cannot doubt that its unusual size and prosperity were due to a 'special relationship' with Minoan Crete, and that much of the shipping in Akrotiri harbour would have been *en route* to or from that island. Thera constituted a natural link between Crete, the other Cycladic islands and the Greek mainland. Ships stopping there may also in some instances have been travelling further afield, in the circular pattern around the eastern Mediterranean indicated for a somewhat later period by the wreck found at Ulu Burun on the south coast of Turkey, with its mixed cargo indicating links with Egypt and the Syro-Palestinian coast.

By chance the excavations have hit upon a rich area of the town, where houses were occupied by wealthy and important people. As in Crete itself, we have no means of discerning whether merchants, traders, shop-keepers or entrepreneurs of any kind could operate independently of a centralized power. It may seem unnecessary to postulate control from the Cretan palaces, for which there is no direct evidence. A palace or its equivalent at Akrotiri may, though, remain to be found.

We are fortunate indeed that chance has preserved for us the wonderful wall-paintings of this island, and should perhaps pause to consider how lucky we are to be able to see the skilled, thoughtful, even inspired works of people who lived their lives so remotely from us, three and a half millennia ago. What did they mean to the people who painted them and the people who viewed them? The question inevitably brings us to a consideration of religion.

Minoan Religion in the Neopalatial Period

The difficulties of addressing the topic of religion in the Late Minoan period hardly need stating. As for the earlier periods, we can identify, with greater or lesser degrees of certainty, places and objects with religious significance. To these can be added a much broader range of representational evidence, mostly from wall-paintings and from the engravings on seals. It remains, though, a process famously compared by Martin Nilsson, the pioneering scholar of Minoan and Mycenaean religion, to interpreting a picture-book without a text. We can only tread cautiously on such uncertain ground.

Colin Renfrew, in his book *The Archaeology of Cult: The Sanctuary at Phylakopi*,[9] makes a fundamental attempt to bring a rigorous approach to the analysis of archaeological material of potential religious significance. His rational formulation is helpful in a field that has been beset by the implicit assumptions of 'the beholder', and gives a useful framework for an appraisal of the evidence. He quotes a definition of religion from the *Shorter Oxford Dictionary*: 'Action or conduct indicating a belief in, or reverence for, and desire to please, a divine ruling power…. Recognition on the part of man of some higher unseen power as having control of his destiny, and as being entitled to obedience, reverence and worship.' He then goes on to draw the distinction between the beliefs of a religion, which cannot be recovered archaeologically, and the actions arising from those beliefs. These include the creation or choosing of special places for religious observance, the rituals enacted and the materials or paraphernalia of the cult. It is the results of these actions that we can hope to see in the archaeological record. Naturally they bear a direct relation to the beliefs from which they spring, but reconstruction of the framework of beliefs will always be a difficult process. Plausible suggestions can be made, and those based on anthropological evidence for known belief systems will perhaps carry most weight. Nonetheless the world offers a wide variety both of belief systems and indeed of cult practices. Suggestions about Minoan religion will not usually be susceptible to absolute proof.

We can proceed by attempting to recognize areas for use for cult purposes, whether natural or man-made. The evidence may include the formalized use of a natural space or the formal arrangement of a built environment, with some evidence for the focusing of attention on a particular spot: the equivalent of an altar in a Christian church. The focus of attention is likely to have had some material form or image symbolizing or suggesting the presence of the deity. A cult statue might fulfil this purpose, but equally a simpler symbol could be in place: the equivalent of a Christian cross. Evidence for participation in worship of the deity is likely to be seen in the form of cult apparatus – special vessels and the like – while the dedication of offerings is particularly likely to be visible in the archaeological record.

The danger of circular arguments is obvious, but some identifications both of actual shrines and sanctuaries and of iconographic representations of rituals or deities can be made with confidence, particularly when a number of these factors are demonstrably present. We can use the evidence from these to help with the interpretation of sites or objects where the picture is not so clear.

CULT PLACES

In the neopalatial period some of the larger peak sanctuaries saw new buildings and a greater number and range of offerings, though many smaller sanctuaries fell out of use. This may indicate increasing centralization of religion, with fewer but larger shrines more directly linked to the palace centres. The sanctuary on Mount Juktas, for example, was approached directly by a Minoan road from Knossos. A neopalatial building just outside the circuit wall perhaps acted as a way-station for visitors and as a place of manufacture for votive items. Within the enclosure a major building programme of MM II–III had seen the construction of megalithic terraces around an altar with extensive traces of burning. The sanctuary building was remodelled during the neopalatial period, though the focus of activity remained essentially open-air, centred on a deep natural chasm in the rock. A range of finds still included many figurines, along with stone vessels such as libation tables, seal-stones and bronze votive tools.

Sacred caves continued to be used, and received rich offerings in the neopalatial period, while in several caves cult was newly established at this time. Indeed, the major caves continued to receive votive offerings both in the Minoan period and in later antiquity. The Idaean cave and the Psychro cave are examples. The former was used from the end of the Neolithic period

94 The entrance to the Idaean cave on the Nidha plateau. The cave is so high that the entrance is blocked by snow for a proportion of each year.

down to the Roman era, the latter had votive offerings from Minoan to Late Geometric and Archaic times. Both were associated with the childhood of Zeus. Evans identified Psychro as the Diktaian cave, Zeus' birthplace, and this seems entirely reasonable as it is situated on a mountain called Mount Dikte in modern times. However, Hellenistic sources clearly place both the Diktaian cave and Mount Dikte in the far east of Crete, in the area of Palaikastro, for which an identification with Dikte can reasonably be claimed. The situation is further complicated by the existence of a Linear B tablet at Knossos recording an offering to Diktaian Zeus. Arguably this should more probably be a 'Dikte' in the Lasithi area, since place names from the far east of Crete do not otherwise appear in the tablets.[10]

The confusion remains. Hellenistic writers do, though, sometimes place the birth of Zeus in the Idaean cave — and it seems more than likely that the god was worshipped in many parts of the island, and many shrines were associated with his birth or early youth.

Other cult places were inside the palaces and houses, and it is possible that there was a tendency to concentrate activities within the palaces at this time, to bring religion very directly under palatial control. Some ceremonies may have been partly secret, or at least hidden from the general populace. The Throne Room complex at Knossos is essentially a hidden environment. It has plausibly been suggested that a ritual of 'enacted epiphany' took place here, in which a priestess dressed as the goddess 'appeared' on the gypsum throne flanked by the painted griffins. A select group of people seated on the benches in the Throne Room itself and its ante-room may have seen her, and offerings were probably made in the lustral basin that is part of the Throne Room complex. There may have been indirect participation by a larger group of people gathered in the Central Court. The Central and West Courts of the palaces were doubtless used for large-scale gatherings, and fresco representations give us some impression of what these were like.

GODS AND GODDESSES

Does the iconographic evidence, rich as it is in ritual scenes, allow us to recognize the deity or deities worshipped by the Minoans? We can see certain rites and at least begin to guess at their motivation, but what god or gods were thought to preside over them? The question is not easy to answer. In some depictions a deity seems to be present, but we must admit at the outset that we have great difficulty making the identification securely. Indeed, some scholars have even questioned whether the Minoans ever represented deities anthropomorphically. They point to the fact that on the gold signet-rings that are among our best evidence for cult scenes, ritual activities – apparently intended to summon the deity – include ecstatic dancing, shaking of trees and clasping of large boulders. In these scenes the presence of the deity is possibly indicated by birds, butterflies, chrysalids and symbols such as double-axes and sacral knots. If so, the 'human' participants could be truly human: priests, priestesses or worshippers. But the question is complicated by the fact that a priestess might assume the role of the goddess in an 'enacted epiphany' as described above.

In spite of this, some figures do seem to stand out because of their gestures or contexts as non-human. Perhaps most obvious are the small hovering figures that again feature on the gold signets. These are usually, but not exclusively, female, and their scale and position differentiates them from the human participants in the scene. Many commentators feel that they represent the deity, who is summoned by the ritual actions of the human worshippers.

Other representations show a male or female figure using commanding gestures. These often dominate the animal world. An example is the well-known sealing from Knossos showing a female figure on a mountain-top extending her staff, flanked by lions and attended by a male figure in a conventional position of prayer. Her identification as a goddess is widely accepted and seems fairly secure.

Let us turn first, then, to representations that might show a goddess. An important female figure is often depicted in a setting that emphasizes a connection with nature. Her natural background is outdoor landscape with flowers and trees, and she is frequently portrayed with animals or birds. Sometimes these approach her, or, as in the sealing mentioned above, they may flank her symmetrically. She is clearly a 'Mistress of Animals', who dominates or subdues the natural world.

Sometimes the goddess is attended by adorant animals, such as lions or monkeys, or mythical creatures like the griffin, with which she is often associated. Her human attendants are usually female. Like the goddess herself, these women wear the flounced skirt and bare breasts of Minoan formal dress – underlining again the potential difficulty of separating representations of

ABOVE
95 Drawing of a cult scene on a gold signet-ring from the Isopata cemetery, Knossos. Women seem to be engaged in ecstatic dancing, perhaps to encourage the 'epiphany' or appearance of the deity, who may be represented in the small hovering figure above them.

deities from priestesses or worshippers. Very often, though, the goddess is seated, and is clearly receiving offerings from her human – and indeed sometimes from her animal – attendants. The fresco showing saffron-gathering from Thera is a remarkable example of this. The goddess is seated on a tripartite platform, in 'court dress' and bedecked with jewellery, including necklaces of ducks and dragonflies. She receives an offering from a monkey who stands before her, while a griffin guards her back. The women gathering and offering saffron are also in 'court dress', though with less elaborate jewellery and coiffures.

The Thera goddess has a snake in her hair, and this links her to the faience 'snake-goddesses' from the 'Temple Repositories' at Knossos that are among the best-known objects from Minoan Crete. One of these two figures has snakes twining round her arms, the other holds snakes aloft, and has an animal, perhaps a cat, on her head-dress. Their fame has led to the idea that snakes were commonly shown with the goddess, though in fact the association is quite rare. These figures can be viewed simply as further versions of the 'Mistress of Animals' scheme, though again it remains possible that they are worshippers shown in the goddess' guise.

Snakes may, though, have had connections with the earth and the underworld in Minoan religion. The snakes would therefore link the goddess with this realm. Fish, particularly dolphins, are also shown with her, and connect her to the sea. Birds very often accompany her – indeed a strange series of hybrid representations show her as part-woman, part-bird. Earth, sea and sky are therefore all her domains.

Are we seeing representations of a single female deity or of a number of different goddesses? The view that a single female deity was of over-arching importance in Minoan Crete was first formulated by Evans, who felt that the various ways in which the goddess was shown should be explained as different 'aspects' of a single deity. This view partly arose from the intellectual background of his time, and the prevalent notion that a single 'great mother' goddess dominated early religious thought in a variety of Mediterranean cultures. This now seems simplistic. Scholars are much more open to the idea that more than one goddess may be involved. The iconography does not, however, allow us to distinguish separate female deities consistently.[11]

This brings us to the question of 'one goddess or many'? Other evidence, such as that for variations of cult practice at various shrines, may seem to suggest different deities, but must be used cautiously. We know from later Greek religion that the same goddess could be the recipient of distinctly different assemblages of votive offerings at various regional shrines. We may note, however, that the Linear B tablets of the Mycenaean period from Knossos include not only names of Olympian deities but also some names that seem to be of Minoan form. A tablet in the British Museum, for example, records offerings of oil to a deity named Pipituna, as well as to 'the priestess of the winds'. These are not known from later Greek tradition: they are therefore likely to belong to the Minoan religion, and to suggest that it was a polytheistic system.

The same problems surround the identification of a Minoan god or series of gods. They are difficult to distinguish consistently in the iconography, and there may be some confusion with priests or worshippers. A youthful god does, though, seem to appear. He is usually dressed in the typical Minoan breechcloth with codpiece, and wears a belt. His torso is bare. Like the 'goddess' figure he is often shown with animals, sometimes subduing lions or bulls.

Representations of a youthful figure with flowing locks holding a staff in his outstretched hand seem likely to be gods in some, though

97 Drawing of the 'Master Impression', a remarkable sealing from Chania showing a youthful figure with a commanding gesture standing on the buildings of a town.

not necessarily all, instances. This is the position and gesturing of the 'Goddess on the Mountain' sealing. The so-called 'Master Impression',[12] a remarkable sealing from Chania, shows a figure of this type dominating a town. He wears a breechcloth with codpiece and belt, boots, a necklace and bracelets. Though cautious commentators argue that the 'Master Impression' could show an important chief or king, the similarity to the Knossos sealing, along with his scale and dominant position, make the identification as a deity more probable.

Another male figure with outstretched staff, this time accompanied by a lion, appears on a neopalatial seal-stone from Knossos. An unusual 'Master of Animals' is the youthful figure on the gold pendant in the Aigina treasure. He holds a bird in each hand in the symmetrical 'Master of Animals' pose.

While no certainty is possible, modern examination of the evidence makes the interpretation of Minoan religion in terms of the worship of a 'Great Mother' goddess and her youthful male consort seem outdated. Instead we may postulate a range of gods and goddesses, worshipped in a variety of cult places across the island and sometimes represented in ritual scenes.

The presence, indeed the importance, of women in Minoan iconography cannot be denied. The goddess or goddesses of Crete had female acolytes, and women are shown in privileged positions alongside men in large-scale gatherings that were probably for religious festivals. It would be simplistic to extrapolate from this a society in which women held social and political sway, though it may well be that women in the Greek Bronze Age enjoyed a higher status in society than they were accorded, for example, in the world of Classical Athens.

The LM IB Destructions

At the end of LM IB, in about 1450–1430BC, a devastating series of destructions swept over most Minoan sites. The palaces, with the exception of Knossos, were destroyed, as were most other towns and settlements, and perhaps particularly the important buildings within them. The country houses that had populated the neopalatial Cretan landscape were no more, and the whole human face of the island was changed. Many places were abandoned after this devastation, while other areas were severely depopulated. Recovery would come, but only after a lapse of time. Moreover, many of the arts, crafts and cultural features that had combined to make the neopalatial era so impressive were lost for ever. Minoan Crete would never be the same again.

What were the causes of this island-wide destruction? Were the disasters contemporary at all sites? Why did the palace at Knossos survive unscathed, even though there were destructions there in some areas of the town?

The possible causes can broadly be divided into the natural and the man-made. Devastating earthquakes are the most probable natural cause, and in buildings lit by oil-lamps and often containing large stores of olive oil fires would be an expected consequence. However, the spread of the destruction, from Chania in the west to Zakros in the east, makes it unlikely that earth-quakes could have been the main cause, though they may have been a contributory factor. The possible human agencies that have been suggested are the Knossians, or the Mycenaeans of the Greek mainland. A pan-Cretan takeover bid from Knossos, perhaps in the wake of some natural disasters that had weakened the regional centres, would certainly explain why Knossos itself remained untouched. It is perhaps less easy to see why Knossos, already in a position of pre-eminence, should want to bring the rest of Crete to her knees. Could a 'rival' elite group have taken over there without damage to the palace? And if so would the devastation of the rest of the island have been in their interest? Alternatively, a rebellion by a subject population has been suggested, forcing Knossos to act and to cause widespread devastation.

If the Mycenaeans were responsible, again perhaps in the wake of natural disasters, they presumably took over Knossos as their centre of operations and were happy to observe the rest of the island so weakened that no opposition would arise from outside. As we shall see, the increasing 'Mycenaeanization' of Crete, arguably directly after these disasters and certainly in the LM III period, is a strong reason for postulating some Mycenaean involvement. It has to be said, though, that among the various combinations of factors that could have been responsible we must allow for the coalition of different interested groups – could Mycenaean help have been enlisted by some faction or factions in Crete?

These suggestions have been posed as a series of questions because that, in essence, is what they remain. All we can say with certainty is that the effects of the LM IB destructions in Crete were devastating: that in their immediate aftermath LM II Crete really sees only Knossos as a flourishing centre, and that at some time subsequent to the destructions of LM IB main-land traits arrive on the island that had not been there before. Mycenaeans, whether or not in collaboration with local Minoans, seem to have profited ultimately, and so are likely to have been players in these events.

Chapter Five

FROM THE FINAL PALACE PERIOD TO THE END OF MINOAN CIVILIZATION

THE PALACE of Knossos survived the destructions of around 1450BC that brought an end to so many of the Minoan sites of Crete. By the time of its destruction, traditionally dated to about 1375–1350BC though arguably somewhat later, the palace was almost certainly under the control of the Mycenaean Greeks of the Greek mainland. The evidence for this lies in the fact that in its final period the language of the palace administration was Greek, as recorded on the Linear B tablets. Other indications that Mycenaeans arrived in the wake of the LM IB destructions, and were present throughout LM II, include a change of pottery style within the palace and the presence of so-called 'warrior graves' in the Knossos cemeteries, though the date of the Mycenaean incursion is disputed.

The presence of Mycenaeans, whether as agents of the island-wide destructions of 1450BC or simply as lucky chancers profiting from them at some later date, also explains the growing 'Mycenaeanization' of Crete in the latter part of the Late Bronze Age. The LM II–early LM IIIA2 period is described here as the Final Palace period, which is accurate for Crete, as it encompasses the last stage of Knossos, the longest-lived of the Minoan palaces. However, it is sometimes called the Third Palace period, and extended to include the period of the Mycenaean palaces of the mainland, which continued throughout LH IIIB and came to an end around 1200BC.

In Crete the palace phenomenon ends with the fall of Knossos, though the similarity of the Linear B archive there to those of the mainland palaces, and particularly to that of Pylos, has led some scholars to suggest a date rather later in the fourteenth century for the palace's final days and the archive's preservation. A thirteenth-century, LM IIIB date for the fall of Knossos has even been suggested, partly to allow a greater overlap with the other centres such as Chania and the mainland palaces that also used Linear B. The use of Linear B at Chania can be dated to early LM IIIB, but the Pylos archive dates to LH IIIB2.

A complex literature[1] covers the date of the final destruction at Knossos, and no consensus has yet been reached, though there is fairly general agreement that Knossos was not operating as a palace centre after the very beginning of LM IIIB at the latest. In fact a date for the final destruction early in LH IIIA2, in about 1375–1350BC in absolute terms, remains likely.

Although political power was apparently in the hands of Greek-speaking Mycenaeans during LM II–III, initially they may have formed only a small part of the population, based at Knossos and some of the larger centres, such as Chania. The imposition of Mycenaean mores on older Minoan culture was possibly tempered by the long-standing contacts between the Argolid and Crete during the neopalatial period. Over time further Mycenaean settlers probably arrived, but the strong local Minoan identity was never extinguished and helped to create a rich cultural mix during the LM II–III period. Even when part of the wider Mycenaean world, Crete remained different.

The Final Palace Period

In the Final Palace period (about 1450–1375BC) elements of continuity as well as striking changes are found across the island. In the wake of the LM IB destructions the flourishing network of palaces, villas and towns lay in ruins. Many sites experienced severe depopulation or even abandonment. Charting developments at Knossos itself and elsewhere presents some difficulties. LM II is an undeniably shadowy period. Its definition depends on the appearance of a new and short-lived variety of drinking cup, the so-called Ephyrean goblet. This mainland shape was once thought to be confined to Knossos, but has now been identified at a number of sites that had been battered by the LM IB destructions and were slowly finding their feet. These include Phaistos, Mallia and Zakros, where the settlements continued though the palaces no longer functioned. LM II pottery has also come from Archanes, Tylissos, Palaikastro and so on, though most sites are in a poor way and demonstrate only slow signs of recovery. Most places show real recovery from the LM IIIA period onwards.

The palace of Phaistos was not rebuilt after the destructions of 1450BC and shows only scrappy and uncertain signs of later reoccupation. However, south-central Crete was perhaps not so badly devastated as other regions of the island. Recent excavations have shown that Ayia Triadha and Kommos remained important, as we shall see below. In western Crete Chania quickly revived after the LM IB destructions and flourished throughout LM II–III. Indeed, after the fall of Knossos, Chania may have gained prominence, playing an important role in trade and serving as an administrative centre.

Knossos in LM II–IIIA1

Although parts of Knossos town had been affected by the LM IB destructions, the palace remained unscathed. We can perceive there elements both of continuity and of change. New frescoes were painted on the walls, but they followed traditional themes. Some areas of the palace seem to have retained their previous functions: much of the west wing, for example, was still used for storage and administration. Yet to judge from the numbers of sealings found in the east wing, some of its fine apartments were now used for workaday activities. Mervyn Popham[2] famously likened the Final Palace at Knossos to a stately home taken over by the Ministry of Works in the Second World War, conjuring up a picture of clerks, desks and paperwork occupying previously elegant rooms. Some niceties of palace life certainly seem to have been lost. Also open to question is the extent to which earlier Minoan rituals carried on at this time.

In Knossos town there is re-occupation or re-use of several neopalatial town houses, such as the Royal Villa and the Little Palace. As in the palace itself, changes in function are likely, if sometimes difficult to chart. However, the Unexplored Mansion offers clear evidence for altered use in LM II–III. This elegant building had been constructed in the early part of LM IA, but was never finished or occupied. During LM II a clay fireplace was built in the fine pillared hall and bronze melting took place in or near the mansion.

The Unexplored Mansion burned down at the end of LM II, although some parts of the building were apparently re-occupied. Further fire damage in LM IIIA left the building in a ruinous condition, but even so parts continued to be occupied until some time during LM IIIB, when it was finally abandoned.

The complex history of the mansion can be told in some detail thanks to a careful programme of excavation in 1967–73, followed by a thorough publication.[3] We do not have the same sort of information for the palace itself, and controversy and confusion still prevail. It is, though, tempting to speculate that its fate may have been reflected by the buildings of the town, and it may similarly have seen successive downturns in fortune before the final destruction came.

The Linear B Evidence

Linear B tablets, like those of Linear A, were of unbaked clay, and probably were only ever used for temporary records. Their preservation wherever they are found, both at Knossos and in the Mycenaean palaces of the mainland, depends on their being accidentally baked in destructions by fire. At Knossos groups of tablets were found in various locations throughout the palace. Because they came to light early in Evans' excavations their associations tended to be unclear – they were mixed with debris and stratigraphically difficult to pin down. This has led to many decades of argument about the date and nature of the destruction or destructions that baked them. Mervyn Popham, in a thorough re-investigation of the pottery with which the archives were associated,[4] arrived at a date early in LM IIIA2 for the final destruction of the palace, and this has remained a mainstream view. Could any of the 'pockets' of tablets have been preserved either earlier or later than this? Originally it was felt that all the tablets were burned together in one cataclysmic event that finally ended the life of Knossos as a palatial centre. More recently this assumption of the 'unity of the archives' has been challenged. Certainly the fact that scattered groups of tablets appeared all around the palace site means that each context needs to be examined individually. Unfortunately, clear and undisputed associations of tablets and pottery were rarely recorded, and in most cases no certain conclusion can be reached.

The genesis of Linear B has been a matter for discussion. It is widely accepted that it represents the adaptation of scripts of Cretan invention – Hieroglyphic and Linear A – for use with the Greek language. However, the relationship between the scripts is not straightforward: Linear B owes

98 Two Linear B tablets from Knossos. One records numbers of sheep at Phaistos, the other lists offerings made to various deities.

something to both. It may have been developed in Crete in the LM II period, though the possibility of development at Mycenae should not be discounted.

In any case, the tablets found by Evans trapped in the ruins of Knossos are the earliest to survive, and reveal that the palace had administrative interests in many parts of the island. Among the place names mentioned are Kydonia (Chania) in the west; Phaistos, which was destroyed as a palatial centre at the end of LM IB but which continued to be inhabited; Lyktos, also in southern Crete; Tylissos in the centre of the island; and Amnisos on the north coast, a harbour for Knossos and location of the cave sanctuary of Eileithuia. Mount Dikte is mentioned, and there is a possible occurrence of Lasithi, though this place name is otherwise not attested before the Byzantine period. The extreme east of Crete is not certainly included. It is very likely that the harbour town of Kommos is mentioned, though its name cannot be identified with certainty. The place called Da-wo is closely linked to Phaistos. It may have been in the Mesara Plain, or could be the site that we know as Ayia Triadha (this modern name deriving from the dedication of a nearby church). This would make sense in terms of the obvious importance of Ayia Triadha as an administrative centre in the neopalatial period.

What in detail do the tablets record? Broadly, they are lists and accounts, recording various types of commodities and manufactured goods, livestock and people. At first glance they are rather disappointing as a historical resource. They include no 'historical' documents – no annals or king-lists, no diplomatic correspondence, certainly no literature. The use of writing seems to have been the preserve of a few, and its application very limited: the Linear B tablets have unkindly been compared to laundry-lists. Optimists may hope that one day Linear B texts will be found on miraculously preserved parchment or papyrus, but the conditions in Crete would be unlikely to allow their preservation, even if such documents had ever existed.

In spite of their limited scope, the tablets give us information which would not be retrievable from archaeology alone. A prime example is the importance of the wool industry at Knossos. Textiles are not preserved by the conditions in Crete, and though representations in art show us something of Cretan dress nothing in the archaeological remains would have prepared us for the fact that about one-third of all the Knossos tablets proved to be connected with flocks of sheep and the production of woollen textiles. Clearly this was one of the central activities in the palace. All stages of the process are represented. First come careful records of flocks, often naming their shepherd, their location and sometimes the precise make-up of the flock in terms of the animals' sex and age. Then come tablets recording yields of wool, records of the female textile-workers, who were either servants or slaves, and lists of finished textiles.

Along with the Linear B tablets, numerous clay sealings were also preserved in the final destruction at Knossos. Some nodules were carefully formed round knotted cords and were counter-marked with short Linear B inscriptions. Yet most sealings from the Final Palace are rough-and-ready affairs: lumps of clay attached to sturdy cords or pressed against containers. Since these are usually found broken it is likely that they actually sealed and secured objects. Many were found in the former 'Domestic Quarter' of the east wing, along with tablets, suggesting that this part of the palace dealt with incoming commodities.

Arts and Crafts in the Final Palace Period

Fine products and luxury items continued to be made in the Final Palace period. Although styles sometimes changed to meet the taste of a new clientele, much was derived from earlier Minoan traditions.

POTTERY

Several new vase shapes make their appearance in LM II–III Crete. The Ephyrean goblet was a two-handled drinking cup, which was apparently introduced from the mainland in LM II. Fashions in drinking cups tend to change quite rapidly, however, and the Ephyrean goblet was no exception. In LM IIIA1 it was replaced by a more traditional globular 'teacup' with a single handle. Other new vase types were longer-lived, persisting without significant change throughout LM II–IIIA1. The squat alabastron is another mainland shape, which at Knossos occurs in both pottery and stone. Exceptionally large examples made of gypsum were found in the Throne Room. Vases known as 'Palace Style' jars became very popular. These are large display vases, quite grandiose in style and

99 A Palace Style jar from Knossos decorated with double-axes.

usually with boldly painted decoration. Motifs are various and include floral, abstract or geometric and marine decoration. Interestingly, evidence from Zakros now shows antecedents for these jars in the Marine Style pottery of LM IB. It is therefore clear that the tradition of production began on Crete. Nonetheless the vases were obviously much to Mycenaean taste: smaller versions occur in both Cretan and mainland tombs, and they were certainly produced on the mainland too.

100 A copy of the 'Cup-bearer' fresco from Knossos.

FRESCOES

Substantial remains of frescoes of this period have been found only at Knossos and Ayia Triadha. The walls of the palace of Knossos seem still to have been decorated with some neopalatial compositions, while stylistic elements of the new paintings of the Final Palace period can also be traced back to early antecedents.

Processional frescoes and other figured compositions showing ritual actions were particularly characteristic. Life-size processional figures lined the walls of the entrance corridor on the palace's west side that led to the South Propylon, which was similarly decorated. Male and female figures were shown, some carrying vessels of various types. The so-called 'Cup-bearer' is the only well-preserved figure from the very many that were originally part of this scene.

On a smaller scale, the 'Campstool Fresco', originally in an upper room of the west wing, also bore a number of figures, this time arranged in registers in a manner perhaps influenced by Egyptian art. The figures were seated on elaborate stools and toasting each other with *kylikes* or stemmed goblets typical of LM IIIA. Again a well-known fragment from this composition, showing the female figure known as 'La Parisienne', is much reproduced. Her white skin, red lips and dark eye earned her

101 The gypsum throne in the Throne Room at Knossos with copies of the frescoes showing flanking griffins.

the soubriquet. She wears a garment with a 'sacral knot' tied at the back of her neck.

Equally attractive is the 'Dancing Girl' fragment from the Queen's Megaron – a small figure whose black tresses twirl out around her as she moves. From the same area of the palace a fresco with dolphins perhaps originally decorated a floor.

The miniature frescoes showing bull-jumping are among the most famous Minoan works of art. They differ from earlier compositions in that they are painted as individual bordered panels. If the convention that men were painted in red and women in white was observed in these scenes, both males and females seem to have been involved in the bull-sports. The white figures wear male dress, however, and some scholars have wondered whether youthful males might actually have been shown with pale skin. However this may be, the leaps performed by the athletes are spectacular. They could scarcely have been executed in real life in the way apparently shown.[5] It is interesting to note that the horns of the bulls pass below the arm of the figure to the left in the best-preserved panel. This perhaps implies that some sort of restraint on the bull – though that in itself would have been hard enough to achieve.

The frescoes of the Throne Room at Knossos were probably repainted in the Final Palace period, when the room was remodelled, though they almost certainly follow an earlier scheme. It is interesting to speculate whether a priestess still sat flanked by the attendant griffins on each side of the throne.

Perhaps now the Mycenaean *wanax*, or overlord, took this place. The appropriation and continuation of the old symbols of power and of pre-existing religious rituals would be an obvious mechanism by which incomers could take control and yet still in some measure be accepted by the inhabitants of an island with a long history.

OTHER WORKS

The mixing of influences from the mainland and Crete itself is a feature of most arts and crafts of this period, and we must be aware of the possibility not only of movement of objects but also that craftsmen may have been travelling between the two areas to ply their trades. Products such as bronzes, ivories and seal-stones of similar types are found both in Crete and in rich burials in the Argolid, and this phenomenon is particularly noticeable in the tombs at Dendra. Where unprovenanced material is concerned, the distinction between mainland and Cretan products is often impossible.

Bronze vessels and finely decorated weapons were characteristic of the rich tombs of both areas, but those found in the region of Knossos were almost certainly made there. As we have seen, part of the Unexplored Mansion was used as a bronze workshop at this time.

It seems likely that much of the rich jewellery and many of the elaborate ivories found in Crete were made on the island, though in styles and techniques they have much in common with mainland finds. Tholos tomb A at Archanes contained a fine array of beads in carnelian, gold and cast glass, along with seal-stones and gold signet-rings. The ivory inlays for the footstool found there include large and small figure-of-eight shields and heads of warriors wearing boar's-tusk helmets. All could be Cretan products, though the possibility that some pieces were imported should be borne in mind.

Similar difficulties arise in the study of seal-stones. Close parallels exist in material, shape, technique and iconography between seals found on Crete and contemporary examples from the Greek mainland. The LM II–III period sees some losses from the previously extraordinarily rich tradition. The use of hard stones such as jasper, rock-crystal and particularly amethyst declines, though carnelian remains popular, and agate is by far the most common stone. Lentoids become the dominant shape, in hard and soft stone. Some are very large, and an increase in seal size is sometimes attributed to Mycenaean influence.

The iconographic repertoire of seals also contracts. Some losses, notably of cult scenes, may be attributed to the collapse of neopalatial society. Gains include the hybrid creatures sometimes called 'minotaurs': these have the lower part of a man and the upper part of an animal or animals. The animal element is often a bull, but goats, stags and lions are also found.

Seal ownership and use seems to have declined in this period, with only the richest tombs in the Knossos area containing seals. Some seals and gold signet-rings were clearly 'heirlooms', and had remained in use from neopalatial times. Indeed the famous sealing showing the 'Goddess on the Mountain', mentioned above, was impressed by a LM I signet-ring, though it was found in the final destruction at Knossos.

Burials of the Final Palace Period

New types of burials began to be made in different parts of Crete at this time. They are frequent at Knossos, where extensive cemeteries of the LM II–III period exist, particularly in the area to the north of the palace. Typical Mycenaean chamber-tombs with a long *dromos* or entrance passageway are common. These usually contained three or four burials, and were therefore presumably nuclear family tombs, in contrast to the much bigger, perhaps clan-based communal tombs previously used in Crete. Other tomb types included the pit-cave and a variant of the shaft grave type.

'Warrior graves' are not exclusive to Knossos, but again are particularly frequent there. Personal weapons, obviously belonging to individuals of high status, were put into these graves. Swords, spear-heads and helmets have been found. The swords were sometimes elaborately decorated, and have close parallels in the Argolid. Other features of the burials include the use of biers or beds. If it is correct to see the occupants of these tombs as Mycenaeans the evidence for 'intrusive' mainland culture seems, unsurprisingly, to have been particularly concentrated at Knossos in the first part of this period.

102 Chest-shaped terracotta larnax or coffin with a gabled lid. From the Zafer Papoura cemetery at Knossos.

103 The grave enclosure in the Phourni cemetery at Archanes.

104 Tholos tomb A at Archanes.

Some of the 'warrior graves' also have large numbers of bronze vessels, and this is a feature of other tombs in the Knossos area and, occasionally, elsewhere in the island. Vessels include cauldrons, bowls and jugs, and such grave gifts are also characteristic of contemporary tombs on the Greek mainland, particularly in the Argolid.

The cemetery at Phourni, where there had been little evidence for neopalatial burials, becomes important again as a source of evidence for Final Palace period tombs. A miniature grave enclosure, unique on Crete but reminiscent of the earlier grave circles at Mycenae, contained seven small shaft graves. Some had a roughly worked stele, or grave marker, erected above them. The burials within them were made in terracotta larnakes (coffins), and offerings were left in the shaft of the grave.

Tholos tombs were also used, and tholos A at Archanes is remarkable because it had survived more or less intact from antiquity and was a visible feature of the landscape throughout – indeed it had been used as a shepherd's hut. The excavators revealed a long *dromos* leading to this small corbelled tomb. The tomb itself perhaps shows a fusion of earlier Minoan examples with mainland types. The main chamber was, naturally, empty, but in view of the tomb's later use they were amazed to find an undisturbed side-chamber containing a rich burial. The deceased was probably female, and was in a painted clay larnax. Around this lay pottery and bronze vessels, and the footstool with elaborately carved ivory attachments mentioned above. Jewellery and gold rings, including a ring with a cult scene, had been put into the coffin with the body. The skull of a bull was found walled up in the entrance to the unplundered side chamber, while just outside this entrance a complete but dismembered skeleton of a horse came to light. This find is unique in Crete, though horse burials are attested on the Greek mainland.

Religion in the Final Palace Period

The Linear B tablets give for the first time the names of deities worshipped in Crete: some are Olympian, others Minoan. The worship of the Minoan deities was presumably established in the island before the arrival of the Mycenaeans there – whether any of the Olympian deities was worshipped earlier remains a matter for speculation. It seems likely that new gods were introduced, but also that there was much continuity of older cults, and perhaps a combination of the old and the new.

Many aspects of religious iconography continue the old Minoan traditions, and religious conservatism and continuity may well have been a feature of rural shrines. It seems probable that the cult or cults centred on the palace at Knossos would have been controlled by its new rulers. Nonetheless, as we have seen, the frescoes on the walls at the time of its destruction were based on established Minoan ritual themes. The incomers were no doubt anxious to validate their position by the use of such visual display linking them to the island's past. The manipulation of iconography to consolidate their power was probably matched by a corresponding manipulation and fusion of cult practices.

Shrines in the countryside, including that on Mount Juktas, continued to be used. Some sacred caves, such as the Psychro cave, also received votives at this time.

THE AYIA TRIADHA SARCOPHAGUS

The unique sarcophagus found in a chamber-tomb in the area of Ayia Triadha is justly one of the most famous objects from Minoan Crete. Dating from the LM II–III period, it is made of limestone covered in stucco and painted in fresco technique. The two short sides are decorated with pairs of female figures in chariots, on one side pulled by griffins, on the other by goats. The presence of the griffins, in particular, must suggest that these are goddesses.

Elaborate figured scenes decorate the two long sides. On the best-preserved of these a small building on the right may be a tomb. An armless figure in front of this could be the dead person, receiving gifts of a boat model and two bulls from three male figures in hide skirts. On the left of the scene birds perch on two double-axes on stands from which a vessel is suspended. Into this vessel a female figure in a hide skirt is pouring a liquid, presumably blood, from another vessel. Behind her a female in a long blue robe carries buckets suspended on a pole. In the centre a male figure in a yellow robe plays a lyre.

The other side is less well preserved, but five female figures seem to have approached an altar on which a bull is being sacrificed. The bull is trussed, and blood drips from its cut throat into a conical rhyton below. Beneath the altar or table two goats await their fate. In the background a male figure plays a double flute. To the right a woman offers fruit at an altar. The scene also includes a double-axe stand and a building, perhaps a shrine, with 'horns of consecration' and a sacred bough.

This rich iconography deserves a fuller treatment than can be given here, and reminds us of elements of Minoan ritual already touched upon in various contexts: the stone altar and collecting bowl in the courtyard at Gournia, the sacrifices at Anemospilia, the bull's skull in tholos tomb A at Archanes, and so on. The 'cross-referencing' made possible by the Ayia Triadha sarcophagus seems endless. Perhaps the main point to make, though, is that the cult scenes shown here appear very much rooted in the Minoan tradition. We do not know whether the occupant of the sarcophagus was Minoan or Mycenaean. We might suggest that as the Late Bronze Age progressed the distinction may have mattered less and less – perhaps the third- or fourth-generation 'Mycenaeans' felt quite as 'Cretan' as their neighbours who were from Minoan stock.

Postpalatial Crete

After the fall of Knossos in about 1375–1350BC, Crete lost its pre-eminent position. Yet throughout the LM IIIA2–B period the island retained its individuality, and its material culture displays a rich mixture of Minoan and Mycenaean elements. Around 1200BC many centres were abandoned or destroyed, as they were on the Greek mainland. Thereafter a troubled century saw disruptions and movements of peoples throughout the eastern Mediterranean that brought the Bronze Age to an end.

The Linear B tablets from Knossos list some of the places that remained important during the postpalatial period. Chania (Kydonia) seems to have maintained specially close links with the Greek mainland. Large transport stirrup-jars found at mainland centres prove to be made of west Cretan clay. Some of them even bear marks in Linear B, indicating known locations in west Crete. Chania also seems to have served as a port of call for new long-haul routes between the eastern and central Mediterranean. A few fragmentary Linear B tablets and sealings attest to administrative functions, though whether Chania was the 'capital' of Crete following the destruction of Knossos remains far from clear.

In southern Crete the *stoa* at Ayia Triadha, apparently a kind of warehouse, dates from this period, as do the ship-sheds at Kommos. Like Chania, Kommos seems to have benefited from expanded shipping routes to the central and eastern Mediterranean. Indeed it could be argued that the fall of Knossos had a liberating effect, resolving some problems based on over-centralization and allowing Crete to take a new place in a relatively thriving and stable east Mediterranean world.

Over time, perhaps, more Mycenaeans may have arrived to live there, attracted by the island's natural resources and contributing to its vibrant and still prosperous culture. Though Mycenaean attitudes and habits can be seen in such things as tomb types and burial customs, we should not overstate the extent of Mycenaean influence. Much remained Minoan, in culture and in art. An example of this mixing can be seen in the remarkable and extensive cemetery at Armenoi near Rethymnon.

The tombs there must have served a large settlement, though this has not been found. They were chamber-tombs of Mycenaean type, cut into the soft

rock or earth, with a rectangular or circular burial chamber approached by a long *dromos* or entrance passageway. The tombs themselves were largely undisturbed, and have thus been the source of interesting skeletal information as well as rich finds. They were used for family burials. The dead were placed in clay larnakes or chest-shaped coffins, according to the long-established Minoan custom. These larnakes are themselves among the most exciting finds from the cemetery, and a fine selection can be seen in Rethymnon museum. They are painted in lively style, sometimes with figures of men engaged in activities such as warfare or hunting, sometimes with animals, birds and fish. Plant motifs and a number of religious motifs including double-axes and 'horns of consecration' are also part of their repertoire. The iconography is purely Minoan, with roots deep in the island's past.

A high-status burial of the postpalatial period was found in tholos tomb D in the Phourni cemetery at Archanes, where the burial of a 'princess' – or at least a very high-status female – was discovered. She was decked in an array of fine jewellery, including a diadem of gold beads around her head, and had been laid in the tomb holding a mirror before her face, so that she could enjoy her extraordinary finery in the after-life.

Religion in Postpalatial Crete

We might end this brief and selective survey of postpalatial Crete with a word about religion. Figures known as 'goddesses with upraised arms' have been found at a number of shrines and sanctuaries of LM IIIA–C date. These striking terracotta figures are mostly on quite a large scale: the smallest are only 10 cm (4 in) in height but the largest reach up to 85 cm (33½ in). They have wheel-made skirts and modelled upper bodies, their head-dresses frequently embellished with symbols such as birds, poppies, snakes, and 'horns of consecration'. The figurines are often found in groups: whether all are the same goddess in such instances is unclear.

What is clear is the essentially Minoan nature of these figurines. They bear long-established religious symbols, and they occur only in Crete. This is in contrast to the contemporary wheel-made animal figurines, the production of which seems to begin in Crete, but which are found over a wider area.

The 'goddesses with upraised arms' come from built shrines of the Final Palace and postpalatial periods. The so-called 'snake tube', a cylindrical vessel type with multiple loop handles, is often found in association with these 'goddesses'. The snake tubes similarly are sometimes decorated with symbols such as 'horns of consecration'.

106 'Goddess with upraised arms' from Gazi.

A postpalatial shrine containing such goddesses, called by Evans the 'Shrine of the Double-Axes', was found by him in the palace at Knossos. It is of thirteenth-century date, and must therefore have been built in the ruins of Knossos, perhaps indicating that the palace was still considered to be hallowed ground.

The iconography of the 'goddess with upraised arms' continues into the twelfth century, and indicates the continuation of Minoan cult practices in the 'refuge settlement' sites of this period high up in the mountains. Indeed the Minoan goddess lingers on still longer – small models with upraised arms were still being made in Crete in the tenth century BC.

The troubled twelfth century, which saw the destructions of the Mycenaean centres of power, equally brought upheaval to Crete. In this, the twilight of the Bronze Age, the people increasingly sought the safety of inland sites, away from the sea and its dangers. In the so-called 'refuge settlements' of this period, often clinging precariously to the saddles and sides of the mountains, the last Minoans lived out their days. Perhaps in these mountain fastnesses elements of Minoan life and thought were maintained, to become an element in the island's later history.

Chapter Six

THE MYTHOLOGICAL LEGACY AND THE RECEPTION OF MINOAN CRETE

Mythology

MYTHS ABOUT the earliest age of Crete were both familiar and important in the ancient Greek world. Significant events were said to have taken place on the island – the birth of Zeus, the reign of Minos, the exploits of Theseus. These were part of the generality of Greek mythology, which shaped the Greeks' world view and inspired artists, from the poet to the painter of fine pottery. Characters of Cretan origin, such as Pasiphae, Phaedra and Ariadne, are familiar to us in European art and literature: their stories have been re-interpreted from antiquity to the present day. Europa on the back of the bull, Daedalus and Icarus and their attempt at flight – these are familiar images and well-known tales. But it is perhaps the labyrinth, with its dark passageways and the hybrid man-bull monster at its heart, that remains the most potent symbol. It has acquired metaphorical significance, the maze sometimes representing the twists and turns of fate or the convolutions of the human mind, the Minotaur symbolizing the dark, beast-like side of man's nature. The sense of hidden power and menace is compelling, too, in popular culture: the Minotaur roars again and a modern child trembles along with a comic-book Theseus. The force of the tales has not been lost with the passage of time.

We are heirs, then, to a long tradition of stories about ancient Crete, but are these truly Minoan tales? If they are, how have they been affected by their transmission from Bronze Age Crete to the worlds of Classical Greece and Rome and to the written forms in which we know them? As we have seen,

107 Theseus and the
Minotaur drawn for a
contemporary
comic-book.

the Minoans were not Greek and they spoke a language that remains
unknown. Was this, the language of the Linear A script, the tongue in which
these stories were first told?

The written records do not help us: Linear A is not deciphered, but it
seems that the surviving texts, like those of Linear B, represent writing used
for limited and strictly practical purposes. If the Minoans wrote down either
stories or histories, no trace survives. There must, though, be a strong presup-
position that some of the legends, or elements within them, derive from
Minoan culture and Minoan thought. Some aspects seem to reflect a deep
substratum of myth that we can characterize as pre-Hellenic. Even so, they
have been orally transmitted to later generations in Greek – a language that
we know was used in Crete from at least the fourteenth century BC. The
stories may therefore not just have changed with each re-telling, as is natural
in an oral tradition, but may perhaps have undergone quite fundamental
modifications. They are particularly likely to have picked up Greek cultural
values as they were re-interpreted for a Greek audience. So, for example, it is

possible that the Minoans had a king, or kings, called Minos, but the figure who appears in the stories is in many ways a very Greek kind of king. The challenge is to work out which strands are likely to reflect which part of the story's own history, if the myths are to contribute to our understanding of the Minoan past.

This is a difficult process: indeed it is often impossible. Mythology presents a rich field of study in its own right, but any attempt to give myth a chronology and then to mesh mythological and archaeological evidence is fraught with uncertainties and usually more or less inconclusive in its results. The hard facts that can be derived from potsherds and the remains of buildings are enlivened by the tales, but to seek in archaeology the 'proof' of the stories is to adopt too simplistic an approach; bound to fail, and perhaps consequently to undermine the sort of associations that can usefully be made between the two. These are usually general rather than specific, reflecting the fact that while the myths are both colourful and psychologically suggestive, they are not meta-history, and cannot be treated as such.

This was fully recognized by Thucydides, the great historian of the fifth century BC who gives us our first written account of the early history of Crete. In truth, although much closer in time to his subject matter than we are, he had less information than we have today, because the results of archaeological exploration played no part in his data. All he could do was to take the traditional stories, eschew the supernatural, and rationalize the rest into as coherent a picture as possible. In fact he does not find much to say about early Crete – a less methodical and rigorous mind would certainly have found more.

He records the tradition of the 'thalassocracy of Minos', noting that 'Minos, according to tradition, was the first person to organize a navy. He controlled the greater part of what is now called the Hellenic Sea; he ruled over the Cyclades, in most of which he founded the first colonies, putting his sons in as governors after having driven out the Carians. And it is reasonable to suppose that he did his best to put down piracy in order to secure his own revenues.' Elsewhere he writes: '...after Minos had organized a navy, seacommunications improved; he sent colonies to most of the islands and drove out the notorious pirates.'[1]

Archaeology has borne out the idea of Crete as a sea power ('thalassocracy' means 'rule of the sea') and of Minoan influence in the Cyclades. The Cycladic towns may not strictly have been governed 'colonies', though Phylakopi, Thera and Kea shared a Minoan style of living. (The Carians were inhabitants in Thucydides' time of the west coast of Turkey, where Minoan settlements were also founded. The Carian involvement in the islands is not attested from archaeology.)

Thucydides has no interest in heroes, monsters and beautiful maidens, though there is no doubt that Theseus, the Minotaur and Ariadne were familiar to his readers. We may note that he has no need to explain in his account whom he means by 'Minos', or indeed to mention Crete.

If we look back to the earliest preserved Greek literature, the *Odyssey* and the *Iliad*, we similarly would search in vain for the Theseus story, though familiarity with Cretan legend is certainly implied in the evocative reference to 'the dancing floor which once Daedalus created in broad Knossos for beautiful-tressed Ariadne' (*Iliad* XVIII, 590). The Homeric poems do, though, include interesting references to Crete as a rich and populous place. In the *Iliad* Idomeneus, grandson of Minos, leads the Cretan contingent to the Trojan War:

The illustrious spearman Idomeneus led the Cretans: the men from Knossos, from Gortyn of the Great Walls, from Lyctos, Miletos, chalky Lycastos, Phaistos and Rhytion, fine cities all of them; and other troops that had their home in Crete of the Hundred Towns. All these were led by the great spearman Idomeneus and by Meriones, a compeer of the man-destroying War-god. Eighty black ships came under their commands (*Iliad* II, 645ff.).

The status of the so-called 'Catalogue of Ships', from which this passage comes, has been much discussed. It is widely thought to be an interpolation into the *Iliad*, and of later date than much of the rest of the poem. Since the Homeric poems are the product of an oral tradition they may in any case contain material from any period within the centuries of their transmission – thus from the Bronze Age to the period between about 750 and 650BC when they reached their final form. We know of some, though not all, of the places in this list as important in the Bronze Age. We certainly cannot treat it as a gazetteer of Bronze Age sites. Both Knossos and Phaistos continued as important centres in later times. Nonetheless, the tradition of an important island with many cities and great wealth is encapsulated here, and the number of ships is among the largest quoted for any region of Greece for the campaign against Troy.

Idomeneus mentions his lineage when taunting the Trojan Deiphobus: '...it was Zeus who established our line. He made his son Minos King of Crete; the peerless Deucalion was Minos' son; and I am Deucalion's. I succeeded him as King of a great people in our spacious isle; and now my ships have brought me here to be a curse to you and your father and every-one in Troy' (*Iliad* XIII, 449ff.).

In the *Odyssey* (XIX, 174ff.) the disguised Odysseus pretends to his wife Penelope that he is Idomeneus' younger brother, and claims that Odysseus visited him in Crete: 'Out in the wine-dark sea there lies a land called Crete, a rich and lovely land, washed by the waves on every side, densely peopled and boasting ninety cities.... One of the ninety towns is a great city called Knossos, and there, for nine years, King Minos ruled and enjoyed the friendship of almighty Zeus.' Odysseus, according to his own fabrication, was blown off course on his way to Troy and made landfall on the north coast of Crete 'at Amnisos, where the Cave of Eileithuia is – a difficult harbour to make, the storm nearly wrecked him'. He was stuck there, he claims, by northerly gales for twelve days. It is not surprising that Penelope was taken in by this tale. The circumstantial detail remains convincing even in the twenty-first century, when it is still possible to visit Amnisos, to see the cave of Eileithuia, and to experience the wind that blows the sea into crashing and dangerous waves.

From the beginnings of Greek literature, then, we have the poet Homer assuming that his audience is familiar with Cretan myth, while in the fifth century BC the historian Thucydides makes the same assumption. The stories clearly had wide and early currency. Thereafter a range of writers, in Greek and Latin, used Cretan mythology in their writings. It is from the haphazard survivals of these Classical sources, early and late, that the modern world has pieced together the tradition. Some elements have doubtless been lost, but we can survey the main strands of Cretan myth according to its own internal chronology.

CRETAN ZEUS

Perhaps one of the greatest compliments to Crete, the large, mysterious and brooding island on the edge of the Greek homeland, was the belief that it was the birthplace of Zeus. For Classical Greeks, Zeus was 'Cretagenes' – Crete-born. The story went that Kronos, son of Gaia and Ouranos (earth and sky), was king of the heavens, but had been told by his parents that his child would usurp his position. For this reason he devoured each of his children, to his consort Rhea's distress. When she was expecting Zeus, Gaia took pity on her and hid her in Crete's distant and wild mountains. Here Zeus was born, fed on the milk of the she-goat Amaltheia (who becomes a nymph in some versions of the story) and protected by the Curetes, local armed Cretan demons who clashed their shields together so that Kronos would not hear the infant's cries. When he grew up Zeus defeated Kronos, who vomited forth all his other children – and they became Olympian deities, over whom Zeus would reign. Kronos also spat out the stone that Rhea had wrapped in swaddling clothes and given to him to swallow in place of the infant Zeus: this was placed at Delphi, and became the revered navel-stone of the earth.

Cretan mythology also, uniquely, preserved the tradition of the death of Zeus – not, in fact, the manner of his death, but the position of his tomb. It was said to be on Mount Juktas, the Minoan holy mountain, and indeed in folklore this was supposed to have the profile of the dead (or sleeping) god. This is an essentially un-Greek notion. For the Greeks, Zeus was immortal, as were all the gods by their very nature. The king of the gods could not have died. This is what lies behind the well-known, and apparently gratuitous, insult of St Paul, who in the Bible remarked that 'all Cretans are liars'. It was not an original observation: in fact St Paul was actually repeating something that was commonly said, and had almost the force of a proverb, in the ancient world. It was a reaction to the Cretan tradition of the tomb of Zeus, which was unacceptable to Greek thinking. Thus the fourth-century-BC poet Callimachus says in his 'Hymn to Zeus': 'The Cretans are forever liars: they have fashioned a tomb for you, O Lord, but you are immortal and ever livest.'

It is possible that the tradition of a god who died had been preserved from the Minoan past, and that we can discern, running in parallel with the roots of Greek religion, some elements from Minoan thought and ritual. The Minoan god was perhaps assimilated into the worship of Zeus, but with some remaining unresolved contradictions.

KING MINOS

King Minos was in many respects the single most important figure in Cretan mythology, around whom the stories revolved. In recognition of this fact Arthur Evans named the archaeological culture that he discovered 'Minoan', attaching to the palace at Knossos the name of the legendary king. He took the tradition of King Minos quite seriously, though he recognized the distinction between myth and history. Indeed he speculated that the name Minos might in fact have been a hereditary title, like 'pharaoh' in Egypt.

The stories associated with Minos often include bulls. It was in the form of a handsome bull that his father, Zeus, abducted the Phoenician princess Europa and brought her to Gortyn. A descendant of the evergreen plane tree beneath which, according to tradition, the couple were united is still shown to visitors today. Their children were Minos, Rhadamanthys and Sarpedon.

Minos went on to become the king of Crete, renowned for his just laws, and patron of the master-craftsman Daedalus. Rhadamanthys helped him to rule Crete, while Sarpedon went to Lycia and founded a colony there. This finds an interesting echo in the existence of Minoan settlements on Turkey's west coast. Both Minos and Rhadamanthys were said to have become judges in the underworld after their death: the tradition of Minos' justice was very strong.

The bronze giant Talos, whose lineage is differently quoted in different versions of his story, carried tablets inscribed with the laws of Minos around the Cretan coast. He was killed by the Argonauts, for whom, according to one account, Medea unfastened a pin in his leg and let the precious liquor that was his life-blood run out. The theory connecting the brazen giant with the volcanic island of Thera seems somewhat forced.

There is something characteristically Hellenic about the story of Minos asking for a sign from Zeus to validate his pre-eminent position, then angering the god by failing to sacrifice the sign: the wonderful bull that Zeus sent from the sea. Minos was guilty of an act of hubris – he tried to cheat the god, by hiding the bull in his own flocks and substituting an inferior animal. This is a very Greek concept: the idea that man has his own proper place, and that if he oversteps his allotted sphere and challenges the gods he will pay a high price. Nemesis, retribution, invariably follows. Did the Minoans think like that? It is possible that they did, and that Minoan attitudes fed into what we now think of as typically Greek – the Minoans may not have been so different from their neighbours. Yet if their cultural values were as distinctive as their material culture, we must wonder whether the Minoans would have recognized themselves in the eventual, Greek versions of their tales.

As the story goes on it seems to us to have a very 'Minoan' aspect because of our familiarity with Minoan material culture, in which bulls and hybrid creatures loom so large. The price Minos paid for his hubris was high. Zeus afflicted Pasiphae, Minos' wife, with an unnatural passion for the bull. This was consummated with the help of Daedalus, who made a fake cow for her to hide in. The result was the birth of the Minotaur.

The Minotaur had the head of a bull and the body of a man. Minos hid the shameful creature in the heart of the labyrinth, a dark maze of confusing passageways that was again the work of Daedalus, whose versatility was endless. Minos then demanded a regular tribute from Athens of seven youths and seven maidens to be sacrificed to the flesh-eating monster.

In the story the rationale for this demand is that the Athenians had been responsible for the death of Androgeas, one of the sons of Minos. It is striking, though, that the myth preserves the tradition of a time when Athens was subservient to Crete – a situation which seems more than feasible in view of the archaeological evidence for the early pre-eminence of the Minoans in the Aegean.

The Minotaur's downfall is part of the story of Theseus, prince of Athens and a hero of great importance to the city. Indeed, the Athenians of the Classical period attributed to him not only heroic deeds in which he conquered various villains and monsters, but also the founding of many of their city's social and political institutions.

Outraged at the unfairness of the tribute demanded by Minos, Theseus determined to be among the seven youths and seven maidens taken for sacrifice. He entered the labyrinth and found and slew the monster at its heart.

108 Theseus and the Minotaur on an Athenian vase of the fifth century BC.

He had the help of Ariadne, Minos' daughter, who had fallen in love with him, and had given him her ball of thread to unwind behind him so that he could find his way back through the maze to the light of day. In some versions of the story she also gives him a magic crown of light to illuminate the darkness of the labyrinth. Along with the other youths and maidens of the tribute, the pair made good their escape. The story goes that when they had got safely to Naxos they invented a dance in celebration, known as the Crane Dance, its twisting steps evoking the turnings of the labyrinth. The group dances of modern Greece, where the dancers form a sinuous line and athletic young men leap, turn and twist at the front of it, spring inevitably to mind.

The eventual fates of the figures from Cretan mythology range from the dramatic to the surprisingly low-key. An unforgettable episode is the flight of Daedalus and his son Icarus, attempting to escape from Crete with man-made wings of feathers and wax. Daedalus was successful, but Icarus flew too near to the sun. Their exploit, and the latter's fall, have come to symbolize man's brave and ingenious endeavours against the inevitable limits of the human condition, as well as the impetuousness of youth. Ariadne, abandoned on Naxos, equally gained iconic significance for all deserted women – though the version of the story that has her swept up into the wild company of the god Dionysus as his consort certainly offers some consolation. Minos himself was ingloriously killed in his bath in Sicily by the daughters of King

Kokalos. He was said to have gone there in pursuit of Daedalus, still implacably angry at the part the craftsman had played in the union of Pasiphae and the bull.

The Reception of Minoan Crete

In the latter part of the nineteenth century AD the traditional stories about Crete began to be joined by the material evidence for the island's early culture recovered by archaeology. It was partly the stories themselves that gave the impetus for early excavations on Minos' island. From March 1900, and the beginning of Evans' excavations, it became apparent that the island did indeed have a rich and remarkable early history. The equation of myth and history was implicit in Evans' calling the building he discovered the 'Palace of Minos', but even at the time, and certainly later, the difficulties of correlating the two sorts of evidence were apparent.

The rare written references to Minoan Crete of Bronze Age date give nothing other than the most partial insights into how the culture of the island was seen by contemporary eyes. For Egyptians Crete was 'beyond the Great Green' (an expression perhaps referring both to the Nile delta and the Mediterranean Sea), and though by the Late Bronze Age the characteristic people and products of the island were reasonably familiar, they occupied a peripheral position in the Egyptian world view. Similarly 'Kaptara', the Caphtor of the Bible, is almost certainly to be identified with Crete, though for the peoples of the Near East it was a distant and exotic land. No real evocation of Crete emerges in writing from the Bronze Age world: our legacy is one of remembered and transmitted myth, coupled with the evidence buried in the island's soil and recovered by archaeological excavation.

In the wake of the archaeological discovery of Crete modern voices surged into the vacuum of this voiceless past, and some of these have made a sort of new mythology. A selection of reactions, then, rounds off this book. It is partial, of course, and largely excludes the voices of professional archaeologists, for they would swamp the picture. Perhaps in any case the reception of and reaction to the Minoan world from non-specialists is more likely to illustrate what the impact of its discovery has been. We must, though, start with Arthur Evans, not only because this world was his discovery, but also because his voice was fundamentally influential from the moment he first sank his spade into Knossian territory.

It has become something of a cliché to talk of Arthur Evans not just in terms of his discovering Minoan Crete, but also, to a greater or lesser extent, of 'inventing' it. This arises partly from the extensive reconstructions that he carried out at Knossos. A desire to make his finds comprehensible to a wider audience was a major element in his thinking. He had a compelling and thoroughgoing vision of 'his' Minoans, and his archaeological legacy bore his personal stamp very strongly.

The necessity to look beyond and behind the reconstructions of the buildings, the frescoes and the smaller works of art, to strip them of interpretative reconstruction and to see what Evans actually found has long been recognized. Similarly in his great work *The Palace of Minos at Knossos*, published in four volumes between 1921 and 1936, it is necessary to separate interpretations from facts. The work is a discursive masterpiece, encyclopaedic in its coverage of Minoan Crete and the island's position in the wider world, filled with erudition and the thoughts of a keen and enthusiastic mind. It is also, and necessarily, thoroughly imbued with Evans' character and vision. Elements of his thinking dominated the initial reception of Minoan Crete, and, in spite of many 'revisionist' approaches, some of his attitudes have proved extraordinarily durable.

Perhaps the most pervasive, and the most difficult to discard, has been his general 'feeling' that Minoan Crete was a peaceful, sophisticated and almost Utopian world. It is in this regard that he can be said to have founded a modern Cretan mythology. It has rightly been pointed out that there was some element of pre-determination about this, arising from Evans' own history and temperament. The biographical ground is well covered elsewhere, and will not be repeated here.[2] Nonetheless, Evans' attitudes are the starting-point for any survey of the reception of Minoan Crete. His half-sister Joan Evans sets the mood when she writes in her biography of Arthur:

Time and Chance had made him the discoverer of a new civilization, and he had to make it intelligible to other men. Fortunately it was exactly to his taste: set in beautiful Mediterranean country, aristocratic and humane in feeling; creating an art brilliant in colour and unusual in form, that drew inspiration from the flowers and birds and creatures that he loved. It provided him with enigmas to solve and oracles to interpret, and opened a new world for eye and mind to dwell in: a world which served to isolate him from a present in which he had found no real place.[3]

Evans' own romanticism was usually fairly well buried beneath his often rather dense and contorted academic prose, and is suggested rather than overt in his writings. Nonetheless he allowed himself one flight of fancy in the pages of *The Palace of Minos*. Describing with pride his reconstruction of the Grand Staircase of the palace's east wing – an impressive work by any standards – he writes:

... it revives, as no other part of the building, the remote past. It was, indeed, my own lot to experience its strange power of imaginative suggestion.... During an attack of fever, having found, for the sake of better air, a temporary lodging…on the neighbouring edge of the Central Court, and tempted in the warm moonlight to look down the staircase-well, the whole place seemed to awake awhile to life and movement. Such was the force of the illusion that the Priest-King with his plumed lily crown, great ladies, tightly girdled, flounced and corseted, long-stoled priests, and, after them, a retinue of elegant but sinewy youths – as if the Cup Bearer and his fellows had stepped down from the walls – passed and re-passed on the flights below.

Other writers who were early visitors to the Minoan sites and who saw the newly discovered art of Minoan Crete reacted in a similarly lyrical way. The eminent Cretan writer Nikos Kazantzakis was born in Herakleion in 1883, and was therefore seventeen when Evans began the Knossos excavations. Kazantzakis left to continue his studies in Athens in 1902, and thereafter worked in many different places, but the history of Crete was of fundamental significance to him. He saw the modern Cretan character as deriving directly from the struggles in the island of the more recent centuries, but also as rooted even deeper in the Bronze Age past. He describes the art of Minoan Crete in his *Report to Greco*, an autobiographical work published posthumously in 1961:

Large almond-shaped eyes, cascades of black tresses, imposing matrons with bare breasts and thick, voluptuous lips, birds – pheasant and partridge – blue monkeys, princes with peacock feathers in their hair, fierce holy bulls, tender-aged priestesses with sacred snakes wrapped around their arms, blue boys in flowering gardens. Joy, strength, great wealth; a world full of mystery, an Atlantis which had issued from the Cretan soil. This world looked at us with immense black eyes, but its lips were still sealed.

Henry Miller, the American novelist who was born in New York in 1891 and later lived in Paris, was invited by his friend Lawrence Durrell to spend six months in Greece in 1939, just before the outbreak of the Second World War. He considered Greece a 'holy land' and writes about his time there in *The Colossus of Maroussi* (1941). His account of his visit to Phaistos is ecstatic in tone:

I descended the broad steps of the levelled palace and glanced here and there automatically. I hadn't the faintest desire to snoop about examining lintels, urns, pottery, children's toys, votive cells and the like. Below me, stretching away like an infinite magic carpet, lay the plain of Mesara, girdled by a majestic chain of mountain ranges. From this sublime, serene height it has all the appearance of the garden of Eden. At the very gates of paradise the descendants of Zeus halted here on their way to eternity to cast a last look earthward, and saw with the eyes of innocents that the earth is indeed what they had always dreamed it to be: a place of beauty and joy and peace. In his heart man is angelic; in his heart man is united with the whole world. Phaistos contains all the elements of the heart: it is feminine, through and through.

The beauty of the view over the Mesara Plain from the palace at Phaistos cannot be doubted, nor can the sincerity of Miller's response – but he does perhaps give a reason for the extreme exaltation of his vision when he talks of sharing a drink with the custodian of the site:

I believe the wine was called Mavrodaphne. If not it should have been because it is a beautiful black word and describes the wine perfectly. It slips down like molten glass, firing the veins with a heavy red fluid which expands the heart and the mind. One is heavy and light at the same time; one feels as nimble as the antelope and yet powerless to move.

Romanticism, lyricism, the tendency to project on to Minoan Crete ideas of another Eden – such ways of thinking have imbued many writings about the Minoan culture, both scholarly and popular. They have derived largely from perceptions of Minoan art, and have sometimes conveniently forgotten that few human societies have had entirely peaceful histories. And they have certainly sometimes forgotten that the art itself must be viewed with caution because much of it has been heavily restored. There is an interesting circularity of influences here. The faintly art deco feeling noticeable in the restored Palace of Knossos is doubtless partly due to the early twentieth-century artistic tastes of the restorers. At the same time, the newly discovered Cretan works themselves influenced works created in the art deco style. The mutual influences may be inextricable, but at the very least we should bear in mind Evelyn Waugh's characteristically sharp-tongued remark about the restorers of the frescoes. He said that they 'tempered their zeal for accuracy with a somewhat inappropriate predilection for the covers of *Vogue*'.

Not all commentators agreed that the Minoan world as revealed by Evans was 'humane in feeling'. Dilys Powell, who spent long periods at Knossos in the company of her archaeologist husband Humphrey Payne, had time to wander in the ruins by herself and to soak up their atmosphere. She tells us in her book *The Villa Ariadne* (1973) that she felt 'the pall of history pressing bloodstained and heavy on summer days' and 'as I clambered about the reconstructed passages something sacrificial in the air: one half expected a roll of drums...'

The theme is taken up more strongly by Evelyn Waugh,[4] in a paragraph of remarkable intensity:

I do not think it can be only imagination and the recollection of a bloodthirsty mythology which makes something fearful and malignant of the cramped galleries and stunted alleys, these colonnades of inverted, conical pillars, these rooms that are mere blind passages at the end of sunless staircases; this squat little throne, set on a landing where the paths of the palace intersect; it is not the seat of a lawgiver nor a divan for the recreation of a soldier; here an ageing despot might crouch and have borne to him, along the walls of a whispering gallery, barely audible intimations of his own murder.

The perception of a potential for cruelty in Minoan Crete may perhaps be said to have been supported by the evidence for human sacrifice that archaeology has uncovered. In any case, it has increasingly been recognized since Evans' time that warfare and bloodshed must have been part of the Minoan story. The weapons cannot all have been ceremonial, and the elite society of the palaces cannot have lived in luxury without some human cost.

The 'bloodthirsty mythology' includes the story of the Minotaur and the labyrinth into which the Athenian victims were sent to seek their fate. This was the theme adapted by Lawrence Durrell in his novel *The Dark Labyrinth,* which begins with a group of tourists visiting 'the newly-discovered city in the rock' at an imaginary location in Crete. They become trapped by a rock fall, and the book describes their experiences as they pass through the dark passageways, as well as the various outcomes for each of them. Here the labyrinth is life or fate, and the Minotaur features only as a deep and menacing bellowing, perhaps heard, perhaps imagined.

For the writer and artist Michael Ayrton, too, the labyrinth was a potent symbol, and Cretan mythology a major theme. His writings often returned to the figure of Daedalus, the master-craftsman, with whom he clearly felt an affinity. His visual works included a maze built of brick and stone and Minotaur figures in bronze and other media. These remind us of Picasso's fascination with the Minotaur, often transplanted to the bull-ring, and imbued with a sort of sadness: his hybrid creature has a noble bull's head, but we are always made to feel that he has the heart of a man.

We are venturing here, though, into the realms of artists responding indirectly to the physical remains of Minoan Crete, and perhaps more influenced by the mythology than by the archaeology. We will be firmly brought back to earth by Robert George Collingwood (1889–1943), who became Professor of Metaphysical Philosophy at Oxford and who was also an historian and archaeologist, particularly of Roman Britain. He wrote in a diary of a visit to Knossos in April 1932: 'Knossos – the first impression on the mind of the visitor is that Knossian architecture consists of garages and public lavatories.'[5] He concedes that this may be 'partly due to concrete restoration' but says 'on closer inspection it appears that the first unhappy impression has deeper grounds than these. The modern utilitarian buildings of which Knossos reminds one resemble it, at bottom, because they are designed with no reference to sound canons of proportion, and are therefore undignified and mean, however well or even lavishly constructed and decorated.' He goes on to

109 The rocky outcrop in the centre is the site of Karphi, one of the 'refuge settlements' where the Minoans lived at the end of the Bronze Age.

elaborate on the difference between Minoan and Classical Greek architecture, with its sense of ideal proportion and harmony of relationships. He admits 'the flights of the Great Staircase are impressively constructed', but says it is 'in the sort of way in which a modern architect would make a staircase for a big house – with no taste, no elegance, no sense of proportion'. He describes both Minoan and modern architecture as 'a trade, not a fine art', and continues, 'This is the secret of Knossian modernity. The Cretan artists were modern in the sense of being barbarously utilitarian, not Hellenically Classical, concerned to make a grand and commodious house for a rich man, not to make a beautiful building.'

Collingwood pursues the same themes in discussing small-scale Minoan art, with its 'vivid naturalism, naiveté, outpouring of feelings'. He says, 'In this respect – aesthetically – Crete is not the forerunner of Greece but its antithesis,' and concludes, 'Greece borrows lavishly from her own Bronze Age, but what makes her Greece is not these materials but the spirit she brings to the use of them – the spirit of order and symmetry and proportion. This spirit she in no way owes to Bronze Age Crete, where it is wholly lacking, and whose entire life is, to use the Greek term, barbarous.'

Our modern age of cultural relativism would be less inclined to compare Minoan and Classical art to the disadvantage of the former. Yet Collingwood's analysis is more sophisticated than a simple assumption of the innate superiority of Classical Greece. Instead he is responding to very real differences between the Minoan and the Classical aesthetic. This is a revealing exercise, whatever value-judgements are arrived at from a modern perspective.

110 View of Mount Juktas from the north east, showing the profile of the 'sleeping Zeus'.

The Collingwood passages focus on the legacy of Crete to later Greece and to the modern world, and provide a suitable note on which to end. Mycenaean Greece inherited much from Crete, assimilating Minoan arts, crafts and culture into the earliest stratum of Greek history. The Classical Greeks, as Collingwood suggests, created something quite different in their visual world, though the paintings on their vases and the themes of their plays show how firmly the Cretan past was fixed in their preoccupations. From the Classical Greeks to the modern world Cretan themes remain a constant strand: we still describe complex things as 'labyrinthine', and understand the significance of Ariadne's ball of thread.

Archaeological research, though, takes us back to Crete the island, and shows us a unique place. Linking lands to the south and east with the mainland of Europe, the island in earliest times belonged to neither, but only to herself. The Minoan period is widely described as the richest and most glorious that Crete has ever seen. The Minoans declined and faded, and the island's history moved on. It is easy, perhaps, to view the Minoans as inhabiting an impossibly distant age, and to feel that their concerns and achievements are remote from us. Yet they were people, living in a landscape that we can see, breathing, like us, the thyme-scented Cretan air. We cannot share Minoan thoughts, or enter their mental landscape. Perhaps, though, our experience of their island and our study of what remains to us of their culture can give us some insight into the texture of their lives.

Notes

Introduction

1 A wide variety of guide books is available, but the best for the archaeology of the island is the *Blue Guide to Crete* by Pat Cameron (7th edn in press, publication due June 2002).

2 The Archaeological Museum of Herakleion naturally contains by far the richest and most comprehensive collection of Minoan material, though the regional museums of Crete, particularly in Chania, Rethymnon, Ayios Nikolaos and Siteia, also have interesting collections. Minoan objects can be seen in various museums in Europe and the USA. The collection of the Ashmolean Museum, Oxford, where Arthur Evans was Director, stands out, and the British Museum has a relatively small but quite representative selection, with some fine pieces.

Chapter One

1 Rackham, O., and Moody, J., *The Making of the Cretan Landscape* (Manchester and New York, 1996).

2 An exhibition on this subject was mounted in the National Museum, Athens, and travelled to other venues. The catalogue summarizes the results of the analyses and gives background archaeological information. Tzedakis, Y., and Martlew, H., *Minoans and Mycenaeans: Flavours of Their Time* (Athens, 1999).

3 This can clearly be seen in the displays of the Museum of Cretan Ethnology at Vori, near Phaistos.

4 See the discussion in Shaw, J. W., *Minoan architecture: materials and techniques*, Annuario della Scuola Archeologica di Atene, vol. XLIX, 1973 (Nuova Serie XXXIII, 1971).

5 Dickinson, O., *The Aegean Bronze Age* (Cambridge, 1994), p. 11.

6 Warren, P., and Hankey, V., *Aegean Bronze Age Chronology* (Bristol, 1989).

7 Manning, S., *A Test of Time: The volcano of Thera and the chronology and history of the Aegean and east Mediterranean in the mid second millennium BC* (Oxford, 1999).

8 Dickinson, op. cit., p. 20.

9 Niemeier, W-D., 'Tel Kabri: Aegean Fresco Paintings in a Canaanite Palace', in S. Gitin (ed.), *Recent Excavations in Israel: A View to the West*, Archaeological Institute of America, Colloquia and Conference Papers I (Dubuque, 1995).

10 Manning (above, note 7) gives a full bibliography for chronological questions. The discovery of Minoan frescoes at Avaris led to renewed interest in Minoan relations with Egypt. Papers from a colloquium held in London were published as Davies, W. V., and Schofield, L. (eds), *Egypt, the Aegean and the Levant* (London, 1995); a major exhibition in Vienna was accompanied by the catalogue Barbotin, C. (ed.), *Pharaonen und Fremde – Dynastien im Dunkel* (Vienna, 1994); while the important Crete-Egypt exhibition in Herakleion saw the publication both of a catalogue, Karetsou, A., and Andreadaki-Vlasaki, M. (eds), *Crete-Egypt: Three Thousand Years of Cultural Interconnections* (in Greek), (Herakleion, 2000), and of an accompanying volume of conference papers with the same title.

Chapter Two

1 Branigan, K., *Dancing with Death. Life and Death in Southern Crete c. 3000–2000BC* (Amsterdam, 1993), includes references to earlier studies by the same author.

2 Day, P. M., Wilson, D., and Kiriatzi, E., 'Pots, labels and people: Burying ethnicity in the cemetery at Aghia Photia, Siteias', in Branigan, K. (ed.), *Cemetery and Society in the Aegean Bronze Age* (Sheffield, 1998).

3 Warren, P., *Myrtos. An Early Bronze Age Settlement in Crete* (London, 1972). See also Whitelaw, T. M., 'The settlement at Fournou Korifi, Myrtos, and aspects of Early Minoan social organization', in Krzyszkowska, O., and Nixon, L. (eds), *Minoan Society* (Bristol, 1983).

4 Soles, J., *The prepalatial cemeteries at Mochlos and Gournia and the house tombs of Bronze Age Crete* (Hesperia Supplement XXIV, Princeton, 1992).

5 Sakellarakis, J. and E. (eds), *Archanes* (Athens, 1991). This two-volume publication accompanied a major exhibition on Archanes in the Goulandris Museum in Athens. It includes accounts of the tombs in the Phourni cemetery as well as the Anemospilia shrine and the Minoan remains in the town of Archanes itself, and collects references for all aspects of the archaeology of the region. I am also grateful to Y. Papadatos who kindly gave me information from his study *Mortuary practices and their importance for the reconstruction of society and life in prepalatial Crete: The evidence from Tholos Tomb C at Archanes-Phourni*, unpublished PhD thesis, University of Sheffield, 1999.

6 A more detailed account can be found in Quirke, S., and Fitton, L., 'An Aegean origin for Egyptian spirals?', in Phillips, J. (ed.), *Ancient Egypt, the Aegean and the Near East: Studies in Honour of Martha Rhoads Bell* (San Antonio, 1997).

Chapter Three

1 MacGillivray, J. A., 'The early history of the palace at Knossos', in Evely, D., Hughes-Brock, H., and Momigliano, N. (eds), *Knossos: A Labyrinth of History. Papers presented in honour of Sinclair Hood*, British School at Athens (London, 1994).

2 McGillivray, op. cit.

3 Evans, A. J., *The Palace of Minos*, vol. II (London, 1928), p. 548.

4 Cadogan, G., 'An Old Palace period Knossos state?', in *Knossos: A Labyrinth of History* (see note 1 above).

5 Knappett, C., 'Assessing a polity in proto-palatial Crete: the Malia-Lasithi state', *American Journal of Archaeology* 103 (1999), 615–39.

6 Cadogan, G., *Palaces of Minoan Crete* (London, 1976), p. 35.

7 Schiestl, R., 'Eine archäologische Notiz: eine neue Parallele zum Anhänger aus Tel el Dab'a aus dem Petrie Museum, University College, London', *Ägypten und Levante* X, 2000, 127–8. I am grateful to Dr Stephen Quirke of the Petrie Museum for permission to publish this pendant.

8 The sherds are now in the British Museum, and are discussed in Fitton, J. L., Hughes, M., and Quirke, S., 'Northerners at Lahun: Neutron Activation Analysis of Minoan and related pottery in the British Museum', in Quirke, S. (ed.), *Lahun Studies* (Reigate, 1998).

9 The Tod treasure has been much discussed, but the original publication is Bisson de la Roque, F., Contenau, G., and Chapouthier, F., *Le Tresor de Tod* (Cairo, 1953).

10 Weingarten, J., *The Transformation of Egyptian Taweret into the Minoan Genius*, Studies in Mediterranean Archaeology 88 (Partille, 1991).

11 Rutkowski, B., *The Cult Places of the Aegean* (New Haven and London, 1986).

12 MacGillivray, J. A., *Knossos: Pottery Groups of the Old Palace Period*, British School at Athens Studies 5 (London, 1998).

13 Rehak, P., 'Aegean breechcloths, kilts and the Keftiu paintings', *American Journal of Archaeology* 100, 35–51.

Chapter Four

1 Driessen, J., and MacDonald, C. F., *The Troubled Island. Minoan Crete Before and After the Santorini Eruption*, Aegaeum 17 (Liège, 1997).

2 Immerwahr, S. A., *Aegean Painting in the Bronze Age* (Pennsylvania, 1990), p. 49.

3 Niemeier, W-D., 'Das Stuckrelief des "Prinzen mit der Federkrone" aus Knossos und Minoische Götterdarstellungen', *Mitteilungen des Deutschen Archäologischen Instituts. Athenische Abteilung* 102, 1987, 65–98.

4 MacGillivray, J. A., Driessen, J. M., and Sackett. L. H., *The Palaikastro Kouros: a Minoan chryselephantine statuette and its Aegean Bronze Age context*, British School at Athens Studies 6 (London, 2000).

5 Hood, M. S. F., *The Arts in Prehistoric Greece* (Harmondsworth, 1978), p. 120.

6 Davis, E., *The Vapheio Cups and Aegean Gold and Silver Ware* (Ann Arbor, 1973).

7 A large bibliography exists for Thera. Site reports by Marinatos and Doumas are supplemented by important conference proceedings: *Thera and the Aegean World. Proceedings of the Second International Scientific*

Congress, Santorini, Greece, August 1978 (2 vols, London, 1978 and 1980), and *Thera and the Aegean World. Proceedings of the Third International Congress, Santorini, Greece, September 1989* (London, 1990). A very useful and well-written overview is Forsyth, P. Y., *Thera in the Bronze Age*, American University Studies Series IX, History, vol. 187 (New York, 1997). This briefly discusses all aspects of Thera and gives a full bibliography. Finally there is a beautifully produced publication of the wall-paintings: Doumas, C., *The Wall-Painings of Thera* (Athens, 1992).

8 Rehak, P., and Younger, J., '*Neopalatial, final palatial and postpalatial Crete*' (cited in 'Further Reading', below), and Driessen and McDonald, op. cit. (see note 1 above).

9 Renfrew, C., *The Archaeology of Cult: The Sanctuary at Phylakopi* (London, 1985).

10 This is discussed in Watrous, L.V., *The Cave Sanctuary of Zeus at Psychro: a study of extra-urban sanctuaries in Minoan and Early Iron Age Crete*, Aegaeum 15 (Liège, 1996).

11 Goodison, L., and Morris, C., 'Beyond the "Great Mother": the sacred world of the Minoans', in Goodison, L., and Morris, C. (eds), *Ancient Goddesses* (London, 1998).

12 Hallager, E., *The Master Impression*, Studies in Mediterranean Archaeology 69 (Goteborg, 1985).

Chapter Five

1 Both Dickinson and Rehak and Younger, cited in 'Further Reading' below, summarize the problems and give detailed bibliography.

2 Popham, M. R., 'The use of the palace at Knossos at the time of its destruction, *c*.1400BC', in Hagg, R., and Marinatos, N. (eds) *The Function of the Minoan Palaces*, 4th International Symposium, Swedish Institute in Athens, 10–16.6.1984, Skrifter utgivna av Svenska Institutet i Athen 35 (1987).

3 Popham, M. R., *The Minoan Unexplored Mansion at Knossos* (London, 1984).

4 Popham's early articles included 'The last days of the palace at Knossos. Complete vases of the Late Minoan IIIB period', *Studies in Mediterranean Archaeology* 5 (Goteborg, 1964), and 'The destruction of the palace at Knossos. Pottery of the Late Minoan IIIA period', *Studies in Mediterranean Archaeology* 12 (Goteborg, 1970). He returned to the subject and restated his arguments, answering some criticisms, in 'The final destruction of the palace at Knossos: seals, sealings and pottery: a reconsideration', in Driessen, J., and Farnoux, A. (eds), *La Crète Mycénienne*, Bulletin de Correspondance Hellénique, Supplement 30 (Athens, 1997).

5 Younger, J., 'Bronze Age representations of Aegean bull-leaping', *American Journal of Archaeology* 80, 1976.

Chapter Six

1 Thucydides, *History*, Books I, IV and VIII.

2 Fitton, J. L., *The Discovery of the Greek Bronze Age* (London, 1995), contains a chapter on Evans, and he is the subject of a recent biography: MacGillivray, J. A., *Minotaur: Sir Arthur Evans and the Archaeology of the Minoan Myth* (London, 2000).

3 Evans, J., *Time and Chance: The Story of Arthur Evans and his Forbears* (London, 1943).

4 Evelyn Waugh, *Labels: a Mediterranean Journal* (1930).

5 The relevant part of Collingwood's diary is published in Hood, S., 'Collingwood on the Minoan Civilization of Crete', in *Collingwood Studies,* vol. 2, 1995 (published by the R. G. Collingwood Society).

Further Reading

Dickinson, O., *The Aegean Bronze Age* (Cambridge, 1994), Preziosi, D., and Hitchcock, L., *Aegean Art and Architecture* (Oxford, 1999), and Warren, P., *The Aegean Civilizations. From Ancient Crete to Mycenae* (Oxford, 2nd edn, 1989), are useful accounts covering both Crete and a wider Aegean area. Hood, S., *The Arts in Prehistoric Greece* (Harmondsworth, 1978), remains essential reading, while Vasilakis, A., *Minoan Crete: From Myth to History* (Athens, 1999), is a book widely available in Crete that, in spite of a small format, is well illustrated and takes account of recent research.

Two long and detailed review articles by L. Vance Watrous ('Crete from earliest prehistory through the protopalatial period') and Paul Rehak and John Younger ('Neopalatial, final palatial and postpalatial Crete') originally appeared in the *American Journal of Archaeology* (vols 98, 1994, and 102, 1998), and have now conveniently been republished with addenda in Cullen, T. (ed), *Aegean Prehistory: a Review* (Boston, 2001).

Myers, W. J., Myers, E., and Cadogan, G., *An Aerial Atlas of Ancient Crete* (Berkeley, 1992), is valuable both for stunning photography and for references to site publications. The palaces are discussed in Cadogan, G., *Palaces of Minoan Crete* (London, 1976), and Graham, J. W., *The Palaces of Crete* (Princeton, 2nd edn, 1969) – both excellent accounts, though published before the recent discoveries that have broadened our definition of the Minoan palaces.

The Hieroglyphic, Linear A and Linear B scripts of Crete are published in the following corpora:

CHIC Olivier, J-P., and Godart, L., *Corpus Hieroglyphicarum Inscriptionum Cretae* (Études Crétoises 31, Paris, 1996).
GORILA Godart, L., and Olivier, J-P., *Recueil des inscriptions en linéaire A*, vols 1–5 (Études Crétoises 21). (To this, the following article is a useful addition: Vandenabeele, F., 'La chronologie des documents en Linéaire A', *Bulletin de Corréspondance Hellénique* CIX, 1985, pp. 3–20). Chadwick, J., Godart, L., Killen, J., Olivier, J-P., Sacconi, A., and Sakellarakis, I. A. (eds), *Corpus of Mycenaean Inscriptions from Knossos*, vols I–IV (Cambridge and Rome, 1986–98).

Papers from the Swedish Institute symposium on the function of the palaces have already been cited (ch. 5, n. 2, above). See also: Hagg, R.(ed), *The Function of the Minoan Villa*, 8th International Symposium, Swedish Institute in Athens, 6–8.6.1982, Skrifter utgivna av Svenska Institutet i Athen 4, 46 (1997), and Hagg, R., and Marinatos, N. (eds), *Sanctuaries and Cults in the Aegean Bronze Age*, 1st International Symposium, Swedish Institute in Athens, 12–13.5.1980, Skrifter utgivna av Svenska Institutet i Athen 28 (1981).

The following works on specific themes have also proved useful to me in writing this book. Marinatos, N., *Minoan Religion. Ritual, Image and Symbol* (Columbia, 1993), Barber, E. J. W., *Prehistoric Textiles* (Princeton, 1991), and Gale, N. H. (ed.), *Bronze Age Trade in the Mediterranean* (Jonsered, 1991).

Finally *Nestor: Bibliography of Aegean Prehistory and Related Areas* both exists in printed form and has a searchable online database.

Illustration Acknowledgements

Colour Plates
1   Photographs: J. L. Fitton
2   Photographs: J. L. Fitton
3   Photographs: J. L. Fitton
4   Photographs: J. L. Fitton
5   Photographs: J. L. Fitton
6   Archaeological Museum of Herakleion.
    Photographs: T A P Service, Athens
7   (left) Archaeological Museum of Herakleion.
    Photograph: T A P Service, Athens
    (right) Photograph: British Museum,
    BM Cat Gems no. 3, GR 1934.11-20.5,
    BM Cat Gems nos 5, 13, 40, 39, 86 and 78
8   Archaeological Museum of Herakleion.
    Photographs: T A P Service, Athens

Black and White Figures
Frontispiece: Photograph: British Museum,
    BM Cat Jewellery 815
Map: Kate Morton
1   Photograph: J. L. Fitton
2   Photograph: British Museum,
    GR 1950.11-6.7
3   Photograph: J. L. Fitton
4   Photograph: J. L. Fitton
5   Photograph: J. L. Fitton
6   Photograph: British Museum,
    GR 1907.1-19.30 to 35
7   Photograph: J. L. Fitton
8   Photograph: J. L. Fitton
9   Photograph: J. L. Fitton
10 Photograph: J. L. Fitton
11 Archaeological Museum of Herakleion.
    Photographs: O. H. Krzyszkowska
12 Archaeological Museum of Herakleion.
    Photograph: J. L. Fitton
13 Photograph: J. L. Fitton
14 Photograph: British Museum, selection
    from BM Cat Vases A990-9
15 Drawing: Kate Morton (figurine in

Archaeological Museum of Herakleion)
16 Photograph: J. L. Fitton
17 Plan: Kate Morton, courtesy of P. Warren
18 Archaeological Museum of Ayios Nikolaos.
    Photograph: T A P Service, Athens
19 Photograph: J. L. Fitton
20 Photograph: J. L. Fitton
21 Photograph: J. L. Fitton
22 Photograph: J. L. Fitton
23 Photograph: J. L. Fitton
24 Photograph: J. L. Fitton
25 Photograph: British Museum,
    GR 1907.1-19.1, 3, 8, 9, 15 and 24
26 Photograph: British Museum,
    BM Cat Vases A425
27 Drawing: Kate Morton (seal in
    Archaeological Museum of Herakleion)
28 Drawing: Kate Morton (seals in
    Archaeological Museums of Herakleion
    and Chania)
29 Photograph: J. L. Fitton
30 Photograph: J. L. Fitton
31 Photograph: J. L. Fitton
32 Photograph: J. L. Fitton
33 Photograph: J. L. Fitton
34 Photograph: J. L. Fitton
35 Photograph: J. L. Fitton
36 Photograph: J. L. Fitton
37 Photograph: O. H. Krzyszkowska
38 Photograph: O. H. Krzyszkowska
39 Photograph: J. L. Fitton
40 Drawing: Kate Morton (sealings in
    Archaeological Museum of Herakleion)
41 Photograph: O. H. Krzyszkowska
42 Archaeological Museum of Herakleion.
    Photograph: T A P Service, Athens
43 Photograph: British Museum,
    BM Cat Vases A477
44 Photograph: British Museum,
    BM Cat Jewellery 763 and 765

45 Photograph: British Museum,
   BM Cat Jewellery 762
46 Petrie Museum (UC 34342).
   Photograph: British Museum
47 Musée du Louvre, Paris.
   Photograph: Vronwy Hankey
48 Drawing: Kate Morton (pendant in
   Egyptian Museum, Cairo)
49 Photograph: J. L. Fitton
50 Photograph: J. L. Fitton
51 Plan: Kate Morton
52 Photograph: British Museum
53 Photograph: J. L. Fitton
54 Plan: Kate Morton
55 Photograph: British Museum
56 Photograph: J. L. Fitton
57 Photograph: J. L. Fitton
58 Photograph: J. L. Fitton
59 Photograph: J. L. Fitton
60 Plan: Kate Morton
61 Photograph: J. L. Fitton
62 Photograph: J. L. Fitton
63 Photograph: J. L. Fitton
64 Plan: Kate Morton
65 Photograph: J. L. Fitton
66 Photograph: J. L. Fitton
67 Photograph: J. L. Fitton
68 Photograph: J. L. Fitton
69 Photograph: J. L. Fitton
70 Photograph: J. L. Fitton
71 Photograph: J. L. Fitton
72 Photograph: J. L. Fitton
73 Photograph: J. L. Fitton
74 Photograph: J. L. Fitton
75 Photograph: J. L. Fitton
76 Photograph: J. L. Fitton
77 Photograph: J. L. Fitton
78 Photograph: J. L. Fitton
79 Photograph: British Museum,
   GR 1905.6-18.1
80 Photograph: J. L. Fitton
81 Photograph: British Museum
82 Drawing: Kate Morton, courtesy of
   W-D. Niemeier
83 Photograph: British Museum,

   BM Cat Sculpture A56
84 Photograph: British Museum, GR 1966.3-28.1
85 Photograph: British Museum,
   GR 1918.1-1.114
86 Archaeological Museum of Herakleion.
   Photograph: T A P Service, Athens
87 Archaeological Museum of Herakleion.
   Photograph: T A P Service, Athens
88 Archaeological Museum of Herakleion.
   Photograph: T A P Service, Athens
89 Drawing: Kate Morton (tablets from Ayia
   Triadha in Archaeological Museum of
   Herakleion; nos HT 93a and HT 85b
   in GORILA – see 'Further Reading')
90 Photograph: British Museum,
   GR 1954.10-20.1
91 Photograph: J. L. Fitton
92 Photograph courtesy of Christos Doumas
93 Drawing: Kate Morton (fresco in National
   Museum, Athens)
94 Photograph: J. L. Fitton
95 Drawing: Kate Morton (ring in
   Archaeological Museum of Herakleion)
96 Drawing: Kate Morton (sealing in
   Archaeological Museum of Herakleion)
97 Drawing: Kate Morton (sealing in
   Archaeological Museum of Chania)
98 Photograph: British Museum,
   GR 1910.4-23.1 and 2
99 Archaeological Museum of Herakleion.
   Photograph: J. L. Fitton
100 Photograph: British Museum
101 Photograph: J. L. Fitton
102 Photograph: British Museum,
   BM Cat Vases A746
103 Photograph: J. L. Fitton
104 Photograph: J. L. Fitton
105 Photograph: J. L. Fitton
106 Archaeological Museum of Herakleion.
   Photograph: T A P Service, Athens
107 Drawing: Chris Power
108 Photograph: British Museum,
   BM Cat Vases E441
109 Photograph: J. L. Fitton
110 Photograph: J. L. Fitton

Index

Page numbers in *italics* refer to illustrations.

administration (of goods and produce) and administrative centres 65
country houses and villas 143, 144–5, 162
protopalatial period 68, 71–2, 88
neopalatial period 131, 134, 161–3
Final Palace period 182, 184
postpalatial period 193
see also Chania; Linear A; nodules; noduli; sealings; seals; writing
'Admonitions of Ipuwer' 99
adyton see lustral basins
agriculture 17–18, 29; pl. 1
Neolithic 39
EM I 41
EM II 45, 47, 48
EM III/MM IA 59
prepalatial period 65
storage of produce (food) 17, 67, 68, 70, 133–4, 144, 145, 169
Aigina treasure 93–4, *93, 94,* 107, 157, 178
Ailias 15, 72, 73, 106
Akrotiri, Thera 112, 165–72
frescoes 17, 34, 147, 148, 149, 151, 155, 167, 168–9, *169,* 170–1, *170,* 172, 176
pottery 96, 165, 166, 167
radiocarbon date 33
West House 169–71; pl. 5
Xeste 3: 168–9, *169*
alabastron 185
Amari valley 85, 86
Amenemhat II 98
Amnisos 184, 201
Villa of the Lilies 110, *111*
see also Eileithuia
Anatolia 24, 29, 39, 93, 100, 161, 164
Anemospilia shrine 102–5, *103,* 107, 138
animal bone 103
pottery 103, 104, 105

skeletons 102, 104–5, 106
terracotta feet 103, 153
animals
bronzes of 155
figurines of 59, 195
husbandry 18–21, 41, 47, 48, 59
as motifs/decoration 156, 158
sacrifices 101, 103, 131, 192
on seals 161, 188
see also bulls
Apodoulou 86
Archalochori cave 157
Archanes 45, 53, 61, 131–2, 181
signet-rings 157
tholos tombs 188, *190,* 191, 192, 195
workshops 131
see also Phourni cemetery
archive-rooms 71, 114, 129
archives 133, 163; *see also* Phaistos, First Palace
Argolid 96, 181, 188, 189, 191
Ariadne 197, 200, 204, 211
Armenoi, cemetery 193–4, *194*
arts and crafts
prepalatial period (EM) 45, 60–2
protopalatial period 90–5
neopalatial period 146–7
Final Palace period 188–9
Arvi gorge pl. 1
Asterousia Mountains 23, 42
Avaris *see* Tel el-Dab'a
axes
bronze *163*
metal 61
stone 44
Ayia Irini, Kea 96, 167
Ayia Photia
building 55
cemetery 43–5
Ayia Triadha
EM II houses 48
protopalatial building 132
neopalatial period 74, 131, 132–3, 163
Final Palace period 182, 184, 186
postpalatial period *stoa* 193
clay sealings 133

copper ingots 24, 132
frescoes 126, 132, 149, *150,* 186
Linear A tablet archive 133, 163
Royal Villa 74, 110, 132–3, *132, 133,* 139, 144, 149, 158
sarcophagus 103, 192–3; pl. 8
stone vases 64, 158, *159*
tholos tombs 132
Ayrton, Michael 209

balance-weights 143
beads 51, 61, 188
faience 155
bee-keeping 20
bee-pendant from Chrysolakkos 57, 93, 94; pl. 6
Beirut 97
'bird's nest' bowls 92
blades, obsidian 40, 42, 44
blood sacrifices *see* sacrifices
bone-working 83
bronze *24, 25,* 40, 101, *129,* 156
Bronze Age 23, 27, 29, 30
animal husbandry 18, 19
climate 15–16
see also Early Bronze Age
bronze melting 182
bronzes 51, 101, 132, 146, 154–5, *155,* 162, 188
bronze-workers 134
bronze-working
EM II 45
workshop 82–3, 188
building materials 22–3, 71
bulls 18, 152, *152,* 177
bronze 155, *155*
bull-jumping and bull sports 147, 151, 153, 154, *155,* 158, 161, 187; pls 7–8
bull's head rhytons 128, 137, 158
bull vessel 61
models of 59
in myths 202, 203, 205, 209
skull 191, 192
sacrifices 103, 104, 192
as symbols/motifs 101, 157, 160, 161, 188, 192
burials
Neolithic 39

EM 58
EM I 41–5
EM II 50–4
neopalatial period 145–6, 157, 164
Final Palace period 188, 189–91
postpalatial period 193–5
in pithoi 50, 56, 57, 146
see also caves; cemeteries; house-tombs; larnakes; Mycenae; sarcophagi; tholos tombs
Byblos 64, 97, 99

Canaanite amphorae 164
Caphtor *see* Kaptara
Carians 199
cats 20, 100
cauldrons 156
caves 201
for burials 42, 58, 101
EM I habitation 41
jewellery in 157
Neolithic habitation 39, 58, 101, 173
pit-caves for burial 189
pottery 101
sacred 58, 92, 100, 101, 147, 155, 157, 173–4, 192
sanctuary of Eileithuia 58, 184, 201
cemeteries
EM I 41–5
EM II 50–4
EM III/MM IA 56–7
neopalatial period 140, 146
Final Palace period 180, 189–91
postpalatial period 193–4, *194*
see also Knossos
Central Courts *see* Knossos; Second Palaces
Chamaizi, Oval House 55–6
Chamalevri 17, 86
Chania
as administrative centre 30, 131, 181, 182, 193
Final Neolithic period 39
Final Palace period 181, 182, 184
Kastelli quarter 131
as Kydonia 131, 184, 193
Linear A tablets 131, 163
Linear B tablets 30, 131, 181
palace 66, 67, 85, 86, 131
sealings 133, *177*, 178
shrine 131
chronology 6–7, 25–36
Chrysokamino 23
Chrysolakkos (Mallia), funerary building and pendant 57, *57*, 93, 94; pl. 6
climate 15–16
clothes 106–7, 155, 175–6, 178, 184
coffins *see* larnakes
Collingwood, Robert George 209–11
copper
artefacts 42, 44
ingots 24, 132
ores 23, 24
sources 23, 44, 100
copper-smelting site 23–4

country houses ('villas') 17, 109, 110, 111, 112, 141, 143–5, 178, 181
Linear A tablets 162–3
stone vases 157
crucibles 44
cult places (areas) 58, 130, 144, 168, 172, 173–4
cups
clay *11*, 12
conical 110
gold 157
pottery 50, 60, 79, 91, *91*
silver 97
Cyclades 199
azurite 148
chronology 6–7, 28
contacts with Crete 23, 62
copper 23
figurines 45, 53
grave types 43, 44–5
imports from 50
metal objects 44
pottery 44
silver from 25
stone vase carving 61
turmoil 55
cylinders 62
Cyprus 64
copper 24
pottery 35, 97, 164

Daedalus 197, 200, 202, 203, 204, 205, 209
daggers 60, 107
bronze 44, 61, 82, 156
copper 44
Cycladic 44
EM II 51
dance 43, *114*
Debla 41
deities 58, 59, 101; *see also* goddesses; gods
Dendra, tombs 188
destructions 28
EM II and EM III 55
MM 29, 69, 108, 156
LM IA 110, *111* (*see also* Thera, eruption)
LM IB 30, 110, 131, 178–9, 180, 181, 182, 183
see also earthquakes
Diktaian cave 174; *see also* Mount Dikte
documents *see* Linear A tablets; Linear B tablets
double-axes *24*, 125, 132
metal 61
miniature gold 157
mould for 83
sheet-bronze 145, 156
as symbols/motifs 160, 175, *185*, 192, 194
drinking habits 17–18, 20
Durrell, Lawrence 209
dyes 17, 20

Early Bronze Age 17, 23, 29, 32, 36, 37, 38, 40, 44
climate 15
foreign relations 62–3
painted plaster 147

seals 161
Early Minoan (EM) period 28, 37
caves for burials 58
copper-smelting site 23–4
seal-stones 18
'teapots' 20
wine 18
Early Minoan I (EM I) 40–5
burials (cemetery) 41–5
metal-working 44, 61
pottery 41, 44, 60
tholos tombs 41, 42–5
Early Minoan II (EM II) 45–54, 55
cemeteries and tombs 43, 50–4
EM IIA 48, 52
EM IIB 48, 49, 60, 63
metal-working 45, 61
pottery 46, 48, 50, 51, 52, 53, 60, *61*
seals and sealings 47, 48, 51, 63
settlements 45–50
Early Minoan III (EM III) 28, 54
Early Minoan III/Middle Minoan IA (EM III/MM IA) 54–7
cemetery 56–7
foreign relations 62, 63–4
pottery 28, 54, 56, 61
settlements 55–6
earrings, metal 93, *93*, 157
earthquakes 25, 29, 49, 105, 108, 109, 135, 156, 179
in Akrotiri 165, 166–7, *166*, 169
Egypt 205
art 151, 153, 186
cats 20
chronology 6–7, 26, 27, 28, 31, 33–4, 35, 36, 54
contacts with Crete 38, 63–4, 96–8, 99–100, 164
contacts with Thera 170, 171
cross-dating 27
faience 155
frescoes 148, 149
gold 25, 100
jewellery 94–5, *95*
pigments 148
pottery 35, 91, 96–7, 160, 164
scarabs 62, 63–4, *64*, 100
seals and motifs 92, 93
silver bullion in 98
sistrum clay model 64
vessels *27*, 61, 129
writing 26, 88
Eileithuia, cave of 58, 184, 201
elite groups 67, 83–4, 135, 145, 161, 179, 209
embalming materials 99–100
'enacted epiphany' 136, 174, 175, *176*
Ephyrean goblet 181, 185
Evans, Arthur 22, 28–9, 31, 54, 112, 122–3, 131, 137, 148, *177*, 183, 184, 202, 205–7, 208

faience 61, 155–6, 157; *see also* beads; plaques; snake-goddesses; vases
figurines (statuettes)
bone 53

bronze 154
clay 101, 106–7
Cycladic 45, 53
ivory 141, 153, 154
marble 53
stone 39, 42, 51
terracotta 39, 40, 46, *47*, 59, *59*,
    61, 107, 195
Neolithic 39, 40, *40*
EM II 51, 53
EM III–MM IA 59, *59*
neopalatial period 132, 141,
    151–6, 173
postpalatial period 195
see also sculpture
Final Neolithic period 39, 40, 41
Final Palace period (LM II–early
    LM IIIA2) 180, 181–93
arts and crafts 188–9
burials and cemeteries 188,
    189–91
frescoes 186–8; pl. 8
pottery 185–6, 191
religion 191–2, 195
sarcophagus 192–3; pl. 8
see also Knossos palace
First Palace period (First Palaces)
    29, 37–8
foundation of palaces 54, 55,
    64–5, 66–108 (*see also*
    protopalatial period)
destruction of palaces 29
see also Knossos palace; Mallia
    palace; Phaistos
fish-bone 48
fish-hooks 20, 44, 143
fishing 20
flax 17
footwear 107
foreign relations
prepalatial period 62–4
protopalatial period 95–100
fortifications 56, 67, 77, 87
Fournou Korifi 86
frescoes (wall-paintings) 11, 20, 34,
    206, 208
pigments 148–9
protopalatial period 76, 92, 147
neopalatial period 112, *114*,
    115, 116–17, *117*, 118, *121*,
    122, 126, 131, 132, 136, 137,
    138, 139, 141, 147–51, 153,
    157, 167, 168–9, 170–1, 172,
    174, 176; pl. 7
Final Palace period 148, 182,
    186–8, *186*, 192; pl. 8
see also Akrotiri (Thera); Knossos

Galatas palace 110, 111, 127,
    130–1
Gazi, figurine *195*
'genius' 93, 100, 158
geography/geology 13–16; pl. 1
gilding 157
goddesses 136, 141, 152, 168, *169*,
    175–7, 178, 191
terracotta figurine 46, *47*, 61
see also 'snake-goddesses'
'Goddess on the Mountain' 175–6,
    176, 178, 189
'goddess with upraised arms'
    195–6, *195*

gods 177–8, 191, 202
Olympian deities 177, 191, 201
gold 50, 63, 134, 157
Egyptian 25, 100
gold-working 61–2
Gournia 55, 86
EM II houses 48
Governor's House 142, *142*,
    143, 144
'palace' 112
shrine *142*, 143, 192
town 140–3, *141*
grape- (wine-) presses 21, *21*, 145
grapes 17, 41, 45, 47, 167
Greece (Greek mainland) 30–1,
    210–11
chronology 6–7, 28
contacts with Crete 63, 95, 96,
    164, 171
Dark Age 30
disruption 55
Greek language 89, 180, 183,
    198
sanctuaries 153
seals 161, 188
see also Greek mythology;
    Mycenae
Greek mythology 105, 197, 198–9,
    200, 201, 202, 203, 209
griffins 93, 94, *95*, 136, 175, 176,
    187, *187*, 192
gypsum
alabastron 185
as building stone 22, 71, 132
for carving 152, *152*
veneers 22, 126, *133*

harbours 15, 50, 141, 171
Harvester Vase 64, 158, *159*
Hazor 97
helmets 189
boar's-tusk 18, 146, 188
Herakleion 39, 69
museum 10, 24, *24*, 25, 90
Poros cemetery 146, 157
herbs 17, 20, 167
Hieroglyphic script 71, 72, 84,
    88–9, *89*, 90, 161, 183; pl. 7
honey 20
'horns of consecration' 125, 140,
    168–9, 192, 194, 195
horses 19
horse skeleton 191
house-tombs 51, *52*, 56, 57, *57*,
    146
human remains (skeletons)
children's bones at Knossos 105,
    138
skeletons at Anemospilia 102,
    104–5, 106
in tholoi 43
human sacrifice 102, 104–5, 209

Icarus 197, 204
Ida (Mount Ida) 13, *15*, 73, 86
Idaean cave 145, 173–4, *174*
Ierapetra isthmus 13, 48, 49, 78,
    85, 86, 143
incense 20
ingots
bronze 128, *129*
copper 24, 132

iron *see* ring
Isopata, tombs 146, *176*
Istron area 39
ivory 52, 61, 63, 87, 100, 134, 188
elephant tusks 128, *129*
hippopotamus 62
relief 136
workshop 137
see also figurines

jewellery 50, 51, 52, 61–2, 93–5,
    146, 157, 162, 188, 191, 195
Juktas *see* Mount Juktas

Kamares cave, sanctuary 58, 73, 86,
    90, 96, 101; *see also* pottery
Kaptara (Caphtor) 99, 205
Karpathos 96
Karphi *210*
Kasos 96
Kastri, Kythera 63, 96
Kazantzakis, Nikos 207
Kea 95, 164, 199
Ayia Irini 96, 167
Linear A tablet 163
shrine 152
Keftiu 22, 100
kernoi 47
kilts 94, 107
kings 135, 178, 199
rooms at Knossos palace 123–5
Knossos palace 10, 13, 209–10
Archanes as 'summer palace' of
    131
excavations 205–7
Minoan chronology 28–9
in myths 200, 201, 202
'state' 85–6
textile (wool) industry 18, 71,
    184
Neolithic settlement 29, 39, 40,
    40, 68
EM I occupation 41
EM III/MM IA settlement 54,
    55, 58
First Palace (protopalatial
    period) 28–9, 66, 67, 68–72,
    69, *70*, 77, 81, 83, 88, 91,
    101, 109
building stone 22, 71
Central Court 70, 71
destruction (MM) 69, 156
fresco 76, 147
Linear A tablet 8, 89, 163
paved causeway 76
pottery 67, 85, 91, *91*
script 71–2, 88
store-rooms 70
West Court 70, 71
Second Palace (neopalatial
    period) 66, 69, 71, 109, 110,
    111–12, *113*, 134, 135, 144,
    145
banqueting hall 127
building stone 22, 71
Central Court 111, 116–17,
    117, 118, *118*, 174
east wing 122–5, *122*, 182,
    185
entrances 121; pl. 2
frescoes 112, *114*, 115,
    116–17, *117*, 118, *121*, 122,

126, 136, 137, 138, 147–51, *151*, 206, 208; pl. 7
 Grand Staircase 71, 122–3, *122*, 206–7, 210
 Hall of the Double-Axes 71, 123, 125
 light well 125
 lustral basin 118, 174
 Queen's Megaron 71, 123, *123*, 187
 sealings 175, *176*, 178, 189
 seal-stone 178
 shrine 118, 156
 South Propylon *121*, 122
 southern section 121–2
 statues and figurines 153, 154, 156
 'Temple Repositories' 118, 156, 176; pl. 6
 Theatral Area 115
 Throne Room complex 70, *70*, 81, 118, 174, 185, 187, *187*
 west wing 117–18, *117*
 workshops 125
Final Palace period 73, 148, 181, 182–5
 cemeteries 180, 189, *189*
 destruction of palace 30, 139, 180, 181, 182–3, 192
 frescoes 148, 182, 186–8, *186*, *187*, 192; pl. 8
 Linear B archive 30, 174, 177, 180, 181, 183–5, *183*, 193
 palace 180, 182, 191–2
 pottery 180, 183, 185, *185*
 sealings 182, 185; pl. 7
 west wing 182
postpalatial period, 'Shrine of the Double-Axes' 196
restoration 112, 122, 150, *151*, 208; pl. 2
Knossos town 69, 72–3, 135–9, 178
 'Caravanserai' 130, 136
 cemeteries and tombs 30, 72, 73, 146, 191
 children's bones (funerary ritual?) 105, 138
 destructions 105, 138–9, 178–9
 EM II houses 45, 48
 Final Palace period 182–3
 House of the Frescoes 137, 149, 151
 Kephala hill 54, 68–9
 lime kilns 138
 Little Palace 128–9, 137, 138, 139, 182
 Royal Road 71, 72, 115, 137, 138; pl. 3
 Royal Villa 136, 182
 signet-rings 157
 South House 135–6, *136*, 149, 157
 Stratigraphical Museum 72, 138
 town houses 72–3, 83–4, 110, 112, 122, 125, 135, 182
 Unexplored Mansion 137–8, 139, 182, 188
 valley *14*, 15
 workshops 137, 156, 188
Kommos 74, 86, 110, 141

Final Palace period 182, 184
postpalatial period ship-sheds 193
Koumasa, bull vessel 61
Kouphonisi, shells 20
Krasi, tholos 43
Kydonia 184, 193
Kythnos 23, 24, 44

Lahun (Egypt) 96
lance-head, bronze 104
larnakes (coffins), terracotta and clay 50, 52, 57, *189*, 191, 194
Lasithi plain and plateau 13, 39, 77, 86–7, 184
Late Bronze Age 15–16, 18, 19, 24, 27, 32
 seals 161
Late Minoan (LM) period 6–7, 20, 28
 LM I 34, 136, 142
 LM IA 29–30, 33–5, 109, 110, 131, 135, 137, 149, 182 (*see also* pottery)
 LM IB 34, 35, 109, 110, 111, 138, 149, 186 (*see also* destructions; pottery)
 LM II 34, 35, 179, 180, 181, 182, 184, 185–6, *and see* Final Palace period
 LM IIIA 139, 182
 LM IIIA1 34, 185
 early LM IIIA2 *see* Final Palace period
 LM IIIA2 34, 183
 LM IIIA2–B *see* postpalatial period
 LM IIIB 139, 181
lavatories 125, 171
Lavrion, Attica 24, 25, 96, 98
Lenda *42*, 63, *64*
Lera cave 39
Lerna 96
libation tables 92, 118, 162, 173
light-wells 125, 126, 145
lime kilns 138
lime plaster 48, 148
Linear A (tablets) 71, 72, 80, 81, 82, 88–90, 129, 131, 133, 134, 161–3, 165, 183, 198
 on other objects and pottery 90, 92, 162, 163
Linear B (tablets) 9, 17, 18, 20, 30, 89, 90, 174, 177, 180, 181, 183–5, *183*, 191, 193, 198
 inscriptions on nodules 185
loom-weights 46, 56, 70, 143, 169–70
lustral basins (*adyton*) 118, 125, 131, 135, 137, 145, 168, 174
 Quartier Mu 81, *81*, 102
Luvian language 161
Lyktos 184

Mallia palace
 EM III/MM IA palace and defensive walls 55, 56, 57
 First Palace 66, 67, 68, 77–8, 83, 87, 88, 101
  pottery 85, 86, 87
  script 72, 88
 Second Palace 78, 109, 111, 112,

115, 118–19, *120*, 140; pl. 4
 banqueting hall(?) 127
 building stone 22
 Central Court 118, 119, *119*, 126
 entrances 121
 oil processing 126, *126*
 rhyton 158
 shrine 102
 gold sword 107
 shells 20
 'state' 85, 86–7
Mallia town 78–80, 107, 139–40, 181
 cemeteries 79, 140
 EM II houses 48
 frescoes 92, 139
 'hypostyle crypt' 77, 79–80, *79*
 Linear A archive (clay tablets) 80, 81, 90, 163
 Quartier Delta 140
 Quartier Mu 78, 80–4, 90, 100, 102, 109
 sanctuaries and shrines 140
 town wall 77
 see also Chrysolakkos
marble 22, 53, 152
Mari 24, 99
'Master of Animals' gold pendant 94, *94*, 107, 178
medallions 81, 89
Melos 95, 96, 164, 167
 obsidian 40, 50, 62
merchant class 83, 84
Mesara Plain *10*, 39, 73–4, 86, 141, 184, 207, 208
 tholos tombs 41, 42, 43, 45, 50, 52, 56, 63, *64*, 155
metals 9, 23–5, 97, 164
metalwork 44, 156–7
metalworking 44, 45, 61, 169
Middle Bronze Age 6–7, 19, 23, 24, 29, 32, 37, 54, 55
Middle Minoan (MM) period 6–7, 20, 28, 29
 MM IA 17, 28, 54, 58, 63, 66 (*see also* protopalatial period)
 MM IB 54, 55
 MM II 69, 80 (*see also* protopalatial period)
 MM IIB 76, 105
 MM IIB–IIIA, pottery 105
 MM III 33–4, 109–10, 131, 135, 137, 156
 MM IIIA 105
 MM IIIB 135
Miletos, Turkey 96, 164
Miller, Henry 207–8
mill installations 168
Minos 26, 135, 197, 199, 200, 201, 202–5
Minotaur 188, 197, *198*, 200, 203, *204*, 209
Mochlos 15, *23*, 45, 49–50, 55; pl. 2
 cemetery (house-tombs) 50, 51, *52*, 56, 146
 EM settlement 49–50
 jewellery 50, 61
 neopalatial period 141
 silver vases 62
Monastiraki 67, 85, 86
mortar, stone 101

moulds
  for pottery 82, 91
  stone, for metal objects 83
mountains 13–15
  sacred 58, 73
  see also peak sanctuaries
Mount Dikte 13, 174, 184
Mount Juktas 13, *14*, 101
  shrine/sanctuary 58, 70, 102–5,
    103, 173, 192, 202, *211*
Mycenae (Mycenaean Greeks) 18,
    30, 138–9, 164, 179, 180, 181,
    193, 196, 211
  burials 164, 189, 191, 193–4
  helmet 146
  Linear B tablets 183
  pottery 34, *35*
  seal size 188
  Shaft Graves 156, 157, 161, 164
  Treasury of Atreus 152, *152*
Myrtos-Fournou Korifi 45–7, *46*,
    49, 54, 58
Myrtos-Pyrgos 55, 86, 87, 144,
    163
mythology 25, 26, 105, 197–205,
    206

Near East 27, 31, 34, 63
  art 151
  contacts with Crete 38, 63–4,
    97, 164
  documents 90
  sealings 88
  stones for seals 92
  writing 26, 88
Neolithic (and Final Neolithic)
    period 15, 16, 28, 29, 38–9,
    40, 41
  animals 18, 19
  caves for habitation 39, 58, 173
  figurines 40, *40*
  painted plaster 147
  pottery 39, 40
neopalatial period (Second Palace
    period) 6–7, 29, 67, 83, 90,
    109–79
  arts and crafts 146–7
  burial customs 145–6
  cult places 173–4
  gods and goddesses 175–8
  'libation tables' 92
  Linear A 89
  population 73
  pottery 67, 159, 164, 165; pl. 6
  religion 101, 172–8
  seal-impressions 110
  sealings, clay 90
  shrines and sanctuaries 60, 112,
    140, 147, 155, 173, 177
  trade and exchange 164–72
  women's clothes 107
  writing and administration
    161–3
Nerokourou, country house 144
Nirou Khani, 'villa' shrine 110,
    144, 145
nodules 89, 162, 185
'noduli' 87–8, 143, 162

obsidian 40, 42, 44, 50, 62
oil 97
  perfumed 17

processing 126
olive oil 179
  processing 17
olive presses 21, *21*
olives 17, 41, 45, 47, 167

Pachyammos, cemetery 146
palace towns *see* Knossos town;
    Mallia town; Phaistos; towns
palaces 17, 25, 29, 37, 38, 41, 47
  foundation of (First Palace
    period) 54, 55, 64–5, 66–108
  destructions 178–9
Palaikastro 55, 85, 110, 141, 181
  flask pl. 6
  ivory statuette 141
  shells 20
parchment/papyrus documents 90,
    163, 184
Pasiphae 197, 203, 205
Patrikies 55
peak sanctuaries 56, 58–60, 70, 92,
    96, 100, 101, 106, 173
  on chlorite rhyton 158, *158*
  model animals at *18*, 19
  at Profitis Ilias 77, 101, 140
  temenos 58
pendants 51, 52, 56, 61, 157
  bec-pendant 57, 93, 94; pl. 6
  'Master of Animals', gold 94, *94*,
    107, 178
  silver 94–5, *95*, 98, *98*
Petras
  palatial building 67, 84, 111,
    130–1, *130*
  pottery 85
  pumice 110
  script and archive 72, 88, 89
Petrie, Flinders 94, 96
Petsofa, peak sanctuary *18*, *59*
Phaistos 13, 55, 69, 76, 77, 200,
    207–8
  Ayia Photini area 77, 139
  pottery 76, 77, 91, *91*, 159, *160*
  'state' 85, 86
  town 77, 139, 181, 184
  Final Neolithic period settle-
    ment 39
  EM I 41
  EM II, houses 45, 48
  EM III/MM IA 55
  First Palace (protopalatial
    period) 66, 67, 68, 73–6, *75*,
    76, 88, 91, 101, 111
    altar 104
    destroyed 76
    Linear A archive 72, 88,
      89–90, 163
    sealings 76, 88, *88*
    shrine 101
  Second Palace (neopalatial
    period) 74, 77, 109, 111, 112,
    115–16, *115*, *116*, 121,
    125, 126, 163, 182; pl. 3
    'ante-room to the store-
      rooms' 119, *119*, 121
    and Ayia Triadha villa 131,
      133
    banqueting room 127
    Central Court 121
    state (main) rooms 125, 126,
      127

Theatral Area 115, *115*, 116,
    121
Phalasarna 15
Phourni cemetery 50, 51–3, *53*,
    56, 64, *190*, 191, 195
Phylakopi, Melos 96, 167, 199
pillar crypts 135, 136, 137, 145
pins, metal 157
Pipituna, deity 177
pithoi (storage jars) 46, 70, 78,
    103, 169
  pithos burials 50, 56, 57, 146
  Second Palaces 114, 117, 118,
    126, 129
plant remains 17, 41, 48, 167
plaques, faience 125, 155, 156,
    168; pl. 6
plaster (painted) 48, *49*, 126, 143,
    147
Platanos, tholos tomb *51*
Poros, Herakleion, cemetery 146,
    157
postpalatial period (LM IIIA2–B)
    6–7, 193–6
  cemetery and burials 52, 193–5,
    194
  Mallia, house 139
  red deer 19
  religion 195–6
potters' turntables 46, 54, 143, *143*
potters' wheels 82, 90–1
pottery
  appliqué decoration 82, 91, 100,
    104
  barbotine decoration 61, 91
  chronology 28, 29
  clay beds 23
  residues 20
  scripts on 89, 90, 162, 163
  sea motifs 20
  Neolithic 39, 40
  Early Minoan 58
  EM I and EM II 41, 44, 46, 48,
    50, 51, 52, 53, 60, *61*
    Ayios Onouphrios style 60
    Lenda style 60
    Pyrgos Ware 44, 60
    Vasiliki Ware (mottled) 48, 60,
      61
  EM III 28, 54
  EM III/MM IA 54, 56, 61
  protopalatial period 67, 77, 85,
    86, 87, 90–2, 95, 96–7, 98, 156
    Kamares Ware 73, 76, 90, 91,
      91, 96–7, 101, 156, 159
  neopalatial period 67, 159, 164,
    165; pl. 6
  LM IA and LM IB 33, 159–60,
    166
    Floral Style 128, 159–60, *160*
    Marine Style 128, 160, 186;
      pl. 6
  LM II 181
  LM IIIA2 34
  MM IA 54
  MM III 159
  Final Palace period 185–6, 191
    'Palace Style' jars 185–6, *185*
  Cypriote White Slip 35
  Cyprus 164
  Mycenaean 34, *35*, 180
pottery production 46, 134

workshops 82, 91, 160
Powell, Dilys 208
prepalatial period 37–65
 arts and crafts 60–2
 foreign relations 62–4
 metalworking 61
 pottery 60–1, 61
 religion 57–60
 seals 56, 62, 62, 63, 87–8
 stone vases 50, 51, 61
 see also Early Minoan I, II, III/
  Middle Minoan IA
priestesses 125, 136, 171, 174, 175,
 176, 177, 187
 skeleton 102, 104, 106
priest-kings 148, 150, 151, 154,
 207; pl. 7
priests 125, 135, 175, 177
 ring 104–5
 skeleton 102, 104–5, 106
'princely gift-exchange' 97, 99
Profitis Ilias, peak sanctuary 77,
 101, 140
protopalatial period (First Palace
 period) 6–7, 29, 48, 66–108
 appearance of people and
  clothes 106–7
 arts and crafts 90–5
 Ayia Triadha building and tombs
  132
 faience 155
 figurines 101, 106–7
 foreign relations 95–100
 frescoes (wall-painting) 92, 147
 jewellery 93–5
 Mallia town 139, 140
 painted plaster 147
 pottery 67, 73, 76, 77, 85, 86,
  87, 90–2, 95, 96–7, 98, 101,
  156, 159
 regionalism 67, 72
 religion 60, 100–8
 sculptures, stone 92
 seals and seal-stones 92–3, 105
 'states' 85–7
 swords 78
 vases, stone 92
 writing 71–2, 87–90
Pseira 15, 39, 110, 141
Psychro cave 58, 173, 174, 192
pumice 34–5, 110, 166
Pylos 181

Qatna 97
Quartier Mu, Mallia 78, 80–4, 90,
 102
Qubbet el-Hawa, Egypt 96

radiocarbon dating 32, 33
refuge settlements 30, 196, 210
regionalism 28, 38, 67, 72
religion
 prepalatial period 57–60
 protopalatial period 100–8
 neopalatial period 172–8
 Final Palace period 191–2, 195
 postpalatial period 195–6
Rhodes 96
rhytons (ritual sprinklers) 125
 chlorite 103, 158, 158
 silver 157
 stone 128, 137, 158–9

rings
 gold and silver 157
 silver and iron, priest's 104–5
 see also signet-rings
rock-crystal 23, 82, 92, 158, 188
rock-cut tombs 23
rock shelters 42
'roundels' 131, 162
Royal Villa see Ayia Triadha;
 Knossos town

sacred caves see caves
sacred (sacral) knots 160, 175, 187
sacred mountains see mountains
sacrifices (blood sacrifices) 136,
 143, 169
 of animals 101, 103, 192
 human 102, 104–5, 209
saffron 17, 147, 153, 167, 176
sanctuaries
 Greek 153
 Linear A inscriptions 162
 stone vases 157
 EM III/MM IA 58
 protopalatial period 67, 73, 81,
  100–2, 106
 neopalatial period 112, 140,
  147, 155, 157, 162, 173
 postpalatial period 195
 see also peak sanctuaries
sarcophagi 56, 103, 192–3; pl. 8
scarab beetles 59
 Egyptian 62, 63–4, 64, 100
 Minoan 63–4, 64
scripts see Hieroglyphic script;
 Linear A; Linear B; writing
sculpture (statues) 151–6
 stone 92, 152, 153
 terracotta 103, 152–3, 154
 wooden 103–4, 153
 see also figurines
seal impressions 47, 76, 81, 88, 89,
 110, 162
sealings (clay)
 EM II 47, 48
 'Goddess on the Mountain'
  175–6, 176, 178, 189
 'Master Impression' 177, 178
 protopalatial period 72, 89
 neopalatial period 90, 131, 133,
  143, 163, 175, 177, 178
 Final Palace period 182, 185
 see also seal impressions
seals and seal-stones 11
 EM II 47, 48, 51, 52, 62, 63
 prepalatial period 54, 56, 62, 62,
  63, 65, 87–8
 protopalatial period 68, 72,
  87–8, 89, 89, 92–3, 98
 neopalatial period 146, 147,
  152, 154, 161, 163, 172, 173,
  178; pl. 7
 Final Palace period 188–9
 agate, with priest 105
 carving 23, 92–3, 152
 cats 20
 pigs' tusks 18
 workshop 80, 82
 see also stamp-seals
Sea Peoples 30
Second Palace period 29, 48; see
 neopalatial period

Second Palaces 67, 68, 69–70
 archive-rooms 114, 129
 banqueting halls 127–8, 129
 Central Courts 111, 114, 116–17,
  118, 118, 119, 126, 127, 174
 cooking areas 127
 entrances 121
 functions in 133–5
 layouts 114–33
 light-wells 125, 126
 store-rooms 114, 117–18, 117,
  119, 129, 134
 Theatral Area 115, 116
 West Courts 114, 115, 174
 west facade 114–15
 west wings 117–21, 129
settlements
 Neolithic 39–40
 EM II 45–50
 protopalatial period 66
 neopalatial period 112
 see also towns
shellfish 20
shells 20, 48
 models of 156
ship-sheds 193
shrines 58
 Linear A inscriptions 162
 sculpture in 103, 152–3
 stone vases in 157
 in towns 102, 140, 170
 in villa 110
 EM II 46
 protopalatial (First Palace)
  period 67, 75, 92, 100, 101,
  102–3
 neopalatial (Second Palace)
  period 109, 110, 112, 118,
  128, 131, 141, 142, 143, 156,
  157, 162, 170, 173, 177
 Final Palace period 191, 192,
  195
 postpalatial period 195–6
 see also Anemospilia
signet-rings, gold 147, 157, 159,
 161, 175, 176, 188, 189
silk production 170
silver
 exported 97–8
 mines 96
 objects 52, 62, 156–7
 sources 25, 44
 see also cups; pendants; rings;
  vases; vessels
sistrum/rattle 64, 158
Siteia valley 13, 144
skeletons see human remains
Sklavokambos villa 145
snails 20, 48, 138
'snake tube' 195
'snake-goddesses', faience 118,
 156, 176; pl. 6
spiral decoration 63–4, 91, 97, 129,
 147, 159
springs 78, 130, 136, 142
stamp-seals 48, 62, 92; pl. 7; see also
 seals and seal-stones
'states' 37, 67, 85–7
statues see figurines; sculpture
steatite 82, 137, 158, 161
stirrup-jars 193
stone, as building material 22–3

stone vases *see* vases
storage of goods and produce 17,
    47, 67, 68, 86, 87–8, 133–4,
    144, 145, 169
store-rooms
    EM II 46, 48
    in First Palaces 70, 72, 80, 86,
        87, 88
    in Second Palaces 114, 117–18,
        117, 119, 129, 134
    in villas and country houses
        144, 145
swords *24*, 44, 99, 107, 189
    bronze 78, 156
    gold 107
Syria 24
Syro-Palestinian coast 63, 64, 93,
    96, 164, 171
    pottery 91, 97, 164

tablets (clay documents) *see* Linear
    A; Linear B
Taweret, goddess 93, 100
Tel el-Dab'a (Avaris) 34–5, 94, 151
Tel Kabri (Israel) 34, 151
Tel el-Amarna 34, *35*
'temples', terminology 134–5
textile production 18, 46, 71,134,
    169–70, 184
textile workshops 99
textiles 97, 99, 153, 184
Thera 95, 96, 199, 203, 165–72;
    pl. 5
    eruption (Late Bronze Age) 27,
        29–30, 31–6, *32*, 109, 110–11,
        165–7, 169
    frescoes *see* Akrotiri
    Linear A tablets 163
Theseus 197, *198*, 200, 203–4, *204*
Third Palace period 180; *see* Final
    Palace period
tholos tombs 41, 42–5, *42*, 50–1,
    51, 52, *53*, 56, 63, *64*, 86, 132,
    155, 188, *190*, 191, 192, 195
    paved areas 43, 57
Thucydides 199, 200, 201
tin
    sources 24–5
    trade 99, 100

Tod treasure 96, 98, *98*, *99*, 156
tokens, clay 89
tombs *see* house-tombs; tholos
    tombs
tools 21, 41, 132, 143
    bronze 25, 29, 40, 51, 61, 136,
        156
    votive, bronze 173
town houses 155
    Knossos town 72–3, 83–4, 110,
        112, 122, 125, 135, 182
    Phaistos 139
'Town Mosaic', on plaques 125,
    155, 169; pl. 6
towns
    destroyed 178
    nonpalatial 140–5
    and palaces 67, 68–84
    see also Knossos town; Mallia
        town; Phaistos
trade and exchange, neopalatial
    period 164–72
Traostalos 101
Trypeti 47–8
Turkey 64, 95, 96, 164, 202
Tylissos
    cauldrons 156
    copper ingots 24
    Linear A tablets 163
    villa 112, 144, *144*, 181, 184

Ugarit 64, 97, 99
Ulu Burun, wreck 171
urbanization 109
User, statuette of 100

Vapheio, gold cups 157
vases
    faience 156
    gilded stone 157
    pottery 44, 50, 60, 61, 146, 159
    production 83
    silver 62, 156–7
    stone 23, 44, 50, 51, 61, 83, 92,
        132, 152, 157–9
Vasiliki 48–9, 55
    'Red House' 48–9, *49*
    see also pottery
Vathypetro, villa *21*, 144, 145

vessels 21
    bronze 156, 188, 191
    gold 157
    silver 96, 98, 136, 156–7
    stone *27*, 101, 128, 143, 162, 173
villas *see* country houses
vine cultivation 17
votive offerings 59, 153, 156, 173,
    174, 177, 192

wall-paintings 92; *see also* frescoes
'warrior graves' 146, 180, 189, 191
Waugh, Evelyn 208–9
weapons 25, 99, 189
    bronze 29, 40, 50, 146, 156, 188
    see also daggers; swords
weaving 134, 169–70
wine 18, 97
wine-press *21*
workshops
    MM IA 63
    palaces 99, 114, 125, 134, 156
    towns 80, 82–3, 131, 137, 139,
        169
worshippers 59, 154, 155, *155*,
    175, 176, 177
writing 9, 26, 65, 198
    protopalatial period 68, 71–2,
        87–90
    neopalatial period 161–3
    Final Palace period 184
    see also Hieroglyphic script;
        Linear A; Linear B

Zakros 84, *84*, 181, 186
    burials 106
    copper ingots 24
    Linear A tablets 163
    palace 15, 66, 67, 84, 85, 101,
        111, 112, 115, 118, 119, *124*,
        128–30, *128*; pl. 4
    shrine 128
    stone vases (rhytons)/vessels *27*,
        103, 157, 158, *158*
    town 130
    'treasury' *129*
    water features 129–30, *130*
Zeus 174, 197, 200, 201–2, 203
Zominthos 145